Twelve Great Clashes that Shaped Modern America

From Geronimo to George W. Bush

Anthony Arthur

John Broesamle

PEARSON
Longman

New York San Francisco Boston
London Toronto Sydney Tokyo Singapore Madrid
Mexico City Munich Paris Cape Town Hong Kong Montreal

For Brady, Duncan, Jane, Julia, Nell, Olivia,
and Tyler: our future

Executive Editor: Michael Boezi
Executive Marketing Manager: Sue Westmoreland
Project Coordination, Text Design, and Electronic Page Makeup:
   WestWords, Inc.
Senior Cover Design Manager/Cover Designer: Nancy Danahy
Cover Designer: Base Art Co.
Cover photos from left to right: CORBIS; AP/Wide World; AP/Wide
   World; CORBIS
Senior Manufacturing Buyer: Dennis Para
Printer and Binder: Courier Corporation
Cover Printer: Phoenix Color Corporation

Please visit us at www.ablongman.com

ISBN 0-321-41826-3

1 2 3 4 5 6 7 8 9 10—ptr code—09 08 07 06

Contents

Preface

Pick up any newspaper or turn on any television news program, and you quickly notice that it includes stories on wars, political fights, battles over the environment, and a dozen other disputed issues. Abraham Lincoln spoke of America's defining characteristic as "eternal struggle." Today, no less than in Lincoln's time, life often seems to be a welter of violent clashes, shouted slogans, and complicated ideas that lack meaning or pattern.

When viewed in the perspective of history, though, these quarrels and confrontations can be seen as elements of an ongoing struggle to define the country's identity and purpose. We offer here some insights into 12 great controversies that shape today's headlines but whose sources lie in the past. In each instance, our focus is on a classic dispute between two or three people who represent the opposing sides in these controversies. We are writing about contentious, committed individuals who stand for something outside themselves. Taken together, their stories make up a coherent, if selective, portrait of the United States over the past century and a half.

The first guiding idea of this book, then, is that we see issues through the lens of personality, by which we mean the mysterious yet revealing complex of character, ideas, and emotions that make people what they are. The figures we have chosen intrigue us both because of their actions and their beliefs. We present them as they were (or are), complex flesh-and-blood human beings. Some of them had deep flaws. We do not attempt to "sanitize" them, feeling that to try to clean up the messiness of the past debases the study of history itself. This book contains no saints.

Our second theme involves the dichotomy of American history: the opposition of what *should* be and what *can* be. Many of our chapters pit an idealist against a realist—John Muir the idealist, for example, against Theodore Roosevelt the realist, or

Woodrow Wilson against Henry Cabot Lodge, or (arguably) Clarence Thomas against Sandra Day O'Connor. In every confrontation we describe, ideas mattered, and in every instance, ideas had consequences.

Half of the lives we treat ended on a note of failure or immense frustration. Yet in time, perhaps long after their death, many were vindicated. Either because the passage of years has changed perspectives on them or because of startling new revelations, some figures are viewed today in quite a different light from the way their contemporaries saw them. No doubt perspectives will continue to change.

To our first two themes, add a third: the democratic tendency toward compromise. All of the people we portray were (or are) remarkably strong-willed. They took firm stands on one side of an issue or the other. Yet the upshot of their disagreements was that America proceeded along a *middle* course. If the disputants could not arrive at compromise in their own time, their successors did. What keeps America, or any democracy, from spinning out of control internally is that most conflicts are at least partially resolved, somewhere short of unconditional surrender. The very fact that issues of the past continue to vex us today suggests that *full* resolution is an ideal that will never be achieved. We will still live in a state of ongoing debate and compromise. That any kind of achievement is possible is due to the capacity of ordinary citizens, along with their political and judicial representatives, to weigh the positions taken by very persuasive advocates.

Some of the people we portray are genuine legends, larger than life. Neither Geronimo, Eugene Debs, Theodore Roosevelt, John Muir, Booker T. Washington, W. E. B. DuBois, Woodrow Wilson, Franklin D. Roosevelt, nor Douglas MacArthur now has any American equivalent. But they are not museum figures. We show within these pages that their clashes of will not only helped to shape the world of today, but that they shared our own hopes and fears as well.

ACKNOWLEDGMENTS

We wish to thank all who have helped us in writing this book by sharing their knowledge and commenting on our chapters: John S. Baick, Susan Ford Bennion, Alan Bloom, Simon M. Caron, Kathleen S. Carter, Michael P. Gabriel, Jessica Gerard, Ron Good, Roderick Greene, Deborah Clarke Grosvenor, Leslie Heaphy, James Hedtke, Juli Jones, Marc Larson, the late David Lavender, William E. Leuchtenburg, the late James D. Loebl, Constance M. McGovern, Michael R. Nichols, Justin Nordstrom, Phillip Payne, William L. Peck, Patrick D. Reagan, Robert W. Righter, Mansfield D. Sprague, Susan A. Strauss, Carolyn J. Vondriska, Bill Wilmer, and Irvin D. S. Winsboro.

1

I Never Do Wrong Without a Cause

Geronimo, George Crook, Nelson A. Miles, and the Ownership of America

The encounter occurred in March, 1886, at a place called the Canyon of the Tricksters. Everything about this Apache terrain spelled danger. Three years before, the United States army had tracked down the Apaches in Mexico's Sierra Madre. Struggling along canyon walls, pack mules lost their footing and plunged hundreds of feet with their loads. This time the Apaches had positioned themselves on top of a rocky volcanic hill with ravines all around it for quick escape. America's canniest Indian fighter, Brigadier General George Crook, was about to meet with Geronimo, the last of the great North American Indian warriors. Geronimo's name alone aroused almost supernatural fear throughout the Southwest. He was unpredictable, uncontrollable, and violent. Each man had a small escort; if anything went wrong, both sides were ready to shoot.

Chased by both the U.S. and Mexican armies, among the last Indians still resisting white domination, Geronimo's band of

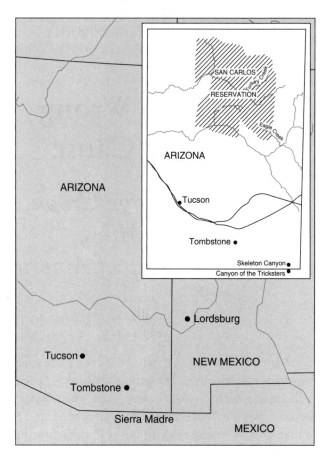

FIGURE 1.1 Geronimo Country.

Chiricahua Apaches had already passed the point of exhaustion. Most of them wanted to surrender. Crook's immediate task was to convince the whole band to give up without inadvertently touching off a firefight. In the Southwest, though, killing Apaches was just what many people wanted. The Arizona press ridiculed Crook's softness toward the Apaches, along with his conviction that Indians—including Geronimo—actually had rights.

As Geronimo's words filtered their way through translation, one of Crook's officers wrote them down. A photographer stood by. "I want to talk first of the causes which led me to leave the reservation," Geronimo told Crook. "In the papers all over the world they say I am a bad man; but it is a bad thing to say so about me. I never do wrong without a cause." Crook showed a poker face. He appeared entirely indifferent whether the Indians surrendered or not. The choice was theirs, he said—they could take the easy way by surrendering, or else the hard way, being tracked down and killed like hunted animals. Extremely wary, Geronimo held back. The other Chiricahua leaders, though, trusted Crook. His words might seem as hard as hammer blows, but then Crook always spoke that way, and he had never lied to them. After mulling it over for several days, the entire band gave up.

Crook had abundant reason for his quiet satisfaction. Even if the army sent thousands of troops after just a few determined warriors, he knew, the chances of actually catching or killing them were slim. The Apache "has the eye of a hawk, the stealth of a coyote, the courage of a tiger—and its mercilessness," wrote a journalist at the time. "He knows every foot of his savage realm better than you know your own parlor." Pressed by the army, the Indians would simply slide south into the Sierra Madre "as if the hills and valleys were a greased pole." Later they would rematerialize, ambushing settlers or army patrols. Better to bluff the Apaches out, Crook thought, than try to kill them one by one.

But within a day of the surrender Geronimo—together with 21 men, 14 women, and 6 children—fled anyway, virtually the last American Indians resisting conquest. Soon Geronimo faced a new general, Nelson A. Miles, who brought down on his tiny band the full wrath of the United States government. Geronimo and his followers were finished; they began calling themselves Indeh, meaning The Dead. They would die—but neither how nor where they might have expected.

✧ ✧ ✧

By the 1880s, the American Indians' losing battle to retain a grip on their tribal lands had entered its final phase. Since the first European settlement, the story had been one of steady retreat. The struggle pitted white, Western concepts of progress against the Indians' very different belief systems. The tribes held that no individual or group could own the land, any more than they could own the oceans. Indians thought of resources in terms of animals and plants that were renewable and pursuable; if the buffalo herds on the Great Plains traveled hundreds of miles, the Indians could easily travel with them, killing those they needed for food and clothing, confident that the herd would renew itself in succeeding seasons.

Whites, though, wanted to convert the communally held tribal "oceans" into private property, split them up, and, in the term we now use, *develop* them. Whites intended to capitalize not only on renewable resources (Oregon timber, California irrigation water) but on nonrenewable ones as well (South Dakota gold, Arizona copper). And this, in turn, required a permanent imprint on the land—railroads, barbed wire, and telegraph lines, not to mention forts, towns, and cities.

Whites tended to regard Indians as stone-age relics; in a common nineteenth-century expression, they "stood in the way of progress." The goal, then, was to get the Indians out of the way. It became the essence of U.S. Indian policy to move tribes on to reservations, peacefully if possible but by military force if necessary. General William Tecumseh Sherman put it succinctly: "We have provided reservations for all [Indians], off the great roads. All who cling to their old hunting grounds are hostile and will remain so till killed off." The public rarely objected to using force against a hostile tribe. In time, the logic went, the Indians would become "civilized" and Christianized, and would begin to think and act more or less *like* whites. Until they succeeded at raising crops or running livestock, reservation Indians would be fed by the government. Meanwhile, the military must carefully control them.

To the Indians, reservation life spelled confinement, the abandonment of ancient ways, an agonizing separation from the bones of their ancestors, and, often, death. Reservation land commonly amounted to waste land; and when, as often occurred, the government consigned a tribe to a reservation located far from its historic domain, the Indians began dying of diseases to which they lacked immunity. Inevitably, the military ran into problems in carrying out Washington's reservation policies.

The United States army, a million strong at the end of the Civil War, had plummeted to just 38,000 by 1866. When this kind of shrinkage has occurred following great wars, a core of talented career officers has typically stayed on, as if occupying a vacant hotel. Among these officers in the 1870s and 1880s, attitudes toward the Indian ran the gamut from outright contempt to genuine sympathy, mixed with a good deal of ambivalence. Like other Americans, officers commonly expressed admiration for the Indian's physical toughness, courage, and fighting qualities. General Sherman himself, the Indians' fiercest antagonist— he once called for "extermination" of the Sioux "men, women and children"—had been named for a famous warrior, the Shawnee chief Tecumseh. General Philip Sheridan, charged with orchestrating the Indians' defeat, openly sympathized with them: "Alas for the poor savage! along came nineteenth century progress, or whatever it may be called, to disturb their happy condition. . . . We took away their country and their means of support, broke up their mode of living, their habits of life, introduced disease and decay among them, and it was for this and against this they made war. Could anyone expect less?" Whatever the private sympathies of individual members might have been, the military was charged with carrying out national policy under trying circumstances. Understaffed and divided, pulled this way and that by cultural and political concerns, the army found itself running what would later be called a counterinsurgency (or peacekeeping) program to get the Indians under control with the least bother and bloodshed while keeping white interlopers off the reservations. Strategies and tactics varied according to the situation and the officers in charge.

The whites' sympathetic admiration for their Indian adversaries tended to focus on those whose noble profiles, such as that of the Sioux chief Crazy Horse, reminded them of the ancient Romans, or whose words, such as those of Chief Joseph, took on a grand dignity. Geronimo did not fit into either of these categories. By the mid-1880s, Geronimo had become the army's most relentless enemy. Born around 1829 somewhere in what is today either Arizona or New Mexico, Geronimo's proper if improbable Apache name was Goyahkla (meaning "One Who Yawns"). In 1848 the Treaty of Guadalupe Hidalgo split these lands from Mexico, making them part of the United States. In 1851 Mexican irregulars killed Geronimo's mother, his first wife—he would have nine altogether—and his three children. Afterward, the vengeful Geronimo would continually raid Mexico, taking a keen delight in killing Mexicans indiscriminately. It was the Mexicans who assigned the name Geronimo to him,* and Mexican mothers frightened their children into behaving by dropping Geronimo's name in their ear.

In many ways, Geronimo was and remains an enigma, and it is far easier to account for the army's actions than for his. Stocky, of medium height, he wore a fixed scowl. He was a medicine man, a spiritual figure. He could break unpredictably into outbursts of rage. He loved to gamble. Neither the chief of his band, the Chiricahua Apaches, nor a great speaker, his qualities of leadership grew instead out of a humorless pride, a keen and logical intelligence, and a single-minded determination to preserve the ancient Apache ways.

---

*Geronimo's biographer, Angie Debo, wrote: "Each time he emerged, the Mexicans began to cry out in terror, 'Cuidado! Watch out! Geronimo!' (Perhaps this was as close as they could come to the choking sounds that composed his name, or perhaps they were calling on St. Jerome.) The Apaches took it up as their battle cry, and Goyahkla became Geronimo."

Born in 1828, George Crook was a contemporary of Geronimo. Although the two had much in common—intelligence, single-mindedness, willingness to take risks, tenacity in battle—Crook was colorless almost to the point of invisibility. Once glimpsed, Geronimo's photographic image remains indelible, a frontier settler's darkest nightmare. In contrast, apart from his height, somewhat over six feet, Crook's image slides to the back of the memory, almost disappearing. He resembled millions of other middle-class Victorian men. A great listener and learner, Crook rarely disclosed much about himself or his intentions. Quiet, independent, a little distant, he shunned the glitter of publicity. Instead of an elegant uniform, he dressed whenever possible in plain civilian clothes; in preference to galloping white chargers, Crook rode mules. He had a passion for hunting quail, deer, grizzly bears, and other creatures, and he had the hunter's ability to think like his quarry. Eventually Crook's greatest quarry would become Geronimo.

Between his graduation from West Point in 1852 and the outbreak of the Civil War nine years later, Crook fought Indians in California and Oregon. Intrigued by his tribal opponents, Crook made a study of their ways and traditions. The injustices he saw other whites inflicting on them gnawed at him. His study of the tribes was interrupted by the Civil War, during which he earned repeated promotions for valor and learned lessons he would later apply to defeating the Indians. The chief lesson he and other strategists took away from the Civil War was the need to move beyond the "mere" battlefield toward ruthlessly obliterating an opponent's physical resources and thus its will to fight. The monumental example of the new approach was Sherman's march through Georgia and the Carolinas in 1864–65, during which his tough, ragged troops carved a swath of destruction hundreds of miles long. Sherman did not intend to fight any oftener than necessary nor to kill civilians at all, but he did intend utterly to destroy their livelihoods and physical property along with liberating their human property, the slaves. In effect, Sherman was inventing today's military strategy—minimal infliction of death, maximum destruction of infrastructure. At the time, this approach caused shock and dismay in the South.

Nelson A. Miles became another military star during the Civil War, but a star rising on a different course from West Pointers such as George Crook. Tall and good-looking, an easy talker, Miles had clerked in a Boston crockery store before the Civil War broke out. In 1861 he borrowed money, recruited and equipped a company of volunteers, had a tutor train him in tactics, and entered the war as a first lieutenant. By the following year, he had risen to colonel. Dashing and valiant, he was wounded repeatedly in battle and won a Medal of Honor. Besides intelligence, great courage, huge ambition, and a staggering ego—Theodore Roosevelt called him a "Brave Peacock"—what particularly distinguished Miles was aggressiveness. He could also show indifference to the niceties of military protocol. When the Confederate president, Jefferson Davis, was captured, Miles had him clamped into leg irons.

✧   ✧   ✧

Following the Civil War, a huge surge of white migrants pouring into the West set tribe after tribe on the warpath—Kiowa, Sioux, Cheyenne, Arapaho, Comanche, Apache. Crook and Miles became important agents of Washington's policy of forcing the Indians to accept permanent, fixed reservations. They also became symbols of Washington's warring attitudes toward the Indians—Crook the sympathizer, Miles the stern antagonist.

Separated into half a dozen tribes (sometimes called divisions), before the arrival of whites the Apaches had controlled an enormous domain in modern Arizona, New Mexico, and northern old Mexico. The tribes were split into bands, the bands into groups composed of several extended families. Under Cochise, their fierce and skillful chief, during the 1860s the Chiricahua tribe managed through relentless fighting to clear most of southeastern Arizona of white settlers. Towns such as Tucson and Tombstone became as isolated as dots on a map. The Apache menace seemed so intractable that General Sherman unsuccessfully recommended pulling both the settlers and the army out of Arizona and handing the then-territory back to the Indians. Well-armed with rifles, superb horsemen, Apache warriors typically fought in bodies ranging from a few braves into the hundreds. They utterly terrified whites. The Apaches would routinely kill any adult captive, whether male or female. They dashed babies' heads against trees. Older white children, though, who could survive without their mothers, were adopted (whites would say kidnapped) into the band. Some of these children would later become influential members of the tribe.

Apache atrocities in turn generated white atrocities. White Arizonans wanted one of two things: the Apaches either had to surrender unconditionally or face total annihilation. A Tucson newspaper demanded killing Indians "until every valley and crest and crag and fastness shall send to high heaven the grateful incense of festering and rotting" Apaches. When enraged Tucson vigilantes went on a rampage in 1871, hacking and clubbing to death from one hundred to one hundred and fifty Apaches (mostly women and children) who supposedly fell under army protection, the incident aroused sympathy for the tribe around the nation. A local jury, though, expressed its appreciation for the vigilantes' actions and immediately acquitted them.

That same year, the army dispatched Crook to Arizona. Determined to push the Apaches onto reservations, he studied their ways as he had those of the West Coast tribes. Indians communicated orally, and Crook, as always, listened to them carefully. A fellow officer recalled that "the Indians evinced an awe for him the first moment of their meeting; they did not seem to understand how it was that a white man could so quickly absorb all that they had to teach." Unlike other people both inside and outside the army who shared his sympathy with Indians, Crook did not believe that tribal willpower could be broken just by kind words and warm feelings. Before fair treatment could start, any hostile tribe would first have to be broken by force. This meant crushing the Apaches militarily. "These tigers of the human race," Crook wrote, "resented anything like an attempt to regulate their conduct, or in any way to interfere with their mode of life."

Despite clamor for action from the Arizona press, Crook recognized that chasing down Apaches using conventional military formations would prove next to impossible. Apaches thrived on surprise raids and ambushes. They preferred to choose the terrain and timing of their attacks, strike fast, then flee, scattering in every direction, as difficult to pursue as blowing sand. Apaches could cover 100 miles a day on horseback; when large forces confronted them, they would sometimes eat their horses before fleeing on foot. As one officer put it, "they knew how to disguise themselves so thoroughly that one might almost step upon a warrior thus occupied before he could detect his presence. Stripped naked, with head and shoulders wrapped up in a bundle of yucca shoots or sacaton grass, and with body rubbed over with the clay or sand along which it wriggled as sinuously and as venomously as the rattler itself," the Apache made an extraordinary guerilla.

Crook had his own weapons and techniques of attack, honed in his earlier Indian campaigns. Provisioning soldiers in the conventional way from massive, slow-moving wagon trains, he realized, impeded speed and mobility. Instead, he hit on a major if mundane innovation—mule trains. Actually an old army form of transportation, Crook radically improved on it with better mules and equipment as well as more competent "mule skinners." His methods proved so successful that as late as World War II, American troops would still rely on these stubborn, sure-footed animals to supply them in mountainous terrain.

Another weapon in Crook's arsenal was provided by the Apaches themselves, who did not limit their animosity to whites and Mexicans. Different groups of Apaches carried on blood feuds. Why not, then, pit Apaches against one another? The army had historically aligned friendly Indian "scouts" against hostiles.

Using Arizona Indians now to hunt their fellow tribesmen, or, even better, to chase members of their own band within the tribe, would further erode unity and psychologically unhinge those being pursued. As Crook himself put it: "Nothing breaks them up like turning their own people against them. They don't fear the white soldiers, whom they easily surpass in the peculiar style of warfare which they force upon us, but put upon their trail an enemy of their own blood, an enemy as tireless, as foxy, and as stealthy and familiar with the country as they themselves, and it breaks them all up."

With this in mind, Crook began recruiting hundreds of Apache scouts. In November, 1872, he launched his offensive, crushing the hostile bands in a campaign whose decisive elements were scouts and mule trains, each used for unremitting pursuit. Across the treacherous terrain, Crook himself usually rode on muleback. By April, 1873, the campaign had ended. Three hundred warriors had been killed and hundreds of families concentrated on the reservation. As one scholar puts it, "Crook had done more to break the resistance of the Apache . . . than anyone in perhaps three hundred years." Over the next several years, Arizona experienced an unusual calm.

Meanwhile the army went about applying a version of Sherman's Georgia–Carolina strategy against other tribes that remained hostile, destroying food stocks and in particular undercutting tribal hunting by obliterating whole herds of bison. Occasionally, though, the military overreached. In the summer of 1876, shortly after fighting Crook to a standstill in southeastern Montana, the Sioux and Cheyennes wiped out a command led by George Armstrong Custer along the nearby Little Big Horn River. Custer had launched a cavalry charge against an opposing force of warriors that outnumbered him somewhere between ten and thirty to one.

Such overreaching did not necessarily stop with actions in the field. In 1879 Washington ordered Crook to carry out what he considered hideously unfair orders against the Ponca tribe of

Nebraska. Consigned to a reservation in Indian Territory (now Oklahoma), the Poncas began dying of malaria. When Chief Standing Bear saw his own children succumb, he led part of his tribe back toward their original homeland. As they moved along, the Poncas, who had never fought the whites, begged for food. Reaching Nebraska, they took up farming. Crook received a directive from Washington to put the Poncas under arrest and return them to Oklahoma. He dutifully carried out the arrest but delayed the return. Public sympathy quickly mounted for the Poncas. After meeting with Standing Bear in March, 1879, Crook collaborated in bringing suit on behalf of the Indians. In *Standing Bear v. Crook*—technically the general himself was the defendant—for the first time in U.S. history a court determined "that an *Indian* is a PERSON within the meaning of the laws." Alarmed, the Department of the Interior realized that if it became precedent, this decision might give Indians constitutional rights, and worked to minimize its effects. Regardless, *Standing Bear* was one of Crook's great monuments, and ultimately, the Poncas remained in Nebraska.

✧　　✧　　✧

When Crook had headed north from Arizona to fight the Cheyennes and Sioux, the Chiricahua Apaches seemed more or less under control. Then Cochise died. Now Geronimo became increasingly central to the Chiricahua equation. Following Crook's campaign of 1872–73, Washington had decided to slash the number of Apache reservations from five to one. Crook foresaw catastrophe. Pressured to abandon territory they had been promised and move to the desolate bottomlands that made up the chosen San Carlos reservation in Arizona, Geronimo and others began repeatedly slipping out of government hands. In a flurry of violent adventures, they proved hard to catch and almost impossible to contain as they rampaged back and forth between the United States and Mexico.

In 1876, Geronimo's renegades began killing whites and seizing firearms, cattle, and horses. Eventually recaptured, Geronimo was thrown into a cell at San Carlos, where he languished for months. Along with the Chiricahuas, other formerly free-roaming bands that had traditionally fought with one another were hemmed in at San Carlos, continually under the observation of the white authorities. Ignoring their agreements with the Apaches, these authorities allowed white miners and farmers to grab big pieces of the reservation. Again in 1878, Geronimo broke out, killing more whites, battling soldiers, and fleeing into Mexico, where he joined other rebellious Apaches in the Sierra Madre. This time, apparently weary of being chased by Mexican troops and lonely for his relatives, Geronimo returned on his own to San Carlos to live with his three wives and children. In 1881, again restless with reservation life, Geronimo's small band raced southward, raiding and killing their way across southern Arizona into Mexico. In April of the following year, leading some sixty warriors, Geronimo carried out an astonishingly successful raid on the San Carlos reservation, then spirited hundreds of Apaches into Mexico while fighting off both U.S. and Mexican forces. Hunted down and trapped in a dry ravine, trying to protect their women and children but taking heavy losses, 35 warriors stood off 250 Mexican troops for hours on end. Finally, in the dead of night, the Apaches escaped.

The slaughter in Mexico went on. One of Geronimo's wives, captured in an ambush, was probably sold into slavery. To the north the bloodletting continued as well. In one incident near Lordsburg, New Mexico, a white father (and federal judge) who had come under attack tried to pin down the warriors single-handedly so his wife and son could flee in their buckboard. Killing the father, then catching up with the mother, the warriors promptly killed her too. The boy, six-year-old redhead Charley McComas—of an age to be trained as a warrior—they took alive in keeping with their traditions.

With the local press clamoring for extermination of all Apaches, in the summer of 1882 the army ordered Crook back to Arizona. He proceeded characteristically, touring the reservations, hearing out the chiefs, and agreeing that their complaints had justice. "Indian agents" of the Interior Department's Bureau of Indian Affairs (BIA) were supposed to operate the reservations. Essential to the system were white supply contractors and traders. "With them," Crook noted, "peace kills the goose that lays the golden egg." Crook believed the traders were actually engaging in a conspiracy to encourage the Apaches onto the warpath, forcing the army to maintain a big (and for the traders, very lucrative) presence in Arizona. Whether true or not, this sort of treachery had already become infamous elsewhere in the West. Indian agents may have misled Custer as to how many warriors had left the Sioux reservation, since the agents got paid according to the number of Indians actually on the reservation. In Arizona, crooked agents sold most of the supplies that Washington allocated for the Apaches to other whites while the Indians starved. Indians who blew the whistle on this racket got thrown into prison without charges. The agent at San Carlos became the target of a scorching grand jury report compiled by whites. Declaring themselves "honest American citizens," the jurors called his administration "a disgrace to the civilization of the age."

Armed with the grand jury's findings and the testimony of the Apaches themselves, Crook began moving fast. He put the reservations under direct military authority and evicted predatory whites, including prospectors and liquor dealers. Additional reforms included freer movement for the tribal bands, measures to make them self-supporting, a court system with Apache judges and juries, and a ban on Apache men slicing off the noses of unfaithful wives. The white territorial press lambasted Crook for choosing the wrong side.

Meantime Geronimo's Chiricahuas hid out in Mexico. If Crook wanted to catch them, he would have to probe the very heart of the Apache sanctuary, the Sierra Madre. Securing permission from Mexican authorities for the pursuit, Crook moved across the border in May, 1883, with a mixed force of 45 white cavalrymen and 193 Apache scouts. Apaches would track down other Apaches, with the regulars in support. Inching their way along indistinct trails between the towering peaks, they passed through forests and across rushing streams where bullets could fly at any second. When at length they located his camp, Geronimo was away capturing Mexican women to trade for Apache captives, including one of his wives. Half the Chiricahuas had surrendered before their fiercest warrior reappeared. Crook coolly explained to the hostiles that they could give up or not; that if they wanted to continue the fight, he would track down every last one of them again. Surrender or shoot it out—the decision was up to them. Crook casually stepped out of camp by himself at one point, as if inviting ambush. ("It is not advisable," he observed, "to let an Indian think you are afraid of him even when fully armed. Show him that at his best he is no match for you.")

Crook had demonstrated an ability to locate and pursue the Indians virtually anywhere, even places they considered impregnable, and this demoralized them—as Crook well knew it would. Some of the Apaches actually felt relieved to have the opportunity of giving up; the women, in particular, wanted an end to the slaughter, and they helped persuade the men. At length Geronimo acceded. Besides Geronimo's surrender, Crook wanted information about young Charley McComas, whose kidnapping had become a cause célèbre in Arizona. Geronimo said he would personally hunt for the boy, but Charley never reappeared. Accounts of his fate vary: Charley may have been murdered by an angry Apache, or killed by a stray bullet; or he may have survived into adulthood. No one living today knows.

After more than a month in Mexico, Crook finally returned with 325 Apache fugitives, putting to rest rumors that he had suffered Custer's fate. Geronimo himself came in early in 1884. Crook again joined battle against corrupt civilians on the reservation, but in 1885 his position eroded when the Interior

Department got administrative control back from the military. Crook responded forcefully, if undiplomatically, to press clamor to exterminate all the Apaches. The problems the settlers faced, he said, were due more to crooked whites, who should presumably be honorable, than to the Indians, who were admittedly untrustworthy. His analysis was condescending to everyone but the army: "It should not be expected that an Indian who has lived as a barbarian all his life will become an angel the moment he comes on a reservation and promises to behave himself, or that he has that strict sense of honor which a person should have who has had the advantage of civilization all his life." A lot of whites, on the other hand, were "vampires who prey on the misfortunes of their fellow men. . . . Greed and avarice on the part of the whites—in other words the almighty dollar—is at the bottom of nine-tenths of all our Indian troubles." "Bad as the Indians often are," Crook declared, "I have never yet seen one so demoralized that he was not an example in honor and nobility to the wretches who enrich themselves by plundering him of the little our government appropriates him."

Crook had promised the Apaches peace, decent land, and official forgiveness regardless of what Arizona's white population thought. Geronimo agreed to obey orders, but he wanted his people to have land off the reservation, at a place called Eagle Creek. Settlers had already claimed Eagle Creek. When Crook sent the Chiricahuas to another, less desirable locale—not Eagle Creek but Turkey Creek—Geronimo's suspicions swelled. Still, Turkey Creek was better than the San Carlos bottomlands. Geronimo's band, numbering some six hundred and fifty now, moved to Turkey Creek and planted out the land in corn, squash, and melons. But plain farming was not the ancient Chiricahua way; besides, the warriors resented Crook's regulations banning alcohol and wife-beating.

Once again, in May, 1885, Geronimo slipped off the reservation. This time he took just a quarter of the Chiricahuas with him (42 men and 92 women and children), the few still willing to defy the army. Almost immediately the renegade band began killing whites in the accustomed manner, but this time they faced an entirely new threat. Among the scouts Crook sent after them were not just other Apaches but other *Chiricahuas,* who captured Geronimo's wives and five of his children and sent the rest of the hostiles flying. Hiding out in Mexico's Sierra Madre without their families, the warriors' spirits began to flag. As always Geronimo wanted to fight on, but the others did not. The moment had arrived for yet another meeting with Crook. And so in March, 1886, the general and the warrior talked again, in the Canyon of the Tricksters, and reached yet another agreement. The Chiricahua renegades would surrender, rejoin their families, and be sent to Florida for a maximum of two years. After that they could return to Arizona.

And then, one final time, Geronimo and a small band of Chiricahuas disappeared.

✧   ✧   ✧

Crook was the army's best strategist against the Apaches, but when Geronimo slipped away, Arizonans mounted a withering attack on him. The army's current commanding general, Philip Sheridan, suspected that Crook had gone soft and did not like Crook's reliance on Apache scouts, whom Sheridan distrusted. Sheridan informed Crook that the terms to which the Indians had agreed before Geronimo's break must be cancelled. The Apaches would have to surrender unconditionally, and any who resisted must be shot. Crook, insulted, had his back to the wall. He had most of the hostiles in hand, but they had given up based on the two-year provision. Crook would not double-cross them. To do that would violate both his own code of honor and his way of dealing with Indians. So he wired Sheridan, "I respectfully request that I may be now relieved from . . . command." Sheridan wasted no time in transferring him back to the Great Plains.

Crook told the assembled Apache leaders: "You have been very faithful. I have made many enemies among my own people by being honest and square with you." Then he was gone. As the new commander of the army's Department of Arizona, Sheridan named a man after his own heart, Nelson A. Miles. Long jealous of Crook, who had been promoted ahead of him, by now the one-time Boston store clerk could lay equal claim with Crook to being the army's premier Indian fighter. Like Sheridan, Miles dismissed Crook's approach to the Apaches as soft. Miles called the Chiricahuas "the lowest, most brutal, and cruel[est] of all the Indian savages on this continent." He wanted to upstage Crook not by conciliating them but by suppressing them once and for all, using maximum military force and, if necessary, killing every last Apache who remained hostile. To do the job—to round up three dozen remaining warriors, women, and children—the army assigned Miles some five thousand troops, 2,000 more than Crook had had. Five thousand men amounted to practically a quarter of the U.S. army, spread all the way from southwestern Arizona to southeastern New Mexico. Miles also deployed a high-tech British army invention used in colonial India. This was the heliograph, a mechanical mirror apparatus mounted on a tripod so as to catch the sun. Taking advantage of the brilliant desert light, heliograph stations on mountaintops could flash messages in Morse code about Apache sightings that troops could read up to thirty miles away.

Miles sent after Geronimo a picked force composed mostly of regulars, with some Apache scouts as guides. These men labored across 2,000 miles of scorching, rattlesnake-infested terrain without success. Another mobile force tried again, quite fruitlessly. With six months gone and no enemy Chiricahuas killed, Miles was compelled to adopt Crook's strategy by using more Apache scouts—and, finally, to parlay with the hostiles just as Crook had done. Miles sent an officer whom Geronimo respected to confer with the warrior in Mexico. The officer gave Geronimo Miles's ultimatum: "Surrender, and you will be sent with your families to Florida, there to await the decision of the President as to your final disposition. Accept these terms or fight to the bitter end." Meantime, the president wanted blood. Sick of all the trouble Geronimo had put the army to, Grover Cleveland ordered that nothing "be done with Geronimo which will prevent our treating him as a prisoner of war, *if we cannot hang him, which I would much prefer*" [italics in original]. White Arizonans wanted to try Geronimo for murder in the territorial courts, which no doubt would have produced the outcome Cleveland desired.

Though he favored shipping the Apaches east, the injustice of exiling them to humid, "sickly Florida" was too much even for Miles to stomach. Regardless, in late summer, 1886, after Miles had lured them together for a head count, nearly six hundred Chiricahua and other suspect Apaches from the San Carlos reservation found themselves piled into rail cars bound for Florida. Among them were most of Crook's loyal Chiricahua scouts.

Then, in early September, Miles met directly with Geronimo at a place with the forbidding name of Skeleton Canyon. Geronimo had insisted on this; he would surrender to no less than Miles himself. Geronimo's penetrating eyes reminded Miles of General Sherman, who resembled a bird of prey. By now, Geronimo was down to 17 men. That their families had already been shipped to Florida had undermined whatever remained of the hostiles' fighting spirit. Miles talked warmly and guaranteed Geronimo fair treatment; the Chiricahua families, he said, would be reunited.

And so, yet again, Geronimo agreed to give up. This time, though, Miles—wary of suffering Crook's fate—handled Geronimo more or less as he had treated Jefferson Davis. After an army band played "Auld Lang Syne," a train sped Geronimo and the others eastward. They wound up incarcerated in Florida alongside Crook's betrayed scouts.

Robert M. Utley writes that "the real hero of the army's Apache campaigns remains George Crook," both for the enlightened way in which he treated the Apaches and because "he devised and carried out the only military techniques that ever seriously challenged Apaches in warfare." "No army officer of the late nineteenth century ever matched Crook's record in Indian affairs," agrees Jerome A. Greene. Yet while Crook, with all his subtlety and courage, had succeeded at bringing in every hostile Apache except Geronimo and a small remnant of followers, it was Miles who ultimately subdued the great Apache warrior by discarding Crook's humanitarianism and forbearance. To Crook's proven techniques Miles had added one final, critical innovation: deporting Geronimo's people, and finally Geronimo himself, three-quarters of the way across the continent. Absent exile, the cycle of escape and surrender would probably have gone on until Geronimo was killed or finally died of old age. Considering Grover Cleveland's widely shared sentiments, the wonder in retrospect is that Geronimo survived capture at all. Even under Miles, the army protected him against the civilians, including President Cleveland.

When Washington consigned the Apaches and his faithful scouts to Florida, Crook grew livid. Wretched conditions and disease at Fort Marion—Miles himself called it "a second black hole of Calcutta"—aroused widespread publicity. In violation of the surrender agreement, families were split up. By 1888 federal authorities had shifted the prisoners to Alabama, but as in Florida, they continued to die of illness. Taken off to boarding school for training in the ways of the whites, the children, too, sickened and succumbed. By late 1889, a quarter of the Chiricahuas in captivity were dead. At least move the Apaches to the less lethal Indian Territory, Crook demanded. Play fair with them, keep agreements with them: "No one else in the world is so quick to see and to resent any treachery as is the Indian."

In a move which doubtless astounded many, Crook allied himself with the Indian Rights Association. The Indians, he insisted, could govern themselves. Give them citizenship and the vote. Give them jury trials and the right to bring lawsuits. Give women equal protection. Educate the Indians. Help them become commercial farmers. In general, bring them patiently along in the direction of what Crook always regarded as the vastly more advanced nineteenth-century mainstream civilization. Many of these innovations Crook had already begun when he oversaw the Apache reservations. His faith for the future lay in the fundamental belief that Indians could, and must, abandon tribalism and become more or less like whites.

In January, 1890, Crook visited the Chiricahuas for the last time at their barracks near Mobile. A lieutenant who accompanied him observed that "the Apaches crowded about the General, shaking hands, and laughing in their delight." Then Geronimo approached. "I don't want to hear anything from Geronimo," Crook remarked to the interpreter. "He is such a liar that I can't believe a word he says. I don't want to have anything to do with him." Geronimo retreated, as he had so many times before. One need not search very deeply for the sources of Crook's reaction. Four years before, Geronimo had disappeared after making peace. This led indirectly to the Chiricahuas' mass exile to Florida. Now, quarreling with Miles and bitter that Miles had captured the glory of finally bringing Geronimo to ground, Crook was also angry that the government had undermined his credibility with the Apaches; he could neither end their exile nor ease their plight. For all his understated calm, Crook needed a full measure of credit from both the conquerors and the conquered. Ironically, the greater gratitude seems to have come from the Apaches stranded in Alabama.

The battle for Indian rights, following years of hard frontier duty, had undermined Crook's health. In March, 1890, as he mounted a new public campaign in behalf of the Chiricahuas, a heart attack killed him. In a valedictory that must have galled Miles (who resolutely opposed Crook's Indian rights initiatives), William Tecumseh Sherman lauded Crook as the army's greatest Indian fighter and Indian overseer. Red Cloud, chief of the Oglala Sioux, offered a different valedictory: "General Crook came; he, at least, had never lied to us. His words gave the people hope. He died. Their hope died again. Despair came again."

By this time, the final phase of Indian suppression was ending. In 1889, Crook had persuaded the Lakotas of South Dakota to surrender 11 million acres previously set aside for them; otherwise, he warned, Washington would simply step in and seize the land. After they relinquished it, to Crook's fury, Washington actually slashed the supply of beef to the Lakotas. The starvation that ensued helped produce one of the last great nineteenth-century tragedies of the Plains Indians. A prophet named Wovoka proclaimed that Indians who performed the "ghost dance" and wore the "ghost shirt" would live to see the rise of an Indian messiah. Whites would vanish. The buffalo would return. And, so Wovoka declared, Indians who adhered to his faith could not be killed by bullets. Inevitably, these preachments made the military edgy. In the winter of 1890, the Seventh Cavalry—Custer's regiment—faced down a Sioux band at Wounded Knee, South Dakota. Apparently an Indian fired a shot, perhaps by accident. Bedlam broke out, and by the time the Wounded Knee massacre had ended, 144 Sioux and 25 troopers lay dead. As regional commander, Miles had tried hard to avoid just such a calamity by negotiating (as Crook would have done) with the Indians. Livid, he unsuccessfully filed charges against the colonel in command.

Meanwhile Washington's Indian policy was taking a decisive turn away from such slaughter and toward assimilation. A woman and her book played a big part in raising the consciousness of whites about deplorable conditions on Great Plains reservations: Helen Hunt Jackson's *A Century of Dishonor* (1881) was the *Uncle Tom's Cabin* of the Indian reform movement. The reformers' plans combined converting Indians from "paganism" to Protestantism, providing them with educational and health services, and giving them vocational training. Moving Indian children away from the reservations, their families, and their tribal traditions played a central role in assimilation policy. By 1900 the government was running hundreds of boarding and day schools in order to convert Indian children into white children.

Breaking down tribal identities proved hard to achieve, though, partly because of basic economic realities. Just as the nation entered the urban-industrial age, where the real economic opportunities lay, the government wanted to turn the Indians into conventional farmers. And how could Indians take up agriculture on barren land such as the San Carlos reservation? Regardless, in 1887 Congress passed the Dawes Severalty Act, under which reservations were to be split up. Each head of an Indian family would receive an allotment of 10 to 160 acres as private property; any remaining lands would be sold off. Crook and likeminded reformers wholeheartedly supported the legislation as a way to set the Indian on a path out of the Stone Age. Others, though, saw Dawes less idealistically as a method of stripping the Indians of their land. Before Dawes, the tribes owned 216,000 square miles, held communally; after four decades under Dawes and vast purchases by whites, tribal landholdings had plunged about two-thirds, to 75,000 square miles.

In 1894 the government finally transferred the Chiricahuas to Fort Sill, Oklahoma. Still they died, homesick for their native lands, as if they could only safely live in Arizona or New Mexico. Geronimo regretted that he had ever surrendered. "We are vanishing from the earth," he declared, but he survived. In 1905, Geronimo rode up Pennsylvania Avenue in Theodore Roosevelt's inaugural parade, attracting more attention than anyone but the president himself. A few days later, Geronimo spoke with the Great White Father, explaining to Roosevelt the plight of his people and pleading for their return to the old hunting grounds. He was sorry, Roosevelt replied, but warfare would only erupt again. "It is best for you to stay where you are." One day in February, 1909, Geronimo, drunk, toppled from his horse. Pneumonia followed. He died in the last place he might have imagined 20 years before, an ordinary hospital bed. Finally, in 1913, the

261 Chiricahuas who had survived 27 years as prisoners of war were allowed to return to New Mexico.

For Geronimo's and Crook's nemesis, Nelson Miles, the years following Geronimo's capture brought even greater fame and celebrity. In 1895 President Cleveland named Miles commanding general of the army. In a superbly effective campaign, Miles seized Puerto Rico from the Spanish in the war of 1898. Miles retired as commanding general in 1903, then tried unsuccessfully for the Democratic presidential nomination the following year. He wanted to run against Roosevelt, with whom he had feuded over military policy. With his showman friend, Buffalo Bill, Miles dabbled in motion pictures. Miles's applications for active duty in World War I were rejected. He died at 85 in 1925.

✧   ✧   ✧

For two generations after Miles's death, Washington debated Indian policy, veering back and forth between Dawes-type assimilation programs and greater tribal autonomy. In 1924 the Indians received blanket U.S. citizenship. The reservations, though, remained mired in poverty, malnutrition, disease, infant mortality, alcoholism, illiteracy, unemployment, and emotional depression. Now and again prospects brightened, especially during World War II, when defense plant jobs abounded for urbanized Indians. Navajo language codes employed in the Pacific proved unbreakable by the Japanese. American paratroopers shouted the fearsome Apache leader's name "Geronimo!" as they jumped behind enemy positions.

Meanwhile, the way Indians were portrayed changed in literature and film. Early Hollywood Westerns, for example, tended to depict the Indian with ambivalence at most, if not as a bloodthirsty marauder. After the 1960s, movies involving Indians were written so as to wring every last ounce of guilt out of predominantly white audiences. The director John Ford struck a fine balance between these extremes in his 1948 classic, "Fort

Apache." Ford pits a George Crook-like officer (John Wayne) against his Custeresque superior (Henry Fonda). Wayne wants honest negotiations with the Apaches; Fonda opts for fighting and gets his men slaughtered in a cavalry charge. Moral ambiguity pervades the film. The Apaches torture and kill whites but do so in part, at least, because other whites have abused them. The true villain is not Cochise or Geronimo but a white trader with a rigged scale who specializes in selling Indians whiskey and rifles.

During the 1960s and early 1970s, the political activism that swept through American society inspired younger Indians toward protest and rebellion. Assimilationism had gotten them nowhere, the activists insisted; Indians remained worse off than any other group in the country. Militants "captured" Alcatraz and Wounded Knee and demanded the return of ancestral lands. Claims for the righting of old wrongs piled up on court dockets. In 1972 Alaska Indians received a settlement of just under a billion dollars for lost territory.

In resorting to the courts, Indians had finally found a key to the door. They could take advantage of legal terrain pioneered a century before when General George Crook encouraged Standing Bear to sue him. Indian litigation and activism inspired judicial decisions recognizing the legal sovereignty of the tribes, or "nations," based on longstanding treaty rights. Sovereignty meant, for example, that even a state which banned gambling could not apply this ban to a tribal nation within its borders. Today a third of the 557 American Indian reservations offer commercial gaming of one variety or another, accounting for five percent of the country's $400 billion gambling industry. At the Fort Sill Apache Casino, the Chiricahuas of Oklahoma proudly trace their lineage back to Geronimo as they cordially welcome 175,000 tourists a year for games of chance. Gambling has become the greatest commercial success in the history of the reservation system. Some call it the "new buffalo." A number of tribes whose land abuts population centers or major highways have grown rich from it. This variety of buffalo, though, does not roam everywhere; as with real estate in general, location is everything. The economies, educational and unemployment levels, housing, and health care of more isolated Indian tribes still resemble those in the third world. College attendance is little more than a quarter of the national average.

One wonders what George Crook or Nelson Miles would have thought about Indian casinos. Geronimo, we may suppose, would have entirely approved. He did love to gamble, and by the end of his life was becoming a businessman in his own right. He sold whites bows and arrows, autographs, pictures of himself, the buttons off his coat, or the hat off his head. And after the souvenir hunter had departed, he would sew on more buttons, lift another hat from his collection, and patiently wait for the next customer.

2

A Dance of Skeletons Bathed in Human Tears

George Pullman, Eugene Debs, and the Railway Strike of 1894

Stephen Crane's famous short story, "The Bride Comes to Yellow Sky," begins as a newly married couple travel home by train: "The great pullman was whirling onward with such dignity of motion that a glance from the window seemed simply to prove that the plains of Texas were pouring eastward." The nervous husband, anxious to make conversation, praises the dramatic efficiency of the train: "You see, it's a thousand miles from one end of Texas to the other, and this train runs right across it and never stops but four times." Equally stunning, Crane writes, were "the dazzling fittings of the coach"; the bride's eyes "opened wider as she contemplated the sea-green figured velvet, the shining brass, silver, and glass, the wood that gleamed as darkly brilliant as the surface of a pool of oil. At one end a bronze figure sturdily held a support for a separated chamber, and at convenient places on the ceiling were frescoes in olive and silver."

Published in 1898, Crane's story perfectly illustrates how George Pullman's name had become part of the American language, an uncapitalized noun synonymous with practical elegance. In the three decades since the end of the Civil War, Pullman's "Palace cars" had transformed train travel in the United States from a dreary, grinding test of endurance into something that increasing numbers of people did for its romance and adventure. By the time of his death in 1897 at the age of 66, George Pullman had earned a securely elevated position in the pantheon of American heroes of capitalism. Or so one might have thought.

In fact, while the cars that bore his name remained popular, Pullman died brokenhearted, reviled by more people than admired him; he had to be buried beneath a massive hidden structure of railroad ties and concrete in order to be protected from vandals who, like most of the workers who had helped him build his empire, despised his memory. His greatest effort had failed—the construction of a town in his own image that would show the way to solve the war between workers and employers, or, as it was usually termed, between labor and capital. Pullman's dream collapsed for a variety of reasons, some of his own making, many beyond his control.

A key architect of Pullman's failure was Eugene Debs, the railway union leader who went to jail because of his role in opposing Pullman. Debs's career as a giant of labor began even as Pullman's virtually ended, with the great railway strike of 1894. It was ironic indeed that Debs's own dream, the American Railway Union, would itself be destroyed in the course of its historic strike against the Pullman company.

The struggle between Debs and Pullman was less a matter of personal antipathy than were some of the others in this volume, and neither man is any longer a household name. But their opposition is unusually instructive today because of the continuing issues that it reflects, among them these: Are labor and management natural enemies? What are the obligations and responsibilities of labor and business to each other, and to the public? What is the role of government in mediating disputes between them?

✧　　✧　　✧

George Pullman, born poor in upstate New York in 1831, went to work at 14 after completing nine years of schooling. Like his five siblings, including two brothers who became prominent Universalist ministers, young George was persuaded that character was the key to success—a conviction he shared with Booker T. Washington and Herbert Hoover, who also have chapters devoted to them in this book. "Character" was not given but earned through honest, hard work; devotion to family; and devout if rather generalized religious obligations. After working briefly as a clerk and then as an apprentice cabinetmaker, Pullman moved houses away from the banks of the Erie Canal when the canal was being widened near his home in Albion, New York. In the 1850s, he landed a contract in Chicago to raise buildings above the rising water level of Lake Michigan; he supervised crews that lifted a whole block of offices using screw jacks and heavy timbers, and won fame for hoisting the four-story Hotel Tremont without cracking so much as a pane of glass.

In the mid-1860s, Pullman perceived and filled the need for a comfortable and reliable way to travel long distances by rail, designing a prototype coach that he called the "Pioneer." Throughout the winter and spring of 1864, he supervised a selected crew of expert craftsmen and engineers as they completed the coach. No expense was spared—the finished car cost $20,000 (this when a sturdy three-bedroom house cost $2,000). Considered a technological marvel of the age, the Pioneer soon achieved another distinction. Its completion and final outfitting coincided approximately with the assassination of President Abraham Lincoln in April, 1865. Pullman arranged the attachment of the Pioneer to Lincoln's funeral train when it passed through Chicago en route to its final destination in Springfield,

Illinois. At a somber pace of ten miles per hour, the train had rolled through the cities and towns and villages of five states. Walt Whitman's elegy, "When Lilacs Last in the Dooryard Bloomed," describes how, past "the countless torches lit, with the silent sea of faces," the train and its "arriving coffin" crept into each "waiting depot." Now, thanks to Pullman's marketing genius and his subsequent energetic advertising campaign, the journey of the martyred president to his final resting place would forever be linked to his beautiful Pioneer.

Unlike his majestic Palace cars, the line of cars made from the prototype Pioneer, Pullman himself was physically unimpressive. He was short and stout, and while a young man, grew a small beard to give his round, pink, unlined face a degree of maturity. His manner with his employees was reserved, and even with his business associates he smiled rarely and was never heard to joke. It was said that he unbent with his wife (at least enough to sire four children). But for all his social awkwardness and reserve, Pullman was industrious and inventive—and much more: before he was 50, his combination of technical expertise, marketing savvy, and business acumen had made his company into an effective monopoly simply because he made and sold the best product of its kind.

The heart of Pullman's success lay in his perception that transcontinental rail travel requiring many days would become common after the Civil War, as it did—and as it remained well into the twentieth century. But hardly less important was his canny refusal to sell his cars to the train companies; he leased them, retaining control over their design, operation, and maintenance and greatly enhancing his profit margin.

Pullman benefited also from his early experience as a practical civil engineer and cabinetmaker. He selected his craftsmen carefully and set them to work as teams, even as he trained unskilled workers in disciplined production and manufacturing techniques that were well ahead of his time. Overseeing maintenance and construction facilities spread over four states from his Chicago offices, Pullman also devised coordinated purchase and use of such essential materials as steel, glass, fabrics, and wood. His was an early instance of the advantages of a vertically run company, and it profited mightily.

By the late 1870s, Pullman was manufacturing sleepers, dining cars, and luxury day coaches that could be adapted to offer virtually every product and convenience needed by travelers for as long as their journey took, even the week-long trek from New York to San Francisco. Passengers could rise from their sleep in one car, stroll to a second for a full breakfast served by liveried waiters, and while away the morning reading in the leather easy chairs of the library in a third. In the afternoon, they could take in an organ recital in the music room or work on their correspondence at roll-top desks. After a fine dinner, during which they might watch the sun set across the Mississippi River or behind the front range of the Rockies, they could enjoy a game of backgammon and an aperitif in the bar, then retire to their freshly turned-back beds and be lulled to sleep by the clickety-clack of the wheels as their little village rolled securely across the continent.

Such travel was not cheap, but many could afford it as the economy resumed its vigor after the Panic of 1873. Accordingly, the Pullman company was healthy and respected in 1879, a time when many industries were notorious for churning out dangerous and shoddy products. George Pullman lived well, in the grandest house on Chicago's executive row, Prairie Avenue, believing that his personal reputation for insisting on the highest quality in everything he did was a significant part of his company's success. His public relations staff energetically burnished the Pullman legend, constantly linking the man with the company: "The reputation for first-class work which this company enjoys is unique," his ads boasted. "It is no exaggeration to say that anything that bears the name of Pullman instantly secures favor and is immediately accepted as the fashion."

Always, though, there was the threat that labor unrest might destroy what Pullman had built. He rode the crest of the enormous wave of commercial energy released at the end of the Civil War, but there were serious undertows within this wave. The Panic of 1873, caused largely by railroad overbuilding, did not bother his niche business—he also owned his own bank and avoided foolish speculation—but workers' unrest and demands increased markedly as times grew harder. Typically, Pullman took the initiative with an innovative scheme to solve the labor problem; untypically, his plan was inspired by a novel.

According to his daughter, Pullman had read and been profoundly impressed by the English novelist Charles Reade's *Put Yourself in His Place*. Published in 1870, Reade's story described a violent struggle in an industrial town between unions and a factory owner who, like Pullman, had himself been a working man. In 1873, perhaps as a result of Reade's novel, Pullman visited the real-life English factory town of Saltaire, the building of which suggested a way of appeasing labor's needs without giving in to its demands for unions. In 1853 Sir Titus Salt, a manufacturer of alpaca woolens, enlarged his plant on the Aire River near Bradford. To house his workers and their families, he built a new town next to the factory. Four thousand people lived in solid stone cottages surrounded by green lawns and flower gardens on paved, tree-lined streets. Salt built a 14-acre park (complete with cricket pitch, croquet courts, and bathing facilities), a Congregational church, a library, a school, a recreational center, a hospital, even a home for the indigent and needy. He retained ownership of all the houses and other structures, and charged sufficient rent as well as fees for his various services to make a small return on his investment. But profit was not his motive. The underlying premise of Salt's experiment was that happy workers meant a trouble-free business operation. Because he was a genial and kindly man who took a strong personal interest in the people who lived in Saltaire, his experiment worked.

Pullman was operating on a much larger scale than Salt when, in 1880, his new town-and-factory south of Chicago was launched, but the principle was the same: openly avowed paternalism as an alternative to fist-in-the-face corporate militancy, fruitful cooperation with workers instead of strikes and boycotts counterpunched by lockouts and blacklists. He was starting fresh, designating for his new town 300 acres out of several thousand he had purchased near Lake Calumet in the late 1870s. Its young architect, Solon Spencer Beman, was thrilled by the opportunity to build a model community from the ground up, as was the landscape designer, Nathan Barrett.

The resulting town was far more impressive than Saltaire, as suggested by what remains today of its 800 original houses and buildings in what is now suburban Chicago. Pullman was unusually perceptive not only for his insistence on the direct connection between esthetics and profitability but for linking happiness with beauty. A lover of classical organ music, he understood the connection between esthetic form and practical function; he wanted his town as well as his business to demonstrate what he called "the commercial value of beauty." He was willing to spend whatever it took on landscaping, ornamentation, and design to make all of the buildings in his town and factory as attractive as they were functional.

For more than a decade, from its origins in 1880 to 1893, Pullman's experimental town was widely regarded as a practical, functioning Utopia. Like Brook Farm and the even earlier New Harmony communities, it was idealistic; but unlike them, it was the result of hard-headed business decisions and thus more likely to succeed. The company welcomed visitors, drawing many from the business and professional conventions that Chicago was beginning to attract. A typical group would be met at the station where Pullman's spur line from the city terminated. A smooth drive in a fleet of elegant carriages called phaetons around the town's blacktopped streets (a typical Pullman innovation, enhanced by cobblestone gutters), then a guided tour of the works themselves, would be topped off by an evening steamboat cruise on Lake Calumet. Those who chose to stay over at the new Florence Hotel (named for Pullman's favorite daughter) might attend a play or concert at the elegant Persian-themed Arcade Theater, said to be one of the finest in the country. If they wanted to take a stroll through the town's leafy neighborhoods before turning in, they could do so in complete safety, for there was no crime—and only one policeman—in the town of Pullman.

By 1885 nearly four thousand employees, mostly men, lived in Pullman. Some were single laborers who occupied block housing, but many of the skilled craftsmen and foremen lived in detached homes with their wives and children. The total population approached 9,000, and included 2,000 women and 3,000 children. One contented employee recalled what his life had been like in Chicago, in "a little cottage" with "mud on all sides of us, two beer saloons within a block, clouds of soft coal, poor sewerage," and "villainous water," along with the constant threat of sudden death from diphtheria and scarlet fever. In Pullman, "I found I could work at wages fully equal to those paid in the city, and that I could rent a whole brick house with water and drainage" for $15 a month. His children were happy and healthy now, and his wife "has seemed like a different woman."

What Pullman fatally lacked as a community, according to labor leaders and their sympathizers, was democracy—and the freedom to be less than perfect. Its inhabitants were said to be, in the words of a popular song of the time, birds in a gilded cage. There was no mayor, no city council: all the decisions concerning governance came from the company. Inspectors visited the homes to make sure they were kept clean, and fined or evicted those who failed to comply with the company's standards. Sometimes new residents, particularly recent immigrants, "lacked a decent concern for appearance," as Stanley Buder writes in summarizing the company's concerns: "In the evening they would be seen lounging on their doorsteps, the husband in his shirtsleeves, smoking a pipe, his untidy wife darning, and half-dressed children playing about them. They were soon made aware that they were expected to appear in public properly attired and that the park, not their stoops, was the place for relaxation." Image and appearance were indeed reality for Pullman; he had faith in the power of an esthetically ordered environment to change character and behavior: "On a broad avenue lined with cozy houses, with flowers and lawns on every hand, and scrupulous neatness everywhere maintained, a man of the dullest mind would feel ashamed to appear in public in his shirtsleeves or barefooted."

Living in Pullman's town was thus like riding in his Palace coaches: a public more than a private experience, almost a performance, with certain attendant costs involved. One key difference between the two experiences was that people only occasionally took long train journeys and could choose either to pay the premium for the luxury coach or to travel more cheaply in second class. But people live in their houses full time, not just occasionally, and the second-class equivalents for lodging were at inconvenient distances from their jobs. Moreover, Pullman paid lower wages than most companies (despite the enthusiastic worker's testimony above), even while he justified charging higher rents because he provided such a nice place to live.

Pullman's paternalism was also seen to be compromised by his insistence on treating the town as an investment: everything—the rental of living units and shop space, even the community church—was supposed to yield a return of six percent. Nor would he consider selling his rental units any more than he would sell his cars to the railroads. Workers were also convinced that those who chose to commute rather than live in Pullman were usually the first to be laid off during bad times.

Particularly irksome when those bad times arrived, as they did again in the 1880s, was Pullman's insistence that rents remain uncut even when workers' wages were reduced. Efforts to persuade him to alter his course were fruitless: George Pullman was serenely confident that he knew what was best for his "children," who could do nothing other than quit or complain among themselves. Pullman's town may have been a Utopia compared with the norm, but many of his workers came to think of themselves as prisoners in paradise.

✦   ✧   ✧

The man to whom George Pullman's workers would turn for help, Eugene Victor Debs, was born in 1855 to French immigrants in the western Indiana town of Terre Haute, about one hundred and eighty miles south of Chicago. His ancestors had fought in the French Revolution of 1789, and his father, who revered Voltaire and Rousseau, tutored the boy in French and German. He read Goethe and Schiller, but his favorite book as a boy and for the rest of his life was Victor Hugo's *Les Misérables*. The book's central theme, the redemption of a man who has become a criminal through no fault of his own, captured Debs as firmly as the later Broadway version of the story did American audiences.

According to his first biographer, Ray Ginger, Debs "swore allegiance" to this concept and "talked about it constantly" to everyone who would listen. Consistent with his revolutionary sympathies, young Debs was a freethinker; he won a Bible in a spelling contest but rejected his teacher's command to "read and obey" it, later saying tersely, "I did neither."

Four railroads crossed Terre Haute. Entranced by the roaring engines and lured, as were most boys then, by the romance of the rails, Debs left school at 14 (like Pullman) for his first job, scraping grease from engines. A lean and energetic six-footer with a shock of brown hair and a prominent jaw, he soon was painting the lettering on locomotives. The young Debs was outgoing and generous, sufficiently talented to paint signs freehand for friends and neighbors, seldom asking for payment. At 16 he became a fireman, the hardest work on the railroad short of pounding spikes. He lost his job during the Panic of 1873, which was caused in part by fraud in railway construction as well as overbuilding. He found work in St. Louis in 1874 as a locomotive fireman and continued his solitary reading in an effort to make up for his lost education. A few months later, when a friend slipped under a locomotive and died, Debs's frantic mother implored him to return home to safer work as a grocery clerk. Debs was still only 19, but he had already lived through the Civil War and two depressions. And he had learned, he said later, "of the hardships of the rail in snow, sleet and hail, of the ceaseless danger that lurks along the iron highway, the uncertainty of employment, scant wages and altogether trying lot of the workingman, so that from my very boyhood I was made to feel the wrongs of labor."

Later in that same year, 1874, Debs leaped at the chance to escape the grocery store and become first secretary of the local Brotherhood of Locomotive Firemen (BLF). He continued to read and to study public speaking and soon developed a reputation as a fiery crusader for workers' rights. For several years, he worked within the political system, first as city clerk in Terre Haute and later as a Democratic state legislator for one brief two-year term.

In 1877 Debs took over as treasurer for the BLF and began editing its monthly magazine. It was a period of considerable turmoil, one that the labor historian Philip S. Foner has described in *The Great Labor Uprising of 1877*. The troubles began when the Pennsylvania Railroad, along with several competing railroads, instituted wage cuts of ten percent in July. Protests led by a secret society of the different railway crafts, the Trainmen's Union, resulted in a cascading series of strikes that ultimately stopped the movement of freight on almost all raillines from coast to coast. A general strike was called in St. Louis and then in Chicago, where a police attack on demonstrators and onlookers resulted in 18 deaths. The railroad strike ended in late July. It had been chaotic and disorganized, and had nearly destroyed Debs's union and many others as well. He later took the lessons of the disastrous strikes of 1877 with him to the negotiating table.

Debs was by now a big man physically, six feet two inches tall and weighing 180 pounds, capable of confronting tough railway executives in their suites and demanding fair treatment. But he was no revolutionary firebrand; he "shuddered," he said, when workers "began to burn and plunder the property of the corporations" they worked for. "Our organization believes in arbitration," he said. He had no problem, as late as 1882, accepting the praise of William H. Vanderbilt, president of the New York Central, for his conservative role in the union's leadership.

After leaving his post as city clerk in 1884, Debs traveled widely, trying to drum up membership in his union. The battle lines were being drawn that year and next—the head of the Pennsylvania Railroad (still militant in his opposition to the unions) suggested a "rifle diet" for strikers, while the pro-labor *Chicago Times* wrote about the merits of different kinds of hand grenades applied in the proper places. Appropriately enough, it was in Chicago that the defining moment of the decade occurred in 1886, when eight immigrant anarchists were charged with and ultimately convicted of killing several policemen with a bomb during a labor protest in the Haymarket district. The prior year Debs himself, who was given to occasional fits of intemperance, had let stand an incendiary comment in his union's magazine, claiming, "legitimate warfare in the future is to be in the interest of the weak, the oppressed, those who aspire to be free. Dynamite is to be a potent weapon in the contest." Even so, he remained throughout the 1880s a relative conservative among labor leaders, denying that "there is a natural, a necessary conflict between labor and capital." Those who said so were "very shallow thinkers, or else very great demagogues."

By the 1890s, the labor situation had deteriorated radically. Two decades of increasingly violent strikes reached their apogee in 1892, when steelworkers at Homestead, near Pittsburgh, railroad switchmen in Buffalo, and silver miners in Idaho all were defeated in bloody confrontations with the owners. Millions of workers who had no intention of striking, as well as farmers and small business proprietors, were threatened with starvation as the new Panic of 1893 took hold. John Swinton, a radical journalist, reflected the bitter anguish of many when he asked, "Do we hear cries of distress from a million idle people? The wail of hunger from men, women, and children? The groans of anguish from the multitudes who suffer in many a great city? Do we see hordes of men, mingled with women, looking for work by which they may earn their daily bread? Does strife rage between the workers and the capitalists? Do we hear the tramp of a hundred thousand soldiers, bearing guns, with which they are ready to shoot their own countrymen?"

This was the tumultuous context in which Eugene Debs achieved, in June, 1893, the almost miraculous feat of persuading the dozens of different railroad brotherhoods to join together in the new American Railway Union (ARU) under his leadership. By April of the following year, the ARU was strong enough to close down James J. Hill's Great Northern Railroad, which had instituted a series of wage cuts beginning the previous August. For 14 days, workers from various locals—engineers, firemen, brakemen, switchmen, conductors, telegraphers—froze the Great Northern in its tracks, ultimately forcing it to the negotiating table where arbitration restored their lost wages. It was a huge triumph for Debs and for organized labor.

Just one year later, his ARU would be in its death throes, a casualty of the war between labor and capital that he and George Pullman would inadvertently turn into more than merely a metaphor.

✧   ✧   ✧

The successful formation of the ARU was rightly seen as both a practical and a symbolic watershed for organized labor. It occurred at precisely the same time, and in the same place, as the great celebration of American business, the World's Columbian Exposition. One year late—Columbus had, after all, sailed in 1492—the ambitious world's fair was intended to outshine the Paris Exposition of 1889, the chief memorial of which was the Eiffel Tower. The fair's beautiful White City—the temporary buildings of the exposition were all painted white—would assert not only the primacy of the new world's science and technology but the ascendancy of Chicago as the queen of the prairie. Prominent among its displays was Mr. Ferris's new revolving wheel; from its gently rocking enclosed cars, each of which held 60 people, one could see all of the fair as well as the spiderweb of rail lines that brought an astonishing 35 million visitors to Chicago in a mere 6 months from May through October.

The extraordinary demands of the exposition upon the railroads meant that George Pullman had to turn out several hundred cars and even had to buy more cars from other builders and convert them. In the town of Pullman, throughout the winter and spring of 1893, the surge of orders staved off the depression that was wracking the rest of the country. But by early summer, there were no more orders to fill. The railroads themselves, struggling to cope with shrinking revenues following their excessive expansion, lagged behind on their lease payments for cars already delivered.

On the surface, all was still well in Pullman's town and with his business. Thousands of visitors to the fair were so intrigued by the Transportation Building's meticulous plaster of paris model of the town that they went to see the real thing for themselves. Few had any cause to dispute Pullman's boast that it was a haven where "all that is ugly, and discordant and demoralizing, is eliminated, and all that inspires to self-respect, to thrift and to cleanliness of thought is generously provided." But the tourists were not allowed into Pullman's factories, where they would have seen only an echo of the year's earlier furious activity: from July, 1893 to May, 1894 the workforce in Pullman declined from

5,500 to 3,300, and many of those who remained would have their wages cut by as much as thirty percent. By Christmas of 1893, the White City was dark and cold, the visitors to the fair long gone; and in Pullman, according to Ray Ginger's evocative description, "[a]ll joy [had] passed from life. Sullen, tight-lipped women walked lead-footed through their worries. Men stood day after day by their windows and looked at the dirty black snow in the street—no work, no money, little hope."

What little hope there was came soon from Debs's ARU. By an ingenious (and legalistic) stretch, Debs said Pullman's operation qualified as a railroad company on the basis of the six-mile spur that he had built when his town was under construction and that still transported workers and others. This meant all Pullman employees, including fabric workers and seamstresses, woodworkers and metal fabricators, were eligible to join the ARU—and to expect ARU support if they went on strike. On May 11, 1894, ignoring Debs's advice to go slow and press for arbitration before striking, 3,000 Pullman workers walked off the job; those who chose not to strike were dismissed anyway, and the Pullman factories quickly shut down.

Debs spent the day of May 14 wandering the streets of Pullman, taking complaints from workers, inspecting their houses, trying to gauge the extent of their grievances and their commitment. He returned several days later and assured the strikers that he thought Pullman was a "self-confessed robber" and that they were acting nobly to "avert slavery and degradation." On June 12, he told the ARU convention in Chicago what he believed had caused the strike: "It was work and poverty in Pullmantown, or Pullemdown, until, patience ceasing to be a virtue, and further forbearance becoming treason to life, liberty and the pursuit of happiness," the workers had no choice but to walk off the job. The strikers' demands were, he thought, reasonable. They wanted rents lowered, working conditions improved, and, most of all, a return to their previous wage scale.

The sympathy that Debs conveyed for the Pullman strikers did not yet mean he wanted to commit the ARU to their support. He was frustrated because they had struck before exhausting the possibilities for arbitration with the company. The suddenness of the action meant the workers and their families had no strike fund to draw on, and the ARU had insufficient resources to carry them for long. Many important locals such as the Brotherhood of Railroad Engineers were restive under Debs's leadership and opposed to any expanded strike. On the other side, the General Managers Association—the efficient and coordinated representatives of the different railroad lines—was smarting from the recent defeat of the Great Northern and looking for a way to smash the ARU. The traveling public would react bitterly to any widespread disruption in rail service. And the Cleveland administration in Washington had repeatedly come down on the side of the corporate interests when public safety appeared to be threatened by strikes of any kind.

Thus it was with considerable uneasiness that Debs heard Jennie Curtis, a wan but vibrant young Pullman seamstress, address his ARU members on June 12. Curtis excoriated Pullman as "an ulcer on the body politic" who was conducting "a dance of skeletons bathed in human tears." Irving Stone, best remembered as the author of *The Agony and the Ecstasy,* also wrote a 1947 novel about Debs, *Adversary in the House,* in which he dramatized Jennie's speech as well as Debs's dilemma: if he allowed this charismatic young woman, "slight, black-haired, black-eyed, with pale skin and almost bloodless lips," to remain on the platform, Debs knew that he might lose control of the convention entirely. But he "could not get off his chair, for Jennie Curtis was still standing there, her toes turned in toward each other, swaying slightly at the knees, her shoulders hunched from years over a sewing machine, her fingers clenched and held hard up against her belly." When she pleaded for support from the ARU—"We're fightin' for freedom for workingmen all over the country. We ask you to stand by us and come out with us. Will you come?"—

strong men were moved to tears and rage. Debs realized that his union was determined to go out on strike, and he was compelled to go with them: "He was their leader, he had given birth to this organization . . . if the delegates wanted to go out on a strike he must lead them, for what good is a leader if he will not implement the wishes of his people?"

As Debs's biographers Ray Ginger and Nick Salvatore confirm, the actual events transpired much as Stone described them—the dramatic sequel to Jennie Curtis's talk is indeed hard to exaggerate. Debs did manage to put off the strike for a time, pressing Pullman for arbitration, only to be frustrated by the company's absolute intransigence: its rock-solid position was that management, not labor, determined wages and working conditions. The response of Pullman vice-president Thomas Wickes to one union proposal was typical: Would the company at least consider restoring wages to the May, 1893, level? Wickes replied that the men making the request no longer worked for Pullman, and that they therefore had nothing more to say concerning the company and its policies than "the man on the sidewalk."

Predictable attacks on Pullman's character soon followed. The *Chicago Times* called him a "cold-blooded autocrat" with "small, piggish eyes" and an expression of "supercilious contempt for the world at large, mingled with traces of self-satisfaction at his own comfortable state." John Swinton compared him to his friends the hog butchers, the personification of "extortion, banality and churlishness." But even some of Pullman's fellow industrialists thought he was going too far: Mark Hanna, the New York tycoon who would become famous for helping maneuver Theodore Roosevelt into the White House, wondered aloud, "What, for God's sake," did Pullman think he was doing? "The damned idiot ought to arbitrate, arbitrate, arbitrate! . . . A man who won't meet his men half-way is a God-damn fool."

On June 26, after continued rebuffs from the company, Debs ordered all Pullman cars to be uncoupled from trains on lines worked by the ARU—covering, in effect, most of the western two-thirds of the country. The railroads responded that their contractual obligations with Pullman exposed them to lawsuits if they allowed his cars to be sidetracked. ARU members were fired on the spot and replaced with eager strikebreakers. The great railway strike of 1894 was fully launched.

✧   ✧   ✧

Among the perquisites of George Pullman's position were several elaborately equipped Palace cars that each summer conveyed him and his family—as well as their stable of six horses and a dozen grooms and other servants—away from sultry Chicago to their mansion on the New Jersey coast. Pullman got out of town before the strike began, leaving the mess he had created in the hands of the Managers. Eugene Debs remained, of course. A one-man cyclone of activity, he pleaded for support from other unions, including Samuel Gompers's American Federation of Labor, with partial success. He publicly berated his management opponents even as he secretly maneuvered for negotiations with them. And he appealed for support, or at least tolerance, from a public angry at being inconvenienced.

Few other leaders were better equipped for these difficult tasks. Eloquent testimony survives to show that Debs was personally persuasive when speaking to one or two people but that he was even more effective on the speaker's platform. There he was already the "electric presence" that Upton Sinclair captured so memorably in his 1906 novel, *The Jungle,* which has Debs addressing the striking Chicago meatpackers in 1904: "When he spoke he paced the stage, lithe and eager, like a panther. He leaned over, reaching out for his audience; he pointed into their souls with an insistent finger. His voice was husky from much speaking, but the great auditorium was as still as death, and every one heard him." In a similar tone Debs now told the ARU that "the struggle with the Pullman Company has developed into a contest between the producing classes and the money power of the country." The railroad owners, in the form of the General Managers Association, had come "to the rescue" of Pullman and were willing to "stand by him in his devilish work of starving his employees to death." As of July 1, two weeks into the strike, the union was holding firm, Debs said, "with no sign of violence or disorder." The railroads were on the ropes at this point, he later claimed: "Their immediate resources were exhausted, their properties were paralyzed, and they were unable to operate their trains."

Debs exaggerated the strength of his position, just as his magnetism on stage led his followers to excessive optimism. The Managers had cleverly perceived that the federal government would resist any interference with the passage of the nation's mail. By hooking mail cars to Pullman cars and sending them down the tracks together, the Managers placed Debs in a dilemma. If he allowed his men to stop the trains, he would be violating federal law; if he let the trains pass, mail cars and Pullman cars alike, both the Pullman workers and the ARU would go down to failure. Debs offered to provide crews for mail trains if the Pullman cars were detached, but the Managers of course refused. Instead, they appealed to the United States attorney general for an injunction prohibiting the ARU from interfering with their operations. Ironically, they based their appeal on a provision of the recently passed Sherman Antitrust Act (1890), which was generally perceived as an effort to bring large corporations under a degree of governmental regulation. However, a key provision of the Sherman Act banned any "contract, combination . . . or conspiracy" that restrained interstate commerce. Union leaders assumed that strikes, even though they obviously "restrained" commerce, could not be enjoined by this provision of the Sherman Act.

Unfortunately for Debs, the opposite view was held by President Grover Cleveland's attorney general at the time, a burly and aggressive former corporation lawyer from Boston named Richard Olney. Most of Olney's clients had been railroads, on whose boards of directors, in some cases, he had sat for more than thirty years. As the strike began, he was still on the board of the Burlington company, which was involved in the current dispute—a clear, even flagrant, conflict of interest. Olney condemned a nationwide strike that shut down the railroads as automatically illegal, not a strike at all but a "Debs Rebellion." He was on record as looking for a chance to step in to break the Pullman strike.

On July 1 and 2, Olney got his chance, when several thousand protestors at the Rock Island Railroad yards in Chicago brought all traffic to a halt. There was no bloodshed, simply a clotting of the arteries of transportation. The following day, two federal judges in Chicago issued an injunction prohibiting strikers, and their leaders, from doing anything that might lead to violence or disorder. On the afternoon of July 2, a federal marshal tried repeatedly to read and explain the injunction to the milling crowd. He warned them that unless they quit blocking the tracks and dispersed, they would be liable to arrest for rioting. Jeered and mocked by the mob, the marshal telegraphed Olney, saying the situation was "desperate" and that it was "impossible to move trains here without having the Fifteenth Infantry from Fort Sheridan ordered here now."

Olney had already authorized the deputizing of 5,000 federal marshals in Chicago. Charged with protecting interstate freight and passenger trains as well as the movement of the mails, some of these men were railroad employees, hardly objective officers of the law. Many of the others were vagrants, roustabouts, and thugs—"a very low, contemptible set of men," in the eyes of a *Chicago Herald* reporter.

The unprecedented intrusion of the attorney general into the affairs of the city of Chicago on behalf of the railroads was resented not only by the Chicago mayor and his police chief, who considered that he had the situation well in hand, but by the governor of Illinois, John Altgeld. Altgeld, a German immigrant who prided himself on his liberal and humanitarian sympathies, was reviled by the press and the political and business establishment for having pardoned the surviving four men convicted for the Haymarket bombing deaths soon after taking office in 1893. When he denounced the presence of the marshals and asserted that the Chicago police and the Illinois militia were fully capable of handling the disturbances, Altgeld was disparaged by the famously conservative *Chicago Tribune* as a "lying, hypocritical, demagogical, sniveling . . . sympathizer with riot, with violence."

On the night of July 3, Eugene Debs was sound asleep in his room at the Leland Hotel on Jackson Street. It was a typically hot and muggy Chicago night, and he had left the window open to catch the cooling breeze off Lake Michigan. Shortly after midnight, he was startled by the sounds of shouted orders, whinnying horses, and tent pegs being hammered into the ground. The army had arrived from Fort Sheridan, 25 miles north of Chicago, in the form of the Seventh Cavalry Division's Fifteenth Infantry Regiment. As great a surprise to Governor Altgeld as it was to Debs, the deployment had been authorized by President Cleveland at Olney's request. Though their purpose was to restore order, the soldiers would soon be involved in the worst violence of the entire strike, in part because of the attitude of at least some of the troops. Frederick Remington, the artist famous for his western themes, was then traveling with the soldiers and observed their reactions to the local, largely immigrant population as they deployed near the Union Stockyards. It was a hostile, ugly crowd of bearded foreigners, Remington later recalled, "a seething mass of smells, stale beer, and bad language," shouting their support for the strikers and abusing the soldiers in "Hungarian or Polack." With a disdain that Remington clearly shared, one soldier looked at the crowd and remarked wonderingly to a comrade, "Say, do you know them things ain't human!"

✧   ✧   ✧

"In retrospect," concludes John Papke in *The Pullman Case*, "it is not surprising that the boycott became violent but rather that the violence was slow to begin. With Debs trying desperately to direct 150,000 American Railway Union members, other unions joining the cause, and wildcat strikes breaking out against individual lines, it would have been impossible to prevent violence. With the General Managers' Association sending out spies, hiring strikebreakers, and rerouting their trains to irritate the public, severe social disorder was certain."

On the evening of July 5, an enormous fire, clearly the work of arsonists, destroyed several of the remaining buildings of that hymn to capitalism, the Columbian Exposition. Simultaneous fires broke out elsewhere in different and widespread yards where railcars were overturned and burned. The following day, entire rows of cars, tightly grouped together in an Illinois Central yard beyond the reach of water hoses, were filled with waste paper and axle grease and set afire. Two rioters were shot dead by a railroad agent. By evening an orgy of arson had reduced more than seven hundred cars to smoldering husks: "It was pandemonium let loose," one observer said, "the fire leaping along for miles . . . a mad scene where riot became wanton and men and women became drunk on their excesses." The following afternoon, July 7, soldiers sent out to clear the tracks of debris were attacked by rioters. Struck by stones from the mob, the soldiers charged with fixed bayonets, wounding several. Then, badly outnumbered, the soldiers were ordered to fire at will. By the time police reinforcements arrived and the shooting ceased, 4 rioters were dead and 20 wounded.

Ultimately, more than seventeen rioters would die in Chicago during the disruptions and 40 more in confrontations with federal troops across the country. The strike at its peak idled more than a quarter-million workers, disrupting train service from Minnesota to Texas and from Indiana to California. As had been the case with the 1877 strike, the violence in the Pullman strike was particularly intense in Chicago. Debs and his ARU argued, with varying degrees of plausibility, that they had done everything within their power to conduct the strike peacefully. They insisted that most of the rioters were criminal opportunists, not union members; that no proof was offered to show the exposition arson was committed by union sympathizers; that railroad agents had incited some of the violence; that the railroad yards had been left deliberately unguarded as an incitement to attack; and that the Chicago and national press had exaggerated both the violence and the civil disorder brought about by the strike and the Pullman boycott that had triggered it. No matter: the boycott and the ensuing strike became a public relations disaster for Debs and for the ARU. Even the sympathetic Jane Addams, whose Hull House employees wore the white ribbons that the workers displayed, recalled the strike later with distinctly mixed feelings: she had been unable to visit her dying sister because of it.

For much of the larger public, the strike became a symbol of anarchy and "Dictator Debs" the leader of its "riotous emissaries." He was said to be "as much a criminal as are the outlaws who hold up trains in the far west," or, at best, an alcoholic whose mind was "in a disordered condition." *Harper's Weekly,* a respected journal of the time, caricatured Debs as an emperor wearing a crown and sitting on a bridge labeled "Highway of Trade," below which were pictured stalled trains carrying food and mail. Attorney General Olney pressed for an indictment of Debs for incitement to violence, based on the July 2 injunction prohibiting him from doing anything that might lead to civil disorder. Despite the best efforts of the celebrated Clarence Darrow in his defense, Debs was convicted and sentenced to six months in prison, along with several other union officers. Within a year and a half of the beginning of the strike, his dream of the ARU as a super-union of railway workers "was a corpse," in the words of Almont Lindsay—"killed by one strike and the Federal government."

The Pullman strike marked the crest of labor violence in the United States in the nineteenth century. Debs turned away in disgust from the American system of business as it was then constituted, broadening his role far beyond that of a mere union leader. He became a Socialist, arguing from countless platforms across the country that such essential services as railroads and utilities should be nationalized rather than operated for private profit. In 1912, in the third of his five runs for president as the head of the American Socialist Party, he received six percent of the popular vote. He went to jail again in 1919, this time for two years, for opposing governmental repression during World War I. In December, 1921, Debs was pardoned by President Warren G. Harding at the urging of, among others, Upton Sinclair. Debs died in 1926, respected by progressives for having helped social legislation to come about and revered by radicals as, in Max Eastman's words, "the sweetest strong man in the world."

George Pullman was the declared victor in the war between his company and Debs's union, but his public image, which he had worked for so many years to shape, was shattered. Jane Addams compared Pullman to King Lear for his domineering paternalism, implicitly flattering him as a figure of noble pathos. But even the conservative three-man fact-finding committee appointed by President Cleveland in August, 1894, came away disillusioned after its extensive interview with Pullman. The commissioners agreed that the workers' salary demands were unjustified, given the economic circumstances of the company; but, more significantly, they said Pullman could have averted the strike if he had made concessions on the rent he charged them. Perhaps more than they intended, and certainly more than was justified, Pullman was depicted in the commission's published report as a rich opportunist who took the opportunity of a depression to squeeze his workers.

Pullman's last few years of life were darkened by his Pyrrhic victory over the strikers. His actions answered, in ways that could not have pleased him, the questions that were posed in the opening pages of this chapter. Are labor and management natural enemies? Yes, if management—that is, Pullman—refuses out of hand to consider workers' demands as a legitimate starting point for negotiation. What are the obligations and responsibilities of labor and business to each other, and to the public? Certainly, on Pullman's part, the need at the very least to stay on the scene of the battle he had initiated, rather than vacationing for the summer in eastern resorts—an obligation more than met by Debs and his continued presence in Chicago throughout the strike. Finally, what is the role of government in mediating disputes between management and labor? In this instance, although the violence on the part of the union had justified government intervention to protect the public, the federal government acted primarily in behalf of Pullman and his allies, while the Chicago city government and the state of Illinois tilted toward the side of the strikers. What George Pullman had begun as a grand experiment, even a kind of workers' Utopia, had come to a sad end— a dispiriting conclusion that overshadowed his earlier remarkable successes, particularly his imaginative contribution to safe and comfortable railway travel. Now he worried about assassination—two such attempts were thwarted—and his morbid fear that his corpse would be defiled after his death led him to design a tomb fit for a pharaoh, and one that was just as impervious.

In a final ironic twist, Pullman's successor as president of his company was Robert Todd Lincoln, the son of the man whose murder had helped launch his career and his company so many years before. In 1898, the year after Pullman's death, a court order required the company to divest itself of its real estate holdings, a course of action that Lincoln approved of wholeheartedly. The Pullman Palace Car Company itself lived on until 1969, when it closed its doors 102 years after its birth, an irrelevance in an age of more efficient but far less glamorous interstate highways and jet planes.

By the time the company went out of business, labor and management had reached what many observers took to be a standoff or even a grudging accommodation. A third of the American work force belonged to unions, and during the 1950s and 1960s, wages and benefits reached record highs right along with corporate profits. Since then, though, a massive shift has occurred. While the economy has grown dramatically, as have the incomes of corporate executives, blue-collar wages have fallen in real terms. Just as in the 1890s, unions have come under continual fire. The remaining unionized portion of the work force today is only a fraction of what it was in the mid-twentieth century. When the American Railway Union called its strike a century ago, George Pullman could not threaten to move his Palace car company to China or Mexico. His twenty-first century counterparts can.

3

Cast Down Your Bucket Where You Are

Booker T. Washington, W.E.B. Du Bois, and Equal Rights for Blacks

The words of Booker T. Washington on that sweltering September afternoon in 1895 were simple, direct, and forceful. They described the plight of a ship's crew that was dying of thirst for lack of fresh water. Washington was not an ordained preacher, but he was telling his audience of several thousand listeners a story designed to teach a lesson, a parable of the kind that all of them, black or white, had grown up hearing in Baptist or Methodist Sunday schools. His voice, a rich and reassuring baritone, easily reached the back of the hall at the Atlanta Cotton States and International Exposition, which was filled to capacity. His audience consisted largely of uneasy whites, most of whom had never before heard a black speak to them from a stage, but there were also several hundred attentive Negroes* seated in their segregated section far back from the speaker.

---

*Negroes: Washington's preferred term.

The ship's captain, Washington explained, had signaled another ship approaching his, begging for "Water, water; we die of thirst!" Back came the puzzling advice, "Cast down your bucket where you are." After the same plea met with the same response for the fourth time, the desperate captain obeyed and lowered his bucket where he was. Up rose the life-saving water—the captain finally comprehending that, although he could not yet see land, his ship was sailing through the fresh-water estuary created by the immense flow of the Amazon River into the Atlantic Ocean.

The meaning of this story for himself and "his race," as Washington went on to explain it, was that opportunities lay all about them. They needed only to cast down their buckets, "making friends in every manly way of the people of all races by whom we are surrounded." Specifically, Washington reminded the blacks in his audience that they must be prepared to start at the bottom, as workers, not executives, or as grade-school teachers, not university professors; that they would have to earn the respect of whites rather than demand it as a right guaranteed by law; and that mere proximity to each other did not require that white and black mix socially. To emphasize that point, he introduced his second most memorable image, signaling his own apparent acquiescence to what would become the "separate but equal" doctrine justifying segregation: "In all things that are purely social we can be as separate as the fingers, yet one as the hand in all things essential to mutual progress."

The white members of Washington's audience were similarly enjoined to recognize the worth of the blacks, to acknowledge their loving and loyal devotion in the past. Now whites had to help make blacks prosperous customers and clients for their goods and services, rather than resentful victims of poverty and despair. Let our "sixteen millions of hands help you pull our common load forward," Washington pleaded. The choice was stark: whites could either help blacks to prosper or they could foster the resulting crime and ignorance that would drag them all down together.

Even at the time, Washington's Atlanta Exposition Address would become the "Atlanta Compromise" to some of his sterner opponents who felt that it told whites what they wanted to hear. But to most of those who heard it then or who read about it in the months to come, white or black, this speech was equal in its thoughtful eloquence to the best speeches of an age renowned for platform rhetoric. The awe-struck reporter for the *New York World,* James Creelman, noted that the greatest speaker of the nineteenth century was commonly agreed to be the former prime minister of England, William Gladstone. Yet not even Gladstone could surpass the astonishing performance of this "Negro Moses."

Washington impressed Creelman in part by his sheer physicality. He was then 39 years old and exuded vitality. His "remarkable figure" was "tall, bony, straight as a Sioux chief, high forehead, straight nose, heavy jaws, and strong, determined mouth, with big white teeth, piercing eyes and a commanding manner. The sinews stood out on his bronzed neck, and his muscular right arm swung high in the air, with a lead-pencil grasped in the clenched brown fist." His strong voice "rang out clear and true. . . . Within ten minutes the multitude was in an uproar of enthusiasm. . . . The fairest women of Georgia stood up and cheered. It was as if the orator had bewitched them." This "angular Negro, standing in a nimbus of sunshine, surrounded by the men who once fought to keep his race in bondage," had ushered in a "new epoch."

The reporter had exaggerated his commanding presence: Washington was stocky rather than "bony" and "angular," and looked more like a poor black farmer than a Sioux chief. He had in fact arrived at the exposition grounds in a state of intense nervous anxiety that made him fear he might collapse. He had been given the opportunity, as president of Tuskegee Institute, to speak at the opening of a building constructed for the exposition that would be "devoted wholly to showing the progress of the Negro since freedom," a building "designed and erected wholly" by

black students from Tuskegee. The building was a symbol of
Tuskegee's principles of education under Washington—it was
practical and useful, and thus entirely in keeping with the commercial theme of the Atlanta Exposition. Washington had proved
his own usefulness by lobbying for congressional support of the
exposition. In return, the grateful businessmen of Georgia invited
him to speak. One hand had washed the other.

And yet he knew that he had also been given an opportunity
to fail. A white farmer in Tuskegee warned Washington that
although he had spoken earlier to separate white and black audiences, he had never addressed both groups together. Washington
thought about the farmer's parting shot—"you have got yourself
into a tight place"—and compared himself before his speech to a
condemned man approaching the gallows. Many whites were
hoping he would make a fool of himself, Washington knew; he
had it in his power to "make such an ill-timed address" that any
similar invitation to a black speaker in the South would be pre-
cluded for years to come. If he failed, he would not usher in a "new
epoch" in race relations in America, as he hoped. On the contrary,
he would perpetuate the miserable conditions that now existed.

Washington's careful omission of the truth about black and
white relations in the South provides much of the real drama
behind his Atlanta address. Despite the cheering of the "fairest
women of Georgia" and the rosy aura of friendship emanating
from the white leaders of Georgia sharing the stage with him, and
for all of Washington's protestations about affectionate regard
between the two races, life for blacks in the South was becoming
steadily harder in the 1890s. Legal subterfuges and manipulations
such as literacy tests, designed to prevent blacks from voting, had
eroded the gains brought by Reconstruction following the Civil
War. By 1895, blacks exercised hardly more political, economic,
or social power than they had had as slaves four decades earlier.
But even worse was the fear of lynching from which blacks suffered. Terrorist vigilantes had engaged in a three-decade-long orgy
of lynching. So many gruesome burnings and dismemberings of

blacks were described in local newspapers that to read them today indicates that blacks were living through a kind of American pogrom, one that had the potential to become a racial holocaust. In 1892 alone, the worst year, 156 black men were lynched, mostly in the South. Some sense of the horrors and degradation blacks suffered is evoked by accounts of the excursion trains chartered for holiday parties, with guests sometimes numbering in the thousands traveling to attend lynchings as they would a band concert. Many of the celebrants would buy charred body parts of the victims as souvenirs.

This meant that Washington was talking about blacks casting down their buckets to survive in a white world even as they were drowning in their own blood. He knew this, as did his black and white listeners (as suggested by his earlier mental image of the gallows awaiting him). But he chose to ignore the ugly truth in pursuit of a pragmatic solution to the problem. Blacks had nothing on their side but moral right and Reconstruction-era laws that had once protected them but were now either not enforced or flouted. Whites had everything else: money, power, and numbers. As a Christian and an American, Washington could demand that whites allow blacks to gain the freedom and equality they deserved and castigate them for their sins if they failed to do so. But he had "early learned that it is a hard matter to convert an individual by abusing him, and that this is more often accomplished by giving credit for all the praise-worthy actions performed than by calling attention alone to the evil done." That there *had* been "evil done" was acknowledged by Washington in his address when he cited a hymn linking "oppressor with oppressed," clearly meaning whites oppressing blacks. But he made that reference for the purpose of showing how the races are irretrievably conjoined, as the rest of the hymn continues: "close as sin and suffering joined/ We march to fate abreast."

Washington did have at least two weapons other than the moral club, which he declined to use. One was the compelling fact that his utilitarian, pragmatic philosophy, which he had devoted his life to persuading blacks to adopt as their own, was so clearly in tune with the Protestant ethic of business success espoused by whites. He also believed, as one presumably must believe when living in a democracy, that most people—white and black alike—wanted to behave decently and would do so if given good reason. Blacks should take heart in the fact that "there is something in human nature which always makes an individual recognize and reward merit," regardless of race. Merit could be demonstrated more easily by useful concrete examples than by abstractions, and blacks were as capable as any, perhaps more capable, of providing these examples. Tangible evidence of competence went "a long way in softening prejudices. The actual sight of a first-class house that a Negro has built is ten times more potent than pages of discussion about a house that he ought to build, or perhaps could build."

A more appealing proposition for Washington's white audiences wherever he spoke (and he was much in demand) is hard to imagine: the burden of guilt for centuries of oppression was lifted from the whites, free of charge. In its place was solid evidence of productive benefit to society, provided by the very people they had so grievously abused.

Washington enhanced this appeal to white self-interest with his personal story. Simply put, he was his own best argument for the validity of his view, a stunning example of what his race could do if given half a chance. He had not published his autobiography, *Up From Slavery,* at the time of his Atlanta speech—it would not appear for another six years—but his life story was already widely known by 1895. It was an inspirational story as eloquent, and perhaps as embroidered, in the fashion of nineteenth-century autobiography, as *The Narrative of Frederick Douglass* (1845), the former slave who became one of the great black leaders preceding Washington. Douglass had died the previous February. Many who heard and read Washington's Atlanta speech, and probably Washington himself, regarded it as a confirmation that the torch of leadership had now passed from one generation of blacks to the next. But Washington's achievements transcended race in a way that was not available to Douglass. What he accomplished with Tuskegee was a classic story of entrepreneurial ingenuity in the tradition of Benjamin Franklin and of the rags-to-riches fictional heroes created by the then-popular novelist Horatio Alger. Washington was the embodiment of the optimistic American belief that with "luck and pluck," anyone can succeed and prosper. While nothing could endear a black leader, regardless of his accomplishments, to the so-called mudsill whites, after his speech in Atlanta in 1895, white Republican business and political leaders came to regard Washington as the safe and authorized leader of African Americans. Some of their reasons for doing so were self-serving, but the facts of Washington's rise from poverty to fame were reason enough to admire him.

Born in 1856 in a log cabin in Hale's Ford, Virginia, Washington didn't even know the exact year of his birth until after he wrote his autobiography. Like Frederick Douglass, he never knew anything of his father other than the fact that he was a white man, perhaps related to the farmer who owned his mother. He was ten years old, just beginning grammar school, when he created his own virtual identity.

His teacher required a last name and he didn't have one, so the boy took the surname "Washington"—thereby laying the foundation for himself as the father of his own "nation," as George Washington had been for the United States. Before he could establish this "nation," though, he had to endure years of exacting trials. As a very young boy, he slept on a dirt floor and wore flax shirts—flax was the rough fiber residue left by the process of making linen—that felt like "chestnut burrs, or a hundred small pinpoints" on his soft flesh until the garments became softened with sweat and dirt. For a time, he worked in a salt mine, beginning at 4 A.M. so he could attend school later in the day, until a kind and wealthy widow hired him as a houseboy and encouraged him in his ambition to learn. At age 16, he walked much of the 500 miles from Malden, West Virginia, where his family had earlier moved, to Hampton, Virginia. His goal was to enroll in a new school for black students, the Hampton Institute, where poor boys and girls could learn to be tradesmen, mechanics, and teachers in return for performing menial but necessary tasks—tending furnaces, preparing and serving food, and the like. Before winning admission, he had to show a stern white woman that he could sweep and dust a classroom to her exacting requirements.

Washington was so naïve when he arrived at Hampton that his bed with its two sheets puzzled him—he slept on top of both the first night, under both the second. However, it did not take long for Hampton's visionary leader, Samuel Chapman Andrews, a white man, to see in Washington a leader of his own caliber, and he groomed the boy carefully. Washington worked at several jobs after graduating, including teaching back in West Virginia, before General Andrews, as he was always called, invited him to return to teach at Hampton in 1879. In 1881 black community leaders in the Alabama hamlet of Tuskegee asked Andrews for help in finding a leader for a new school they wanted to start, to be called the Tuskegee Institute. Andrews warmly recommended Washington for the post; the boy who had never seen bed sheets only nine years earlier had become an energetic teacher and administrator. He was just 25 years old.

Most of *Up From Slavery* describes how Washington built Tuskegee Institute from nothing more than a rented church and an idea in 1881 into a flourishing operation by 1901, with 1,400 students; 110 faculty and staff; 66 buildings, all but 4 erected by students; and a campus and fields occupying 2,300 acres. Since the new institute had very little external support from state or local government, it would have to be self-sustaining insofar as that was feasible; this would enable Washington to persuade both the state government and, even more important, wealthy donors to help it. His account of this process in his autobiography followed a pattern of showing through anecdotes and examples how competence wins acceptance.

Washington's favorite and oft-repeated anecdote concerned the efforts of the students to make and sell bricks. Starting from nothing, not even a kiln, and working their way by trial and error through a series of failures, the students at last succeeded in making bricks as good as any on the commercial market. This success taught Washington a critical "lesson in regard to the relations of the two races in the South": that black students needed to prove their education was "not making them worthless. . . . As the people of the neighbourhood came to us to buy bricks, we got acquainted with them. . . . We had something they wanted; they had something which we wanted." Thus was laid "the foundation for the pleasant relations that have continued to exist between us and the white people in that section, and which"—he concluded, with hopeful exaggeration—"now extend throughout the South."

Booker T. Washington was a firm believer in the Great Man theory so prominent in the nineteenth century—no education in books, he said, was "equal to that which can be gotten from contact with great men and women." Fortunately for Washington, many of the great captains of industry (or, less admiringly, robber barons) to whom he appealed for money, such as the oil tycoons John D. Rockefeller and Henry H. Rogers, and Julius Rosenwald, the president of Sears, Roebuck, and Company, were like him: hard-headed realists who could be persuaded by facts, not sentiment. Washington had to be stubborn and to live with rejection: Collis P. Huntington, the "traction magnate" of Los Angeles whose magnificent house and library and gardens are today one of the glories of southern California, brushed Washington off with a paltry two dollars the first time he was approached. Washington persisted in his requests over the years until he persuaded Huntington to donate $50,000. Andrew Carnegie, Tuskegee's greatest benefactor, gave Washington a lump sum of $600,000 to build a library. The key to Washington's success with wealthy donors was that he learned very early to link bequests with specific building or educational projects; he understood that his benefactors detested abstractions as much as he did, and promised them tangible returns on their investment.

During the last 20 years of his relatively short life—he died in 1915 at the age of 59—Washington would become the most famous black leader in the United States. He marched from one triumph to the next, always linked with the Institute that was the symbol of his driving compulsion to make blacks into fully participating members of American society. In 1896 he received an honorary doctorate from Harvard, whose president, Charles W. Eliot, praised him as a "teacher, wise helper of his race, good servant of God and country." In 1901 he dined at the White House with President Theodore Roosevelt (who then felt compelled to assure outraged Southern supporters that the dinner was not a formal occasion and would not be repeated). And in 1903, Andrew Carnegie would elaborate on what had already become something of a cliché, praising Washington as the "modern Moses who leads his race" through education to a Promised Land, not one of milk and honey but of something much better—productive parity with whites.

✧   ✧   ✧

That promised land was certainly not yet possible in the South, where 90 percent of the black population then lived, mostly on farms. It was somewhat more conceivable in the North, where William Edward Burghardt Du Bois was born in 1868, in the small western Massachusetts city of Great Barrington. New England had been the heart of abolitionist fervor before the Civil War, and overt manifestations of prejudice against the few blacks who lived there were still frowned upon as showing bad taste. There were only about fifty blacks in Great Barrington's population of 5,000, which made them relatively invisible and therefore innocuous. Moreover, Du Bois inherited from his white father aquiline features and light skin, and he was marked from his early childhood as intellectually outstanding, so he passed through high school without difficulty. But he did not look back fondly on his early years in Great Barrington; it was then a faltering mill town in the hinterlands, not an intellectual haven like Cambridge, and it was hardly less racist in its underlying attitudes, Du Bois felt, than the South. An unusual combination of abilities—an incisive and analytical mind paired with a poetic and intuitive emotional sensibility—heightened his resentment at racial slights, subtle though they might have been, when he was growing up.

Initially, Du Bois's path resembled Washington's in that both had to settle for less education than their abilities warranted. Though his family was middle class, it lacked the means to send Du Bois to Harvard. He went instead, in 1888, to Fisk College, a black institution in Tennessee. His excellent performance there led to a scholarship at Harvard as a member of the junior class in 1890. It was then that Du Bois began to achieve true academic distinction. While teaching in rural southern classrooms during his summers at Fisk, he had seen at firsthand the kind of poverty that Washington grew up with. He became no less committed than Washington to education as a way out of such conditions, not just for himself but for all blacks. But at Harvard his studies were not, as Washington's had been, in agriculture, applied engineering, and small-business methods in an all-black school. They were in philosophy, literature, history, economics, sociology, and psychology, each of which demanded a mastery of conceptual thinking, of comprehending the rarefied world of abstract ideas—all achieved at one of the most respected colleges in the country, in competition with some of the best minds of his generation, white or black.

Du Bois earned a second bachelor's degree from Harvard College in 1890 and a master's degree from Harvard in 1891, then won a scholarship to study in Berlin for two years. There he mastered the German language and enhanced his understanding of American race problems through a comparative study of similar political and social developments in Europe, Africa, and Asia. Returning to Harvard in 1894, Du Bois completed his dissertation, later published as the first volume in the Harvard Historical Series, *The Suppression of the African Slave Trade in America,* and received his Ph.D. in 1896. That was the same year in which Washington received his Harvard honorary degree, well deserved to be sure but won for his entrepreneurial and humanitarian labors, not for scholarship. Du Bois's earned doctorate rewarded his unparalleled scholarly achievement—he was the first black man to be so recognized by Harvard.

During the next decade, Du Bois achieved a stature in the black intellectual community that matched Washington's with the greater black population. His 1896 research project in Philadelphia focusing on black neighborhoods led to a faculty position teaching sociology at Atlanta University, where for 13 years he led studies into and wrote extensively about blacks in various aspects of their lives, including business, education, religion, and crime.

By 1903, when Du Bois published his most popular work, *The Souls of Black Folk,* his relationship with Washington was one of mutual but wary respect. Washington had tried unsuccessfully three times to hire Du Bois to teach at Tuskegee, and Du Bois had publicly stated his admiration for "the Wizard of Tuskegee" many times. In the opening paragraphs of *The Souls of Black Folk,* he seemed to confirm his high estimation of Washington in a way that promised more praise to come: "Easily the most striking thing in the history of the American Negro since 1876 is the ascendancy of Mr. Booker T. Washington. . . . Today he stands as the one recognized spokesman of his ten million fellows, and one of the most notable figures in a nation of seventy millions."

In fact, this apparent praise is carefully couched: words such as "striking," "recognized," "ascendancy," and "notable" are value neutral, useful evasions that promise more than they deliver. They precede a measured and thoughtful critique that initiated the eventual dismantling of Washington's reputation and earned Du Bois the revered leader's undying enmity and contempt.

The title alone of Du Bois's chapter—"Of Booker T. Washington and Others"—was provocatively magisterial, and his reference to the "unquestioning followers" who constituted "Mr. Washington's cult" was clearly condescending. As Du Bois's tone suggests, their disagreement was in part based upon professional status and social class. Though both were educators, Du Bois was an intellectual, self-defined and proud of it, and he harbored the barely hidden contempt for administrators common to professors then and now. Washington was a practical man who disdained intellectuals as troublemakers who got in his way. Equally important was the fact that Washington lifted himself "up from slavery" into the middle class, while Du Bois, born into the middle class, looked down on it as bourgeois and philistine. Finally, they were distinctively different physically and emotionally. Washington was "thick-set and slow moving," in the words of Francis L. Broderick, with "the assurance of a self-trained man" who always looked "like a farmer in his Sunday best." Du Bois was "slight, nervous in his movements," "witty and convivial" with his intellectual peers but "aloof from the Negro masses." With his fine features and light skin and his elegantly trimmed goatee, he had both the appearance and the manner of a Spanish grandee. On the relatively few occasions when they met, Du Bois recalled later, he and Washington had little to say to each other.

Inevitably, the two men disagreed over the purpose and nature of education, though both saw it as vital. Washington viewed it as a bottom-up device for lifting blacks out of poverty and ignorance. Education should teach what was useful, such as chemistry and biology as they applied to agronomy, and aid in the development of a morally upright character, especially by training teachers for elementary and secondary schools. His mission at Tuskegee was to take the average black boy and girl and turn them into productive and moral citizens.

Du Bois did not object to Washington's "programme of industrial education," as he called it, either then or later. He did object to its dominance, and especially its exclusion of the intellectual or esthetic components of education—for Du Bois, these were key elements in increasing black pride, self-respect, and assertiveness. He argued for a "top-down" structure, in effect—the most important task of education was to find and motivate the best of the black population, the superior "talented tenth" of its men and women, to lead the rest. The ultimate goal of such an education was to challenge America to give blacks what they deserved, not to plead with it for a place at the table.

Du Bois was particularly upset by Washington's scorn for what he regarded as useless distractions, such as the "craze" for Latin and Greek. Washington complained that the white image of an educated Negro was one "with a high hat, imitation gold eye-glasses, a showy walking-stick, kid gloves, fancy boots, and what not—in a word, a man who was determined to live by his wits." In a shrewd rhetorical maneuver that went to the heart of their differing views on education, Du Bois turned one of Washington's most famous examples of wasted effort against him: Washington, he said, had "so thoroughly" absorbed "the speech and thought of triumphant commercialism, and the ideals of material prosperity, that the picture of a lone black boy poring over a French grammar amid the weeds and dirt of a neglected home soon seemed to him the acme of absurdities." What, Du Bois wondered, would "Socrates and St. Francis have to say to this?"

Du Bois also objected to Washington's "hushing of the criticism of honest opponents," a major point that he would repeat more emphatically in the years to come. Washington's influence extended far beyond Tuskegee because national politicians and philanthropists viewed his approval as necessary for any legislation, programs, or appointments they might make that involved black America, and he made the most of his power, sometimes in devious and underhanded ways. More than merely "hushing" those who opposed its dominance, Du Bois and others would charge, the "Tuskegee Machine" under Washington ruthlessly crushed them. The submissive, accommodating face that

Washington showed to whites was, for Du Bois, the stern father's scowl of disapproval for anything less than complete obedience to his wishes.

Du Bois was unaware that Washington's deviousness, as he thought of it, was often employed toward the same ends that Du Bois sought. Washington covered his tracks so effectively that his support of lawsuits against Jim Crow legislation was not discovered until the mid-1960s, when Lewis R. Harlan found the evidence while working on his biography of Washington.*

Even more important than Du Bois's personal or philosophical differences with Washington was a radical change for the worse in the interracial environment in the years following the Atlanta speech. As Joel Williamson notes in *The Crucible of Race,* "the white people with whom Washington had negotiated a modus vivendi in 1895 were, by 1900, rapidly losing control to people who had radically different ideas about the proper state of relations between the races" or, as they were sometimes disparaged, "mudsill whites." Washington persisted in his stance, Williamson says, apparently "psychologically incapable" of altering it, even as "white attitudes of accommodation rapidly melted into universal rejection, and burning and bloody aggression." Du Bois felt that whatever force Washington's argument for accommodation and compromise might have had in 1895 had been crippled by white hostility in the ensuing years.

Du Bois was by no means alone in his criticism of Washington, nor was he Washington's sternest opponent, especially in the North. William Monroe Trotter, a black Harvard graduate who founded the *Boston Guardian* in 1901, charged that Washington was no Moses but a false prophet. In 1903 Trotter was jailed briefly after he angrily heckled Washington in a black church in Boston. Washington, in an attempt at reconciliation, called for a meeting of the opposing factions in New York in January, 1904.

---

*Coauthor John Broesamle was working alongside Harlan at this time on his doctoral dissertation, and recalls how "he and I and the profession were astonished."

Du Bois agreed to attend, arriving with his positions firmly staked out. He wanted identical civil rights for blacks and whites; recourse to the law and the courts when those were denied; compulsory elementary education for all blacks, with both practical and higher levels available to those who were qualified; a black periodical with nationwide circulation; and more academic studies of the black situation.

He also wanted what Washington could hardly be expected to give or even to acknowledge: an end to what Du Bois saw as black self-abasement and self-deprecation. The meeting, predictably, was a failure because of Washington's continued insistence on accommodation. Two years later, Du Bois and Trotter formed what would be called the "Niagara Movement," so named after a meeting of its members in Niagara Falls, Ontario, in 1906. Typical of most groups of intellectuals, the movement was characterized by organizational inefficiency and high-flown rhetoric even in its structure—Washington was said to find its grandly named central body, the Committee of Twelve, "hilariously grandiose." It lasted only about four years, with but a few hundred members, when it was superseded in 1910 by the new National Association for the Advancement of Colored People (NAACP). But the Niagara Movement was extraordinarily important in defining the new stance concerning civil rights for blacks that would ultimately replace that held by the "Bookerites."

Again, the way in which these ideas were expressed was as significant as the ideas themselves. Du Bois argued that, far from being inferior to whites, the black race could take pride in "the beauty of its genius, the sweetness of its soul, and its strength in that meekness which shall yet inherit this turbulent earth." But that meekness did not mean acceptance of injustice: "We must complain. Yes, plain, blunt complaint, ceaseless agitation, unfailing exposure of dishonesty and wrong." In August, 1906, the Niagara Movement met at Harper's Ferry, West Virginia, to honor John Brown as a martyr, and Du Bois took his assertiveness to a new level of intensity: "We will not be satisfied to take one jot or tittle [i.e., "bit"] less than our full manhood rights," he said. Nothing was worse than "the surrender of a people's manhood or the loss of a man's self-respect." In 1907, Du Bois widened the breach with Washington, decrying his strategy of silence as "our great mistake." It was "high time that the Negro agitator should be in the land." Such a role was often unpleasant, but it was essential to "bring forward the dark side" of the picture, to show that "things are bad in order that they may become better." With this speech, Arnold Rampersad says, Du Bois's "brilliant career as an outspoken propagandist of black American, Pan-African, and eventually socialist causes was effectively launched."

In 1910, Du Bois became editor-in-chief of *The Crisis,* the NAACP's monthly magazine. He would hold that post for 25 years, frequently at odds with fellow members, white and black, who seemed to him unjustifiably sympathetic to Washington's gradualism. For his part, Washington did not see much evidence of NAACP sympathy for his position; he criticized its leaders, particularly Du Bois, for persuading blacks that "they can get what they ought to have in the way of right treatment by merely making demands, passing resolutions and cursing somebody."

After 1907, Washington argued his position in his own monthly newspaper, *The New York Age* (yet another instance of how well-financed and extensive the influence of this small-town trade-school president really was). But it took only a year for Du Bois's fiery editorials and commissioned articles to bring *The Crisis* to a position of parity with *The New York Age,* which suggests that there was a hunger among blacks for what Du Bois had to say. Though the circulation numbers in question seem small for a black population numbering more than ten million— 15,000 for *The Crisis,* a few more for *The Age*—the readers included the elite whose allegiance both leaders sought.

Ray Stannard Baker, famous as a muckraking reporter, offers perhaps the most interesting contemporary summary of the differences between Washington and Du Bois. A white progressive sympathetic to both factions, Baker attended an NAACP meeting in New York in early February, 1915. He spent an evening with Washington, who was in town on Tuskegee business, and came away feeling that "he is one of the comparatively few men I have met who always impresses me as being great—somehow possessing qualities beyond & above the ordinary." At the same time, however, after listening to the leaders of the NAACP, Baker said, "I find myself with them, too . . . they emphasize rights, not duties & just as Washington attacks them in an indirect way, so they attack Washington. . . . Agitation for rights is necessary as well as emphasis upon duties. Probably Dr. Washington is attacking the problem from the South in the wisest way; & probably these people are doing the most useful thing here in the North."

✧   ✧   ✧

Although Washington died in November, 1915, his reputation as *the* black leader remained high, particularly with the white community, for decades to come. In 1947 the National Education Association praised him as one of ten men and women who had contributed the most to the development of American education, and he was the subject of flattering magazine and newspaper articles in popular magazines such as the *Reader's Digest,* along the lines of "Booker T. Washington—Apostle of Good Will." But there were strong signs throughout these years that Du Bois had won the battle for the allegiance of his valued top tenth, even as Washington retained that of the white and black middle classes.

Ralph Ellison, whose *Invisible Man* (1952) is routinely included in lists of the best American novels, was an intellectual and artist like Du Bois who attended Tuskegee Institute on a music scholarship from 1933 to 1936 (the curriculum was broadened considerably after Washington's death). The first chapter of *Invisible Man,* frequently excerpted for high school and college anthologies as "The Battle Royal," contains a remarkable depiction of Booker T. Washington and the Atlanta Exposition speech.

Ellison's young protagonist, consistent with the implications of the novel's title, is never named. A recent high school graduate, he is subjected to an evening of painful humiliation by the white establishment of his small southern town. He and several tough blacks hired for the occasion are forced to box each other blindfolded, whirling desperately around a makeshift ring until all are bloodied and exhausted. Their blindfolds removed, the youngsters are humiliated and frightened when a naked blond girl dances for the cheering and jeering audience. When the boys are allowed to leave the boxing ring, they have to scramble for coins scattered on a rug, only to find that the rug is electrified and the coins are worthless brass tokens.

The white businessmen and civic leaders, including the town's ministers, mayor, and the school superintendent, regard these humiliations as harmless teasing, what would today be called a "roast" of an honored guest. The serious business of the evening is the presentation by the protagonist of the excellent speech he has given as valedictorian of the local black high school. The boy—as Ellison consistently represents him—knows that everything rides on his presentation because only through it could his white audience "judge truly my ability." (We may recall how Washington had similar feelings before he gave his speech in Atlanta.) The boy declaims, "We of the younger generation extol the wisdom of that great leader and educator . . . who first spoke these flaming words of wisdom." He recounts the "cast down your bucket" anecdote, to the obvious approval of the audience. The boy, in an act of obvious though accidental rebellion, then commits a nearly fatal error: the acceptable formula for submission by blacks to white dominance had always been "social responsibility," a coded phrase in the South used to oppose "civil rights." The boy gags over the phrase and substitutes in its place "social equality," thinking that nobody in the noisy room is paying attention. Immediate and menacing silence follows. The boy hastily retracts his words and is handed his scholarship to a black college.

Earlier in Ellison's story, the boy's grandfather revealed on his deathbed his true feelings about his life—that though he had seemed to be "the meekest of men," he had been a "spy in the enemy's country," as a black man among whites. He wanted his son, the protagonist's father, to continue as he had, to "overcome 'em with yeses, undermine 'em with grins, agree 'em to death and destruction, let 'em swoller you till they vomit or bust wide open." This degree of fury in his gentle, dying grandfather startled the young boy who witnessed it. After the events of the evening when he had been humiliated by the town's white leaders, he fell asleep and dreamed that the old man appeared and mockingly handed him his scholarship, freshly engraved with letters of gold that read, "To Whom It May Concern: Keep This Nigger-Boy Running."

Ellison's protagonist is a fictional character, not an autobiographical re-creation of his own youth. And yet the fact that Ellison did go to Tuskegee, as well as his obvious qualifications for intellectual leadership, illuminates Washington's declining reputation by the 1950s. Certainly the bitter and sarcastic irony with which Ellison treats the "words of wisdom" of Washington's "Atlanta Compromise" is more devastating than any words against Washington said by Du Bois. The fury of the old man in the boy's dream is a harbinger of the racial discord that would accompany the dramatic progress of civil rights for blacks in the 1960s.

Beginning at the end of that decade, black studies programs, inspired in part by Du Bois's principles and his writings, began to be accepted as experimental exercises in raising racial consciousness. By the end of the twentieth century, such programs were permanent fixtures at many colleges and universities in the country, including Harvard's W.E.B. Du Bois Institute for Afro-American Research—an appropriate honor for the man who, by the time of his death in 1963, had become revered as the "tribune" of his race.

Du Bois's biographer, David Levering Lewis, describes how, over a period of seventy-plus years of mature activity, Du Bois became an editor, a public speaker, an organizer, a novelist, and a historian of major stature through his work on Reconstruction. He subscribed at various times to "virtually every possible solution to the problem of twentieth-century racism—scholarship, propaganda, integration, cultural and economic separatism, politics, international communism, expatriation, third-world solidarity." He was as completely in tune with the rising tide of black nationalism, manifested in black studies programs and black pride movements, as Washington was out of tune with them. Well into the 1990s, favorable references to Washington were as hard to find in the literature of black studies as were negative references to Du Bois.

Not surprisingly, white conservatives who would have felt comfortable with Washington as a team player in the big leagues of American capitalism are less enthusiastic about Du Bois. Gerald Early, for example, writing for the *National Review* in 2000, charged that Du Bois and his followers built their program in part on "the hatred of capitalism as racist and imperialist [and] the defense of any foreign power or ideology that opposes American interests or white racism." Even admirers like Lewis regret that Du Bois's disillusionment with America led him into some bad intellectual company. Fascinated by the Russian experiment with Communism since he had first witnessed it during a visit to the Soviet Union in 1926, he became an outspoken defender of Stalinism during the early years of the Cold War, convinced that, in Lewis's words, "all tactics that contained American capitalism were fair."

In 1951, at the height of the McCarthy era, Du Bois was tried in court as a "foreign agent" for his work with the Peace Information Center, a short-lived leftist advocacy group that the government charged was a Communist front. The case was dismissed, but Du Bois was nevertheless temporarily stripped of his American passport. In 1961, when he was 93, Du Bois joined the tiny American Communist Party—a "Homeric nose-thumbing," in Lewis's words, at a capitalist system "doomed to self-destruction"—and left the United States for Africa. He gave up his American citizenship to become a citizen of Ghana on his ninety-fifth birthday. But he was still an independent thinker. In one of his last recorded comments, he rebuked a man for disparaging another leader as "a Booker T. Washington." "The old man stirred like a tortoise putting its head out of its shell, an observer recalled, and said, 'Don't say that. I used to talk like that.'" Du Bois said his aunt in Great Barrington reminded him years before that he should remember that Washington had come out of slavery, and that "You are fighting for the rights here in the North. It's tough, but it's nothing like as tough as what he had to face in his time and in his place."

Du Bois died in Ghana shortly after that conversation, on August 27, 1963. The following day, on the other side of the world, Dr. Martin Luther King Jr., gave his "I have a dream" speech at the Lincoln Memorial. Just as the Atlanta Exposition speech signaled a transition in leadership from the generation of Frederick Douglass to Booker T. Washington, so King's speech in Washington and the death of Du Bois marked another watershed in African American history. It was one of those historical symmetries, like the deaths of John Adams and Thomas Jefferson on July 4, 1826, that lend force to the cliché that "truth is stranger than fiction."

✦   ✦   ✦

The intellectual battle between Washington the conservative and Du Bois the radical, as they are commonly seen, continues today. Martin Kilson, writing in 2000, opposed them as the "two generic types of modern ethnic group leadership." The first type "focuses on the nuts and bolts of outfitting a group with agencies, mechanisms, networks, and institutions related to modern social development." The second is the "mobilization type which focuses on the character of an ethnic group's status, citizenship rights, human rights, and honor in a modern nation-state society."

Commenting in 1977 on the squabbling between the opposing factions, Ralph Ellison indicated that he was neither so dismissive of Washington nor so admiring of Du Bois as *Invisible Man* suggests. He said Washington had put his finger on a common failing of blacks when he likened them to crabs in a basket—in Ellison's words, "if a Negro threatens to succeed in a field outside the usual areas of Negro professionals, others feel challenged" to drag him back into the basket. Ellison also distrusted Du Bois's notion of a black intellectual elite that dismissed its critics as Uncle Toms—a hazard that Du Bois recognized late in his life—and he deplored what he regarded as the criminality, overblown rhetoric, and the "passionate assertion of the mystique of 'Blackness' that had resulted from Du Bois's formulation."

But it may be wise to look outside the academy or the intellectual world of letters for a perspective on how the long-time antagonists are viewed today. An April 14, 2001, editorial in a southern Texas newspaper, the *Corpus Christi Caller-Times,* spoke approvingly of the San Antonio school board's decision to change the name and focus of the mostly black Main Avenue High School to Fox Technical High School. The name change was designed to appeal to "those students who had finished junior high school and found that the study of ancient Greece, American history and English literature bored them. They would sit in class and count the minutes until they could get out and work on a car with their hands." Regarded with scorn by the more academically inclined black students at their old school, the students at Fox were now where they needed to be, and "all of the same mind; they were eager to help one another as they strived to become auto mechanics, plumbers, carpenters, bricklayers, painters, dress designers, electricians and other skilled workers." The editorial concludes that "Booker T. and W.E.B. were both right," for "each of us has different aptitudes and preferences; different strokes for different folks."

Or at a different level of sophistication, consider the *New Yorker* magazine profile in 2002 by Nicolas Lemann of

Condoleezza Rice, then President George W. Bush's national security advisor and today his secretary of state. Dr. Rice is clearly a brilliant, poised, and accomplished woman by any measure. Born in Birmingham, Alabama, in 1954, she was old enough to remember clearly the battlefield for civil rights that Birmingham had become in the mid-1960s, and she knew two of the four girls who died in 1963 when white extremists bombed a church in that city. A generation earlier, thanks to her parents' status as members of the city's black upper class and to her own talents, Rice might have considered herself in terms of belonging to Du Bois's "talented tenth." However, Rice declined to be thought of as part of any racial or ethnic subgroup; she insisted that "her family was proud, accomplished, self-reliant, and not in need of anybody's help." Indeed, Lemann says, "In the great intellectual divide of twentieth-century black America—between W.E.B. Du Bois, the radical proponent of political change, and Booker T. Washington, the advocate of self-improvement and not confronting the Jim Crow system—the Rices sound as if they were more on the Washington side."

Perhaps the two factions following the paths laid down by Washington and DuBois are finally coming together, as Washington hoped they would a century ago, in 1904. As Nikki Burns, a black journalist, says, "The fight for blacks to obtain economic prosperity while hanging on to their constitutional rights continues today. Black leaders such as the Rev. Jesse Jackson, the Rev. Al Sharpton, Nation of Islam leader Minister Louis Farrakhan and others have mixed both Washington's and Du Bois' approaches in an effort to achieve social and economic progress for African-Americans." Viewed in this light, Du Bois and Washington represent the twin engines of pragmatism and idealism that continue to propel the drive toward black freedom in America.

4

Damn–Dam–Damnation

John Muir, Theodore Roosevelt, and the Environment

For sheer stunning beauty, at the dawn of the twentieth century, few if any of the American West's natural wonders surpassed the Hetch Hetchy Valley.* Countless contemporaries testified that Hetch Hetchy rivaled even Yosemite Valley, just 20 miles to the south. Old black-and-white photographs bear out this claim. Hetch Hetchy was an oblong glacier-carved granite bowl some three and a half miles long by a quarter to three-quarters of a mile across. The sides of the valley towered 2,500 feet almost vertically above an emerald meadow, through which flowed the Tuolumne River, fed by waterfalls spiraling down from the heights. The setting, wrote the great naturalist John Muir, was "a grand landscape garden, one of Nature's rarest and most precious mountain temples," which "goes far to make the weakest and meanest spectator rich and significant evermore."

---

*The meaning of "Hetch Hetchy," an Indian name, is disputed. It may mean "Grass Valley" or the "Valley of Two Trees."

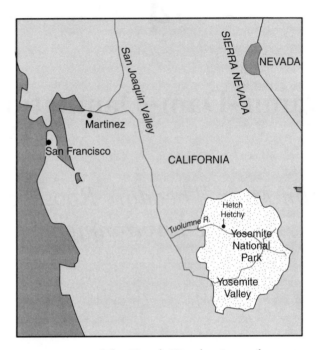

FIGURE 4.1 The Hetch Hetchy Struggle.

Today no Hetch Hetchy Valley remains. Instead, there is a Hetch Hetchy Reservoir. The once-magnificent waterfalls spill part way down into the lake, as if a beautiful maiden's flowing tresses had been brutally hacked off. The reservoir itself is an inky dark hue. When its level recedes, the water line resembles the gray, mottled scum in a bathtub. In seasons of drought, ancient stumps protrude. Signs warning people not to boat or swim seem pointless in a scene so bleak. Few bother to visit Hetch Hetchy at all.

The early-twentieth-century battle over flooding Hetch Hetchy became the prototype for nearly all the environmental struggles that have followed, or that will. It was the greatest environmental conflict of its time. It involved trade-offs and shades of gray. And it pitted the two greatest American environmentalists of their era—perhaps of any era—against each other: John Muir against Theodore Roosevelt.

✧   ✧   ✧

In May, 1903, Muir and Roosevelt went on a famous four-day camping trip together in Yosemite. Planning a western tour, Roosevelt had asked Muir to be his guide: "I do not want anyone but you, and I want to drop politics absolutely for four days, and just be out in the open with you." Muir bought a new yellow suit for the occasion (a man of his era, he always hiked in formal attire). Roosevelt shook off the Secret Service, and the two set out on horseback with a couple of rangers and a packer. They laid out their blankets in the open, awakening one morning beneath a five-inch layer of snow. As he dug himself free, T.R. exclaimed, "I wouldn't miss this for anything." At night they talked around campfires. Roosevelt's knowledge of animals and birds, it turned out, exceeded Muir's. Muir outshone Roosevelt in botany and geology, the inanimate world. Though he regarded most politicians with suspicion, Muir remarked, "I never before had so interesting, hearty, and manly a companion," adding, "I fairly fell in love with him." Roosevelt declared, "John Muir talked even better than he wrote." "The trees and flowers and cliffs are everything to him."

A photograph was taken of Roosevelt and Muir atop Glacier Point, with the walls of Yosemite Valley and the spectacular Yosemite Falls flowing at full volume in the background. It reveals not only the distinctive physical qualities of both men but also something of their characters, dramatically positioned against the same kind of landscape that would lead to their dispute.

During their outing, Muir tried to persuade Roosevelt toward his own brand of environmentalism—outright preservation of landscape for its own sake, specifically the landscape of Yosemite. The nation's unique natural settings must be set aside in perpetuity, and protected forever from commercial exploitation. "I stuffed him pretty well regarding the timber thieves . . . and other spoilers of the forest," Muir later remarked. And on the subject of Yosemite, at least, Roosevelt wound up agreeing with him.

Born in 1838, 20 years before T.R., Muir had become a preservationist through observation. His Scottish parents had brought him to rural Wisconsin as a child. The region's settlers proved so adept at obliterating all traces of natural prairie beneath their plows that today biologists must struggle to re-create even a semblance of the original flora. The Muir family's own manner of impoverishing farm land and moving on gave John an intimate introduction to environmental depletion. As a boy, he hunted and shot a loon. Merely wounding the bird, he turned it into a pet. "No humane being past the thoughtless age of childhood," he wrote, "will wantonly murder any creature." During the Civil War, Muir fled to Canada to avoid the Union draft. No coward, though, he continually took risks in the wild.

In 1868 Muir first encountered California's Sierra Nevada. Awe-struck, he christened it, in a stunningly apposite metaphor, the Range of Light. For six years, he lived in Yosemite Valley, roaming outwards in all directions through forests of pine and giant sequoias, along cascading streams, and up the slopes of glacier-carved granite peaks. Muir's accommodation to life's established conventions proved grudging. In 1880 he finally married, at the age of 42. His new wife was the daughter (and sole heir) of prosperous farmers near the town of Martinez, California. After Muir took over the farming operation, it burgeoned—he was a true Scot, disciplined and industrious. But "I am degenerating into a machine for making money," he complained. "Up there," he once remarked as he pointed to the Sierra Nevada, "is my home."

In May, 1871, when he was 68, Ralph Waldo Emerson visited Yosemite Valley. Muir, somewhat improbably, had set up housekeeping inside a sawmill where he worked. America's leading man of letters and philosopher of nature was fascinated by Muir and returned repeatedly to the mill to talk with the young man about natural lore. Muir persuaded Emerson to camp with him among the sequoias, an agreement that Emerson's handlers disallowed—"Mr. Emerson might take cold." "There is a young man from whom we shall hear," Emerson remarked; "Muir is more wonderful than Thoreau" (Emerson's difficult disciple who had died a decade earlier).

Emerson and Muir never saw one another again, but they did correspond, and the great man's essays, along with the writings of Thoreau himself, markedly influenced Muir. Emerson was the high priest of the religion of nature, and his breathless imagery anticipated Muir's own. In the woods, Emerson wrote, "all mean egotism vanishes. I become a transparent eyeball; . . . I am part or particle of God." Yet, as Thurman Wilkins has pointed out, "Muir immersed himself more deeply and totally in nature (his alpha and omega) than Emerson had ever done." Then too, Emerson was willing to admit the principle of utility or use in connection with nature: "Beasts, fire, water, stones, and corn serve" us all, and steam boilers and railroads were part of the exhilarating march of progress that had taken humanity "from the era of Noah to that of Napoleon!"

By the beginning of the 1890s, Muir had launched his campaign to salvage the newly established Yosemite National Park from "progress"—from still-operating commercial interests, among them ordinary sheepherders, timber companies, and the gigantic Southern Pacific Railroad. A brilliant if florid writer, Muir's pieces on nature meanwhile appeared in national magazines. His first book, *The Mountains of California,* came out in 1894. His campaign to preserve Yosemite marked the high point of his literary fame.

In 1892 the Sierra Club was created, with Muir as its first president. The club dedicated itself to arousing "the support and co-operation of the people and the government in preserving the forests and other natural features of the Sierra Nevada." "The battle we have fought," Muir told club members in 1895, "is a part

of the eternal conflict between right and wrong, and we cannot
expect to see the end of it."

A battle between right and wrong, or good and evil. Though
he declined to affiliate with any religious denomination, in his
own way Muir, as Edwin Way Teale has written, "was intensely
religious. The forests and the mountains formed his temple. His
approach to all nature was worshipful. He saw everything evolv-
ing yet everything the direct handiwork of God. There was a spiritual and religious exaltation in his experiences with nature. And
he came down from the mountains like some bearded prophet to
preach of the beauty and healing he had found in this natural
temple where he worshiped. He spoke with the fire of the old
Covenanters." To Muir, writes Thurman Wilkins, "God and
nature were synonymous."

✧   ✧   ✧

In many ways, John Muir's companion on their 1903 camping
trip could not have been more different from him, despite their
apparent mutual affinity. In 1979, following the American failure in Vietnam and the Watergate scandals, *Newsweek* ran a cover
illustration for a feature story captioned, "Where Have All the
Heroes Gone?" The illustration—inevitably—pictured Teddy
Roosevelt leading the charge up San Juan Hill. On the strength
of a single day of battle in 1898, and in striking contrast to the
pacifist John Muir, Roosevelt became one of America's two or
three most famous soldiers in the period between the Civil War
and World War I.

Over the decades, more than a hundred biographies of T.R.
have appeared. None entirely captures the full man. He was very
likely America's most intelligent twentieth-century president, and
assuredly its most complex. Born to privilege in 1858, Roosevelt
entered public life during the Gilded Age, a time when others of
his class shunned politics as a vile pursuit. Devastated by his
young wife's death in childbirth, in 1884 he retreated to the

Dakota Bad Lands, where he ranched, hunted, and lost a substantial part of the family fortune. As assistant secretary of the
navy under William McKinley, Roosevelt plumped for war with
Spain. When the war came, he abandoned Washington to organize the Rough Riders. Leading the regiment's famous charge up
Kettle and San Juan hills outside Santiago, Cuba, he presented a
choice target. Had Roosevelt died that day, the course of
American history over the following two decades would have
been far less interesting.

Upon his return, Roosevelt was promptly elected governor
of New York. When he demonstrated a particular zeal in clamp-
ing down on some of the state's large corporations, though, the
Republican Party consigned him to the most insignificant office
available, the vice-presidency of the United States. There he
would have remained had not William McKinley succumbed to
an assassin's bullet in September, 1901.

No president has ever embodied more of the ambiguities or
ironies of his time than T.R. did. A Darwinian, he viewed life as
a struggle among nations, social classes, and individuals. He had
a brutal side. After the smoke cleared from San Juan Hill, he
invited bystanders to "look at those damned Spanish dead." As
president, Roosevelt lost the vision in an eye boxing with one of
his aides. Yet Roosevelt's Darwinism was tempered by a sense of
obligation toward ordinary Americans and the poor that went
beyond noblesse oblige. Running at the head of his own third-
party ticket in 1912, he called for social security a generation
before his cousin Franklin would create it as part of the New Deal
(described in Chapter 6).

The most broadly learned of twentieth-century presidents,
Theodore Roosevelt read voraciously, pursuing in greater or lesser
depth the literature and scientific discoveries of his time. He distinguished himself as a historian of naval warfare and the
American West. Yet this bookish intellectual was also one of the
country's most famous outdoorsmen, an advocate of what he

termed "the strenuous life." Apart, perhaps, from Buffalo Bill Cody, Roosevelt became the most famous American hunter of his time. At the age of seven, he grandly founded the "Roosevelt Museum of Natural History." When T.R. walked into a room, declared his sister of his taxidermy skills, "you always hear the words 'bird' and 'skin.'" Had not the horseman, hiker, hunter, soldier, and explorer in Roosevelt prevailed—had he not been happiest in struggle and danger—he might well have become, like Muir, predominantly a naturalist. It was no accident, then, that on their camping trip Roosevelt turned out to know more than Muir about animals and birds.

At his core, T.R. was a brilliant politician, yet a politician who aroused more and more mistrust in the Republican Party. One prominent reason for this mistrust involved Roosevelt's ideas about conservation, which seemed to many to fly in the face of all logic and experience. Traditionally, pioneers, settlers, and business interests had viewed the American continent as a vast buffet. With everything laid out for the eating, they took it as their God-given responsibility to gorge themselves. Visiting the U.S. during the first half of the nineteenth century, Alexis de Tocqueville commented on Americans' compulsion to plunder nature. Haphazardly cutting down trees, wastefully extracting minerals, plowing land until it was exhausted and then abandoning it—all this spelled economic development.

By the turn of the twentieth century, an increasing realization had begun to dawn that America was actually squandering its natural endowment, that even so vast a country might face shortages down the road, and that the time had arrived for a more rational use of resources. This view prevailed most strongly in the northeast, where the squandering had gone on the longest. The most deeply worried included hunters and fishermen who had watched their quarry diminish. As early as 1892, America's leading woman scientist, the New Englander Ellen Swallow Richards, introduced the term "oekology" (as she spelled it) into the language. By contrast, in the less visibly damaged West, a continent away from New England, the full-throated cry to keep on exploiting continued unabated.

The dawning northeastern awareness of environmental degradation profoundly shaped New York's preeminent hunter, Theodore Roosevelt: he called conservation "the most weighty question now before the people of the United States." Beginning in 1901, Roosevelt's administration alerted the country to the dangers of wasting its resources. The new president surrounded himself with early conservationists, and for the first time, Washington developed a comprehensive conservation policy. The first federal wildlife refuges were created, more than fifty all told. ("Is there any law that will prevent me from declaring Pelican Island [Florida] a Federal Bird Reservation?" Roosevelt asked. No, came the answer. "Very well, then I so declare it.")

As president, Roosevelt set out to help restore the bison as a species and expand its range. But less than twenty years previous, in 1883, on a trip out west while a young New York state assemblyman, he had mercilessly driven a guide and himself for a week through continuous downpour to locate and shoot a buffalo. After finally bagging one of the last bulls in Dakota Territory, Roosevelt did a war dance around the carcass. True to his paradoxical form, upon leaving the presidency, Roosevelt soon departed on a hunting expedition to Africa.

In 1908 Roosevelt set up the National Conservation Commission to inventory the nation's remaining natural resources. He doubled the number of national parks (adding, among others, Crater Lake in Oregon and Mesa Verde in Colorado), and established the first 18 national monuments (including the Grand Canyon and what would become Olympic National Park). Roosevelt's Antiquities Act of 1906 allowed a president to declare lands off limits to exploitation due to their "historic and scientific interest." Business interests howled as the administration laid aside mineral tracts and quadrupled the country's forest reserves. Nevertheless, by the end of his term, Roosevelt had enlarged the public domain by 230 million acres—an area larger than Texas, Pennsylvania, and Ohio combined. When the roll of environmentalist presidents is called, indeed, Theodore Roosevelt's name must come first. His conservation achievements rank among the most enduring of his presidency, their implementation entailing constant prodding and fighting. "The conservation of natural resources," Roosevelt declared, was "part of . . . the problem of national efficiency, the patriotic duty of insuring the safety and continuance of the nation." Roosevelt was a conservationist-nationalist.

Yet by conservation Roosevelt did not primarily mean preservation. If the highest and best use of a parcel of land was as scenery—in Yosemite or Yellowstone, for example—then, he reasoned, save it for scenery. But more typical forms of highest and best use were orderly logging, sustainable grazing, or damming a river for water and power. Underlying his conservation philosophy, in other words, was a fundamental preoccupation with resource *management*—the orderly *utilization* of natural resources under federal supervision through a permit system. Historians have termed this "conservation for use."

The leading apostle of conservation for use was Roosevelt's chief forester, Gifford Pinchot. The idea of practicing sustained-yield forestry in national forests had originated with Carl Schurz, secretary of the interior from 1877 to 1881. A German immigrant, Schurz's ideas derived, in turn, from European practices. Schurz and the small circle who agreed with him had been dismissed as alarmists and radicals. Far from being radical, though, to a man such as Pinchot, the notion of husbanding resources for maximum yield over the long term simply amounted to an economic proposition. "The fundamental principle of the whole conservation policy," he declared, "is that of use, to take every part of the land and its resources and put it to that use in which it will serve the most people." Pinchot had observed efficient

European sustained-yield forest management at first hand, and the financial payoffs amazed him. By contrast, the American pattern encouraged government to sell off rich timber and mineral tracts at fire-sale prices, losing all potential for regulated use with the transaction. As part of a regular cycle, loggers would clear-cut and then abandon these tracts.

Pinchot and Roosevelt personified early twentieth-century conservationism—each the son of a wealthy old northeastern family, each the product of an Ivy League education, each well-traveled abroad. They stood at the opposite end of the line from hardscrabble miners and loggers who daily wrested a living from the ground, and they were equally removed from the nouveau riche tycoons who owned the mines and mills. Indeed, the predatory and boorish behavior of the newly rich utterly appalled and antagonized Roosevelt. He and Pinchot found themselves continually squeezed between, on the one hand, extractive interests complaining of government interference, and, on the other hand, "esthetic conservationists" such as Muir, who wanted to preserve nature for its own sake.

Modern readers sensitive to images of gender and power find much to interest them in conservationist rhetoric. The preservationist approach that Muir embraced connoted nurturing, protecting from harm—in a word, mothering. In Victorian America, the image of the esthete (a man with long hair supposedly given to abstractions and removed from reality) and the image of the effeminate were commonly intertwined in the popular mind as well as in political rhetoric. (As late as the 1950s, one would still hear references to the Sierra Club as a collection of "daisy-pickers," and "tree huggers" is a familiar epithet today.) Roosevelt, who succeeded in giving every reform he endorsed a strong masculine cast, did the same for conservation. His kind of conservationist resembled the head of the household, the two-fisted paterfamilias, the man with the "big stick" who apportioned and managed resources—the steward of the land as opposed to the earth mother. In an era that still prized and deferred to manly strength, these connotations of unquestioning love (the feminine) and protective realism (the masculine) surfaced often in the language of both ordinary people and politicians.

In making conservation a national policy, Roosevelt did not entirely depart from precedent. Yosemite and Yellowstone, for instance, had already been set aside. And during the last years of the nineteenth century, under the influence of nascent conservation impulses, presidents had designated tens of millions of acres of land as forest reserves because it seemed like a good idea, without actually adopting any plan as to their future. Muir and his fellow esthetes wanted to save these reserves as outsized botanical gardens, turning them into parks. Western timber interests and their congressional representatives demanded that the reserves be liquidated forthwith. Conservation-for-use advocates such as Pinchot argued in favor of sustained-yield harvesting (successfully enlisting, among others, Theodore Roosevelt). Ultimately, under the 1897 Forest Management Act, sustained yield won out. Pinchot had beaten both the liquidators and Muir. Nor would this prove Pinchot's final victory. He would have yet one more triumph over Muir—one that some say killed the old man.

✧   ✧   ✧

Around the turn of the twentieth century, one American city after another committed itself to the municipal ownership and operation of public utilities. Cities typically did so on the grounds that water and power delivery amounted to a "natural monopoly," and that in order to protect the public, this monopoly should reside in municipal hands.

San Francisco became a case in point. One of the nation's urban gems, with its stately Victorian homes and its magnificent views, San Francisco was supplied by the Spring Valley Water Works (after 1904, the Spring Valley Water Company). Despite the bucolic name, Spring Valley was a private monopoly infamous for high prices, poor service, and graft. When the city sought to purchase a nearby valley as a reservoir site in competition with the company, the company snapped up the valley. A city attempt to buy out Spring Valley's assets came to nothing.

So San Francisco began to look eastward 170 miles, toward Hetch Hetchy. Damming the Tuolumne at the foot of the valley, so the reasoning went, would serve three of the great reform goals of the era: conservation for use (the highest and best use of Hetch Hetchy being to flood it), antimonopoly, and the public ownership of utilities. There were just two problems. Hetch Hetchy was a part of Yosemite National Park, where it bore the designation of "wilderness preserve." And its chief defender was John Muir.

The city's idea left Muir aghast. Although he granted that its walls were "less sublime in height than those of Yosemite," Muir believed that Hetch Hetchy's "groves, gardens, and broad, spacious meadows are more beautiful and picturesque." In 1890 Muir's pleas had led to the inclusion of Hetch Hetchy within Yosemite National Park in the first place. Scarcely had that occurred before San Francisco began its offensive.

"The making of gardens and parks goes on with civilization all over the world," Muir wrote,

> and they increase both in size and number as their value is recognized. Everybody needs beauty as well as bread, places to play in and pray in, where Nature may heal and cheer and give strength to body and soul alike. This natural beauty-hunger is made manifest in the little windowsill gardens of the poor, though perhaps only a geranium slip in a broken cup, as well as in the carefully tended rose and lily gardens of the rich, the thousands of spacious city parks and botanical gardens, and in our magnificent National Parks—the Yellowstone, Yosemite, Sequoia, etc.—Nature's sublime wonderlands, the admiration and joy of the world. Nevertheless, like anything else worth while, from the very beginning, however well guarded, they have always been subject to attack by despoiling gain-seekers and mischief-makers of every degree from Satan to Senators, eagerly trying to make everything immediately and selfishly commercial, with schemes disguised in

smug-smiling philanthropy, industriously, sham-piously crying, "Conservation, conservation, panutilization," that man and beast may be fed and the dear Nation made great. . . . Ever since the establishment of the Yosemite National Park, strife has been going on around its borders and I suppose this will go on as part of the universal battle between right and wrong, however much its boundaries may be shorn, or its wild beauty destroyed.

. . .

These temple destroyers, devotees of ravaging commercialism, seem to have a perfect contempt for Nature, and, instead of lifting their eyes to the God of the mountains, lift them to the Almighty Dollar.

Dam Hetch Hetchy! As well dam for water-tanks the people's cathedrals and churches, for no holier temple has ever been consecrated by the heart of man.

This outcry embodied some of Muir's deepest values: the belief that natural beauty was divinely inspired, prompting him to cast arguments in spiritual terms; a suspicion of "progress" in general; and a particular suspicion of cities. Muir cast good against evil, absolute right against absolute wrong, the cathedral against the capitalist. If "every crystal, every flower" was a "window opening into heaven, a mirror reflecting the Creator," then the opposition became "the Prince of the powers of Darkness."

Initially Muir and the Sierra Club beat back San Francisco's assault on Hetch Hetchy. But in February, 1901, months prior to Roosevelt's presidency, the city quietly slipped a bill through Congress that permitted water development within national parks. The Sierra Club found out about the legislation only after it had passed.

With this act on the books, San Francisco began applying to the Interior Department for specific access to Hetch Hetchy. In 1903 and again in 1905, disinclined to give national parks over to engineering projects, the department turned the city down. A dam, observed interior secretary Ethan Allen Hitchcock, would degrade the valley's "wonderful natural conditions and marvelous scenic interest."

In April, 1906, the San Francisco earthquake struck. After the buildings stopped heaving and collapsing, a mammoth fire devoured most of what remained of the city. With Spring Valley's water mains ruptured by the quake, the inferno raged out of control for three days. A firestorm of outrage now flared up against the company.

Enter Gifford Pinchot. Toward the end of 1906, with a new secretary of the interior—Pinchot's friend James Garfield—coming in, Pinchot signaled to San Francisco's city engineer that the time had arrived to reapply for access to Hetch Hetchy. During the summer of 1907, Garfield attended a high-level meeting on the issue in San Francisco. Like the earlier congressional bill, the meeting was a subdued affair—so subdued that apparently only the dam's proponents knew anything about it. The Sierra Club was on an outing in Yosemite. The city's lawyers and engineers, though, had plenty to say.

In September, 1907, Muir appealed to Roosevelt. He and Roosevelt, after all, had camped together just 20 miles to the south of Hetch Hetchy. The president plainly understood the rising influence of preservationism. At Muir's urging, Roosevelt had advocated and subsequently signed a bill expanding Yosemite National Park. Roosevelt had also asked Garfield to look into other ways of supplying San Francisco with water. Now, in his letter to the president, Muir insisted that the city's water could be located outside "our wild mountain parks" and pleaded that Hetch Hetchy "be saved from all sorts of commercialism and marks of man's works." (Robert W. Righter has pointed out that unspoiled wilderness was never actually in the cards for Hetch Hetchy. As Muir well knew, the valley was going to undergo one form of development or another, either as a tourist destination or as a reservoir.)

Roosevelt, long since an apostle of conservation for use, was increasingly influenced by Pinchot's utilitarian philosophy. Muir's arguments failed to convince either Garfield or Pinchot. The president sent a message to Muir cautioning him that without the political support of the people of California, preservation for its own sake would prove impossible. "So far," Roosevelt told Muir, "everyone that has appeared has been for it [flooding Hetch Hetchy] and I have been in the disagreeable position of seeming to interfere with the development of the State for the sake of keeping a valley, which apparently hardly anyone wanted to have kept, under national control." But "I would not have any difficulty at all [in supporting your position] if, as you say, nine tenths of the citizens took ground against the Hetch Hetchy project." T.R. added: "How I do wish I were again with you camping out under those great sequoias or . . . under the silver firs."

"This Yosemite fight promises to be the worst ever," Muir told an associate. The Sierra Club began a lobbying campaign against the reservoir. San Francisco Mayor James D. Phelan responded that "the 400,000 people of San Francisco are suffering from bad water and ask Mr. Muir to cease his aesthetic quibbling." Every issue related to turn-of-the-century American environmentalism lay on the line, notably preservation versus "multiple use" conservation, and water and power for the people versus sylvan rest and recreation for the people.

Roosevelt placed the final decision in Garfield's hands. Garfield held that "domestic use, . . . especially for a municipal water supply, is the highest use to which water and available storage basins . . . can be put." A referendum late in 1908 showed that San Francisco's voters favored the dam by seven to one. Meanwhile, in May, Garfield had given the city its right-of-way permit, contingent on the approval of Congress. "It was just one of those cases where I was extremely doubtful," Roosevelt wrote, "but finally I came to the conclusion that I ought to stand by Garfield and Pinchot's judgment in the matter." Roosevelt's uncharacteristic hesitation on this occasion is suggestive less of indecisiveness than of ambivalence, for which abundant reasons existed. In the wake of its recent tragedy, though, San Francisco had an added moral claim.

Never before had America seen a conservation battle like this one. Never had the country as a whole debated the question of whether to develop or preserve a wilderness. The dam's opponents put the issue squarely before the entire nation. Leading the attack, John Muir—entering his seventies by now, and financially comfortable—contributed most of the war chest. Yet if the issue divided Muir from Roosevelt, it split other conservationists as well. Even the Sierra Club was angrily polarized, with a minority backing the city. Wrote Muir's friend, the famous naturalist John Burroughs: "Grand scenery is going to waste in the Sierras—let's utilize some of it."

In December, 1908, a few months before leaving office, Roosevelt stated in his final annual message to Congress that Yosemite, along with Yellowstone, "should be kept as a national playground. In both, all wild things should be protected and the scenery kept wholly unmarred." At least one major environmental historian, Roderick Frazier Nash, has concluded that in choosing these particular words Roosevelt was signaling that he had come around to Muir's position against flooding Hetch Hetchy. Roosevelt's unusual public silence about Hetch Hetchy afterward may also imply that he had reversed course.

Early in 1909, a House committee held hearings. Mayor Phelan went for the jugular. "I am sure," he told the committee, that John Muir "would sacrifice his own family for the preservation of beauty." There were in effect two Yosemite Valleys, the reservoirites argued. One (Yosemite) was three times the size of the other (Hetch Hetchy) and had already been protected. Why not, then, sacrifice the smaller valley for the greater good? Congress for the moment dithered over its decision.

In 1909 Muir accompanied Roosevelt's successor, William Howard Taft, on a tour of Yosemite, and escorted Taft's new interior secretary, Richard A. Ballinger, directly to Hetch Hetchy. Taft was not a camper but instead a particularly rotund golfer. Muir found him a lot less companionable than Roosevelt. Even more to the point, Taft, as Muir put it, "refused to regard Yosemite as a place to worship in." But Taft had no love for Pinchot, who criticized him and feuded famously with Ballinger, and Hetch Hetchy was Pinchot's project. Nor did the president, who tended toward legal fastidiousness, feel certain that the executive branch could even grant a city access to federal property. Accordingly, the Taft administration applied the brakes.

Meantime, the war of words went on. Those who declared themselves against the reservoir included the *New York Times* and about a hundred additional newspapers and magazines, outdoor clubs, women's organizations, scientists, college professors, and the president of Harvard. San Francisco's city engineer dismissed them all as a collection of "short-haired women and long-haired men," while the *San Francisco Chronicle* labeled them "mushy esthetes." Also opposed to the dam, though, were hard-headed San Joaquin Valley farmers who did not want San Francisco bleeding off their crop water—and, naturally, the Spring Valley Water Company. Muir found himself accused of being a pawn for the water trust.

And Muir faced another problem. By this time, Yosemite Valley had become familiar, at least by reputation, to millions of Americans. Overuse had already become an issue. Hetch Hetchy, on the other hand, had been visited by only a relative handful of people. In 1908 Yosemite National Park attracted some ten thousand visitors, of whom just 300 got as far as Hetch Hetchy. The very absence of roads and tourist accommodations preserved Hetch Hetchy's beauty, at the same time conferring on the valley an obscurity that made it far harder to defend. To its detriment, Hetch Hetchy had not yet become overrun.

San Francisco bided its time through the William Howard Taft years while accumulating vastly more resources for the Hetch Hetchy struggle than Muir and his allies could ever hope to muster. In due course, the city's patience paid off when the new administration it had waited for took office. This was the administration of Woodrow Wilson.

There is an odd irony here. Wilson was a Democrat, and today it is his party that arouses love or hatred as the political patron of the environment. During the second half of the twentieth century, presidential campaigns would increasingly pit conservationist Democrats against Republican candidates who promised to turn resource management back over to business.

Yet until the 1930s, when New Deal Democrats began to seize the conservation issue as their own, the Democratic record looked very different. The GOP was the conservation party, or at least the party with a conservationist wing. Wilson rarely if ever furrowed his brow over the issue. The new secretary of the interior, Franklin K. Lane—formerly the San Francisco city attorney under Mayor Phelan—had the predictable perspective on Hetch Hetchy. A few weeks after Wilson's 1913 inauguration, the Hetch Hetchy matter went before Congress for final resolution. Preservationists emphasized that alternative sources of water remained available to San Francisco. Indeed—though the preservationists could not know this—San Francisco's chief engineer had received a report from one of the city's young water engineers acknowledging the outright truth of this assertion. So the chief engineer made a point of locking the report away.

The more desperate the reservoir opponents' position became, the harder Muir battled. In the heat of the struggle, his sense of proportion deteriorated; he became rigid and self-righteous, blasting his antagonists as being always and completely in the wrong. It was still good against evil, and more and more Muir the prophet sounded like Muir the fanatic. Then again, there were no two ways about the choice Congress faced, and not a lot to be flexible about. Either Hetch Hetchy was going to be drowned or it wasn't.

Late in 1913, San Francisco's bill passed Congress by overwhelming margins. Wilson declared that he signed it into law "because it seemed to serve the pressing public needs of the region . . . and yet did not impair the usefulness or materially detract from the beauty of the public domain." Calling the outcome "damn–dam–damnation," Muir complained that the Hetch Hetchy battle was "killing me."

It may have been. The fight had exhausted and depleted him, the loss miring him in depression and grief. His health deteriorated; he died the following year. Death in the wake of profound loss was a fate which he shared with Theodore Roosevelt. After 1915, Roosevelt became the preeminent advocate of American intervention into World War I. Raised in their father's warrior tradition, after the U.S. entered that bloodbath, two of Roosevelt's sons were badly wounded; a third, Quentin, an aviator and the youngest, was shot down and killed over France. Theodore Roosevelt's old exuberance never reappeared after that. Just 60, he died in 1919, 5 years after John Muir.

During the 1920s the dam that Muir had fought so hard against was finally completed at the base of Hetch Hetchy, drowning the valley beneath 300 feet of water. In 1928 the Spring Valley Water Company sold out to the city of San Francisco.

There were those at the time—notably San Franciscans— who argued that building reservoirs in the Sierra had the potential to add, as one federal commission put it, "beautiful lakes to the landscape." By combining estheticism with utilitarianism, the reasoning went, you could produce an end product superior to nature's original. Writing in *Sunset* in 1909, one John P. Young, who had recently visited Hetch Hetchy, reflected this sunny view:

> The question has . . . been raised whether the preservation of a scenic gem is of more consequence than the needs of a great and growing community. It is probable that when the crucial time comes the protestants will be wholly silent, for the ultimate conclusion of all who will attentively study the results of transforming Hetch-Hetchy into a great lake must be that the transformation will convert it into a greater scenic wonder than it is at present. It is true that the meadows and trees of the valley would be submerged, but the immense reservoir created would substitute in their place a vastly more attractive feature, which would prove a far more powerful attraction to persons in

search of inspiring scenery than the eliminated beauties have in the past.

To clear up all remaining doubt, Young added: "Some of its present adornments will disappear, but in their place will be substituted that which will make Hetch-Hetchy incomparable and cause it to rank as one of the world's scenic wonders."

Young and others like him argued for a higher form of having one's cake and eating it too. Through modern engineering, the argument ran, you could build better scenery. That this notion might theoretically bear some weight when applied to a place such as Walt Disney World should not obscure the fact that it did not apply to Hetch Hetchy. In the end, Young and other proponents of the improve-on-nature thesis were due for a severe measure of disappointment. San Francisco officials, for example, promised swimming and boating for the masses in preference to access for only a favored or intrepid few. This democratic line of argument did considerable damage to the preservationists' cause. Today signs prohibit each one of those activities.

✧   ✧   ✧

Over the many decades since the Hetch Hetchy battle was fought, variations upon it have erupted again and again, sometimes with similar results, often with different ones. The common characteristic of these clashes has always entailed a trade-off—pristine terrain against development. The battles have typically involved the same antagonists as of old: northeastern (now bicoastal and urban) preservationists against western/ Alaskan resource-extraction interests and their national or international corporate sponsors. Among abounding examples, we will cite an illustrative few.

The first struggle broke out at mid-twentieth century over Dinosaur National Monument in northwestern Colorado. This obscure monument had originally been created to protect dinosaur remains, then enlarged to encompass 100 miles of wild river canyons. The U.S. Bureau of Reclamation developed expensive plans to construct an Echo Park Dam there for storing Colorado River water. Conservationists bridled, and offered a counterproposal—that northern Arizona's seldom-visited Glen Canyon be dammed instead. By 1950 the battle was fully joined. In 1952 the GOP platform, overlooking the conservationist legacy of both Roosevelt and Pinchot, promised "restoration of the traditional Republican lands policy" (i.e., laissez-faire). Eisenhower's new interior secretary, Douglas McKay, was so generous with public lands that he inspired the sobriquet, "Giveaway McKay." His other virtues included an eminently justifiable modesty: "Well you know, I'm just a Chevrolet salesman."

Predictably, Interior endorsed the Echo Park project. Once again, conservationists calling for highest and best use (dams) faced off against conservationists demanding preservation. In his 1954 congressional testimony, David Brower, John Muir's legatee as executive director of the Sierra Club, exhibited before-and-after photographs of what had occurred at Hetch Hetchy.

By now, writes Stephen Fox, "Echo Park had grown into the biggest conservation issue in decades, probably the biggest since Hetch Hetchy itself." This time, with national mobilization, in 1956 the preservationists won—but at what turned out to be a terrific price. Though seldom visited, Glen Canyon was in fact another esthetic jewel. It had been offered up and accepted in trade for Dinosaur. For the rest of his life Brower blamed himself for Glen Canyon's subsequent immersion. Today, filling the canyon and plied by houseboats, Lake Powell snakes across 200 miles of desert. Fantasies of dynamiting Glen Canyon Dam animate Edward Abbey's ribald 1975 novel, *The Monkey Wrench Gang,* and the novel, in turn, has ever since inspired environmental activists operating within the law and without. During the Clinton administration, legitimate dam dismantling (though not on the scale of Glen Canyon) came into fashion.

Along with the tradition of East–West regional differences over conservation, there remains as well a long-standing pattern of controversial presidential initiatives. This executive tradition emerged with Theodore Roosevelt himself. Complaining about Roosevelt's set-asides of forest reserves, in 1907 Congress passed legislation forbidding any further action in six western states without congressional approval. When the bill arrived on his desk for signing, Roosevelt was ready for it. He once declared that "every man holds his property subject to the general right of the community to regulate its use to whatever degree the public welfare may require it." Before signing the bill, Roosevelt created or expanded 32 reserves by executive decree. "We knew precisely what we wanted," Pinchot later recalled. An early director of the National Park Service recounted that "at one point when they ran out of paper, Roosevelt and Pinchot were on their hands and knees in the White House drawing forest-reserve maps on the floor." Their defiant initiative doubled the nation's protected forest land and set off still more howls about federal usurpation.

Decades later, often utilizing Roosevelt's own legislation, presidents would still be setting land aside to both acclaim and outrage. By the 1960s, the balance had tilted to some degree toward preservationism. Lyndon Johnson's administration, better remembered today for civil rights and Vietnam, established a national wilderness preservation system. After four years of prodding from Jimmy Carter, late in his one-term presidency Congress passed the ponderously titled, six-inch thick Alaska National Interest Lands Conservation Act (1980). The area covered—over one hundred and fifty million acres—was bigger than the state of California. As a means of pressuring Congress to pass the measure, the administration took the precaution of withdrawing from development 40 million acres in Alaska and putting them under even stricter regulation than the pending bill called for; if and when Congress acted, the administration declared, then this "insurance policy" would be rescinded. On much of the land that came under final protection, various kinds of use were allowed (oil extraction, timber harvesting—in short, conservation for use). One hundred million acres were set aside, though, for parks and wildlife refuges. By signing the measure, Carter tripled the size of the national wilderness system.

Bill Clinton did not take office with prepossessing environmental credentials. But in 1996, under the authority of Theodore Roosevelt's 90-year-old Antiquities Act, Clinton set aside 1.7 million acres of red rock canyon lands in southern Utah as Grand Staircase-Escalante National Monument. More than twice the size of Yosemite, these lands directly abutted the north side of Lake Powell. No congressional approval was required.

Portions of the new monument had been slated for coal mines and highways, and Utah officials exploded. In the town of Kanab, residents donned black armbands. As always, the locals insisted they knew better than Washington what was best for the land.

Meanwhile, environmentalists lauded Washington. With the Grand Canyon as its backdrop, noted the *Los Angeles Times,* the designation ceremony "took on an almost religious quality. As Clinton and Vice President Al Gore spoke, the overcast sky broke into a bright sunlight that seemed to set the purple canyons in the distance on fire." "On this remarkable site," Clinton declared in an echo of Muir and Emerson, "God's handiwork is everywhere."

Scarcely consulting western lawmakers or propertied interests at all, during his presidency Clinton created 19 new national monuments totaling over five million acres. Apart from Grand Staircase-Escalante, the entire surge of designations came during Clinton's final year in office. In his last, frantic White House days alone, Clinton made wholesale use of the Antiquities Act to establish eight national monuments. Once again, western property owners and lawmakers exploded. President George W. Bush's administration devoted itself to reversing what Clinton had done.

✧　　✧　　✧

Down to the present day, Hetch Hetchy remains the archetype of the environmental hard choice—the choice between competing values. Should agricultural land be built on or farmed?

Should offshore oil drilling occur at the risk of oil spills? Should pristine Alaskan wilderness be punctured for petroleum? Should snowmobiling or mining be encouraged in national parks? Should old-growth redwoods become lawn furniture? And finally, should more canyons be plugged to provide water and power? Hetch Hetchy represented the classic trade-off. Thousands of trade-offs have followed. If anything, the issue is more pressing now than it was then; American problems pale beside what is happening in China's Yang-tze river valley, the Amazon basin, and the Ural Sea.

There remains one last story to tell about Hetch Hetchy. In 1987 the incumbent secretary of the interior—distant successor to Schurz, Hitchcock, Garfield, Ballinger, and Lane—was Donald P. Hodel. A Ronald Reagan appointee, Hodel's credentials as an environmental advocate were so obscure as to have gone quite undetected. Then, suddenly, Hodel suggested draining Hetch Hetchy and returning the valley to its original state. Historian Norris Hundley dismisses Hodel's suggestion as "obviously politically motivated and made to deflect criticism of the administration's poor record on environmental protection." But not everyone saw it that way, and from the embers of the Roosevelt–Muir era a new controversy now erupted.

As an engineering operation, Hodel's idea was entirely feasible. Flushing out Hetch Hetchy's 360,000 acre-feet of water would take a month. Demolishing the dam would require rather more time and money. The *Los Angeles Times* projected what would happen as Hetch Hetchy recovered, with color illustrations showing how the valley might look 10 years and then 100 years out. In a century Hetch Hetchy would resemble the Garden of Eden.

No less than astonished at their new ally—*Donald Hodel?*—the Sierra Club and other environmental organizations quickly endorsed his idea. "I think John Muir will jump out of his grave and applaud," declared the National Parks director. But San Francisco reacted with markedly less enthusiasm. The city still drew drinking water of unusual purity from Hetch Hetchy, not to mention half of its electrical generating capacity. Defending "the farsightedness of San Francisco's water-wise forefathers 70 years ago," the city's Democratic mayor (later U.S. senator), Dianne Feinstein, labeled Hodel's recommendation to demolish "one of America's most efficient water and power systems [in order] to enhance the scenery" as "stupefying," "peculiar," and "essentially ludicrous." Lest she be misunderstood, Feinstein added that Hodel's suggestion was "dumb, dumb, dumb." Neither Feinstein nor Hodel, it turned out, could quite rise to Muir's or Roosevelt's standard of eloquence.

Had the proposition of flooding Hetch Hetchy first come up in the late twentieth or early twenty-first century, it is difficult to imagine any kind of consideration being given to it at all. Never since has a dam of comparable magnitude been constructed in any national park. That proponents encountered the firestorm they did in Muir's time, during the infancy of the American environmental movement, only hints at the walls that opponents would throw up afterward. The problem in 1987, however, was that the dam was an accomplished fact.

In October of that year, Hodel and Feinstein met atop the 420-foot Hetch Hetchy dam and debated dismantling it. The question at issue remained the same as 80 years before: conservation for use versus preservation. On an appreciative note, representatives of the radical environmental organization Earth First! presented Hodel with a gold-colored monkey wrench.

The appeal of draining Hetch Hetchy—at the very least, studying the possibilities—remains strong today. The National Park Service has evaluated the valley's potential recovery process. An organization called Restore Hetch Hetchy has emerged. And the editorial pages of the *New York Times* and the *Los Angeles Times* have weighed in. With a keen eye to its own history, the *New York Times* writes: "In 1913, over the course of the year, this page ran a total of six thunderous editorials opposing the reservoir. . . . Given this editorial pedigree, the least we can do is endorse a feasibility study. It may well lead to something remarkable."

5

The World Must Be Made Safe for Democracy

Woodrow Wilson, Henry Cabot Lodge, and America's Place Among Nations

Hastily scheduled for the afternoon of December 5, 1919, this would go down as one of the strangest interviews ever held in the White House. The interviewers were two United States senators, one of whom, Albert Fall of New Mexico, would do most of the talking. With his drooping moustache, ten-gallon hat, and cigar, Fall looked like an aging poker player about to cut the cards in a frontier saloon. The man Fall would interview was the president of the United States, who, Fall suspected, was hiding something. Specifically, Fall wanted to find out whether the president was conscious, sane, and able to move.

Fall had cause for suspicion. For two months, President Woodrow Wilson, his wife, and his intimate political circle had concealed the truth: a catastrophic stroke had utterly shattered Wilson's health along with his ability to govern. With Wilson's dream of ending great wars for all time through a

League of Nations on the line, the stroke could not have occurred at a more disastrous time.

Fall's team had been dispatched to the White House by the Senate Foreign Relations Committee, chaired by Henry Cabot Lodge of Massachusetts. Lodge hated Wilson. The president's handlers knew that if they tried to turn away Lodge's delegation now, Congress might quickly bring an impeachment resolution claiming presidential incompetence, which Lodge would undoubtedly have relished. Instead, the Wilson circle set the stage for an elaborate play. Lying on his bed beneath lighting dimmed to minimize his cadaverous appearance, with shoulders slightly propped, Wilson was swathed in blankets as high as his chin to conceal the extent of his paralysis. His right arm, which still functioned, remained exposed. But on this particular day, how well would the president's mind function? That no one could arrange for. In order to survive Fall's visit politically, Wilson would have to summon every ounce of strength that remained to him, and then trust to luck.

The press quickly picked up on the importance of what was about to transpire. The New York *World* told its readers that though the ostensible purpose of the meeting had to do with relations between the United States and Mexico, the "actual purpose" was to compel a "disclosure of the president's condition." Over a hundred reporters congregated outside the White House as the senators were escorted toward Wilson's bedroom.

With his good hand, Wilson gave Fall a strong handshake. The first lady started jotting down notes, which conveniently exempted her from letting Fall's despised fingers touch her own. As if reinforcing the impression of his handshake, Wilson lifted a carefully positioned copy of a Senate committee report, remarking thickly, "Despite the stories going the rounds, I can still use my right hand." The president, it turned out, was sharp today; his fluent comments about U.S.–

Mexican relations utterly stymied Fall. Some forty minutes passed. At one point, bending over Wilson and holding the president's good hand, Fall declared:

"We've been praying for you, sir."

According to some accounts Wilson shot back: "Which way, Senator?"

Perhaps Wilson did say this; more likely it is just a good tale. The important thing, though, is what Fall later told the press—that considering his confinement to bed for weeks, the president "seemed to me to be in excellent trim, both mentally and physically." The satisfaction of the two senators with Wilson's condition, reported the *New York Times,* "was accepted as silencing for good the many wild and often unfriendly rumors of Presidential disability."

Only later would the public learn what the senators had failed to perceive: this was the worst case of presidential disability in the nation's history.

✧   ✧   ✧

Woodrow Wilson and his nemesis, Henry Cabot Lodge, had so much in common that, in many ways, to describe the life of one man virtually describes the other. They were contemporaries, Lodge born in 1850 in Boston, Wilson in 1856 in Staunton, Virginia. As an undergraduate, each benefited from an Ivy League education, Lodge at Harvard, Wilson at Princeton. Both studied law but abandoned that field to pursue doctoral studies in history. Even more exceptional, the two men belonged to America's first generation of Ph.D.s, Lodge earning his at Harvard (1876), Wilson at Johns Hopkins (1886). Both became professors and scholars of note. A prodigy, before he even graduated from Princeton Wilson had published an article about American government in the *International Review.* The editor who accepted Wilson's article for publication was Henry Cabot Lodge.

Had their careers continued on their early path, it is easy to imagine Wilson and Lodge as admiring colleagues, the one at Princeton, the other at Harvard, writing books and delivering erudite lectures well into old age. But their careers took a final turn in common that made them brutal enemies. Each man went into politics, though Lodge was decades ahead of Wilson. Entering the U.S. House of Representatives in 1887, advancing to the Senate in 1893, Lodge demonstrated a burning interest in foreign affairs. His consuming desire was to reach the foreign policy pinnacle of Congress—to chair the Senate Foreign Relations Committee.

Three years before Lodge entered the Senate, Princeton had recruited Wilson to join its faculty. Wilson's scholarship easily eclipsed Lodge's. In an age when boundaries between academic disciplines were more fluid than today, Wilson the historian and lawyer became the country's leading political scientist. Pioneering the field of comparative government, he showed a clear preference for British parliamentary democracy over the system laid out in the United States Constitution. "Tolerance," he once wrote, "is of little worth in politics. . . . Government is too serious a matter to admit of meaningless courtesies." In 1902 Princeton's trustees named Wilson president. Again he excelled, ranking among the greatest of all American university presidents. Wilson's leadership of Princeton, though, was marked, and ultimately undermined, by certain characteristics of temperament, notably stubbornness and a refusal to compromise. When Wilson resigned in 1910 to run for the governorship of New Jersey, Princeton's trustees breathed a sigh of relief.

Wilson's self-righteousness, abundantly demonstrated at Princeton, ran as deep as Lodge's political ambition, giving a sense of inevitability to the two men's ultimate, catastrophic collision. Wilson's father was a Presbyterian minister, his mother the daughter of a Presbyterian minister, and he married the daughter of yet another Presbyterian minister. During his childhood, Wilson would practice giving speeches in the empty sanctuary of his father's church. As an adult, he read a chapter of the Bible every day. "I am too intense!" Wilson once complained. Yet in accepting his father's preachments about a world governed by a stern and exacting God, it is difficult to imagine Wilson turning out otherwise. Predestined, they believed, to achieve salvation in heaven, Presbyterians thought of themselves as an elect destined also to improve this world. "America was born a Christian nation," Wilson declared. "America was born to exemplify that devotion to the elements of righteousness which are derived from the revelations of Holy Scripture."

Wilson was driven by principles and ideals, often showing scant patience with mundane details. He saw the world more in stark blacks and whites than shades of gray, with unbounded confidence in his own ability to judge between right and wrong. Though not at heart a cold man, Wilson could come across to strangers like an iceberg. Yet at the same time, he gave highly popular classroom lectures and learned to sway huge audiences on the strength of his rhetoric alone.

When, with astonishing speed, Woodrow Wilson rose from the presidency of Princeton to the presidency of the United States, Henry Cabot Lodge took offense. He would have done so had any Democrat alive entered the White House. Lodge's loyalty to Republican orthodoxy (and to its distant, flinty New England predecessor, the Federalist Party) was the political equivalent of the law of gravity. His scholarship was so tinctured with political bias that, in the words of his major biographer, "some passages in his books read like campaign tracts for the Republican Party." Lodge complained that Wilson—who had jettisoned much of his own earlier conservatism to embrace political progressivism—had not merely changed his mind but had actually abandoned his principles. Wilson, Lodge claimed, "has no intellectual integrity at all."

To Lodge, conservatism and integrity went together. On his mother's side, the Cabot side, he was a product of the old Boston aristocracy. As the saying went, "the Lowells talk to the Cabots/And the Cabots talk only to God." If Presbyterianism formed the core of Wilson's background, Brahmin privilege comprised the core of Lodge's, along with the Federalist and Republican traditions of serving the desires of wealthy mercantile and landowning interests. Dismissing Thomas Jefferson and others of his type as airy theorists, Lodge showed a strong preference for hard facts. In combativeness, rigidity, and aloofness, Lodge could easily match Wilson; he had a gift for making enemies. Very much like Wilson, too, Lodge tended to harbor odd biases and resentments. Over the years, for example, Lodge, the onetime professor, developed a severe distrust of academe, including college presidents such as Wilson as a group (he had fought with Harvard's). At the same time, regarding himself as *the* scholar in Washington, Lodge resented another Ph.D. edging his way into the limelight. Wilson became the first president to hold an earned (as opposed to a merely honorary) doctorate.

✦   ✦   ✦

Lodge and Wilson did not yet hate each other when Wilson was inaugurated in March, 1913. They had met just once. It would take time, and events, to poison their relationship fully.

First came Lodge's knee-jerk opposition to the progressive reform measures pushed through during Wilson's first term. Agonized by ulcers, away from Washington for months, Lodge could only fume as Congress, controlled by the Democrats, lowered tariff rates and passed the Federal Reserve Act. Wilson became an astonishingly successful domestic reformer, signing into law as well the permanent income tax, the Federal Trade

Commission and Clayton Antitrust acts, and major labor and farm legislation. For a time he tempered much of his natural stubbornness, preaching and horse-trading and moving his legislative agenda so ably that political scientists still look to the first two years of his presidency as a (even as *the*) model of presidential effectiveness in advancing a program. Some observers expressed surprise at "Doctor Wilson's" success; after all, hadn't he been just a university president only a few years before? Yes, but for a quarter-century he had been not only the country's leading political scientist but he had also been embroiled in academic street fighting, which could prove as vicious as the so-called real world of Washington politics. Thus Wilson possessed both theoretical and practical political expertise of an exceptionally high order.

His real falling-out with Lodge, though, occurred not over domestic programs but over foreign policy. Lodge had arrived in the Senate on the eve of a monumental transformation in America's role in the world. By the late nineteenth century, the United States already had the greatest potential power of any nation on the globe, but this power remained latent. More than half a dozen other countries (with their empires) dominated world affairs—Britain, France, Germany, and, to a lesser degree, Russia, Japan, Italy, Austria-Hungary, and the Ottoman (Turkish) Empire. The hub of international power was Europe. Except in the Western Hemisphere, where the Monroe Doctrine warned Europeans off, the other big powers could disregard U.S. interests with relative impunity. Americans themselves did not even agree on what these interests were.

This disagreement came to a head with the Spanish-American war of 1898, from which the United States emerged with a troublesome empire of its own in the Philippines. "Isolation is no longer possible or desirable," President William McKinley declared. Before the war, Lodge and Theodore Roosevelt had pushed hard for U.S. naval expansion, including bases and coaling stations. The close friendship between the two men grew out of their shared belief that America must increase its role in the world, enlarge its military, and fully join the ranks of the great powers. Both men applauded the war with Spain. Building on McKinley's record, the Roosevelt presidency (1901–09) fully heralded America's rise to world power. Roosevelt and his successor, William Howard Taft (1909–13), agreed that the U.S. must enter into a cooperative relationship with other big, modern nations. They took guarded steps in this direction. Anticipating a future of peaceful economic competition between basically friendly rival countries, President Taft declared that "modern diplomacy is commercial" (a sentiment coined in the catchphrase "dollar diplomacy"). To many Americans, perhaps to most, a breakdown of diplomacy leading to another great war seemed unthinkable. Civilization, they assumed, had progressed beyond that.

Lodge read Wilson's foreign policy as timid, even cowardly. In actual fact, Wilson's approach to Latin American proved to be anything but timid. He sent U.S. troops to more countries there—Mexico, Haiti, the Dominican Republic—than had any president before him. Like his Republican predecessors, he wanted the U.S. to dominate the region for both economic and strategic purposes. But Wilson's power politics always came with a glaze of moralistic, even professorial, rhetoric: "I am going to teach the South American Republics to elect good men!" In truth, Wilsonian foreign policy espoused two approaches at once: idealism and realism. Wilson the idealist wanted to transform human affairs for the better by implementing abstract principles of right and justice. Wilson the realist used power and force. His opponents took the idealism for weakness, and the realism as never hard-boiled enough.

After World War I, then known as the Great War, broke out in the summer of 1914, Wilson called for strict U.S. "impartiality" and neutrality toward the two coalitions: the

FIGURE 5.1 World War I.

Allies (Great Britain, France, Russia, Italy, Japan) and the
Central Powers (Germany, Austria-Hungary, the Ottoman
Empire). From 1914 to 1917, no statesman worked as hard as
Wilson to bring the conflict to a halt. Calling for a "peace
without victory"—without seizure of territory or the laying on
of indemnities—he fruitlessly urged the warring coalitions to
compromise. In 1916 Wilson ran for a second term as a peace
candidate. "He kept us out of war" went the Democratic campaign refrain. When push came to shove, though, Wilson's
actual sympathies lay with the Allies.

Lodge, on the other hand, took such a one-sided position in favor of Britain and France that he regarded Wilson not just as weak but as unpatriotic and pro-German. A German triumph, Lodge believed, would pose a direct threat to American national security. Wilson's declaration that America was "too proud to fight" and Wilson's talk about peace without victory utterly revolted Lodge. So did Wilson's hesitation about strengthening the American military. Always inclined toward what he regarded as timely, decisive action in foreign affairs, Lodge would willingly risk war in order to guarantee Allied victory. As William C. Widenor has put it, "Wilson in opposing American entry into the war had denied not only the fact of a threat to the national interest but even the primacy of considerations of national interest. His America would contend only for moral principle."

As early as the spring of 1915, the enmity between Wilson and Lodge had gone beyond politics or policies. "I never expected to hate anyone in politics with the hatred I feel towards Wilson," Lodge wrote the militaristic, wholly sympathetic Theodore Roosevelt. Wilson would probably never have permitted himself consciously to hate Lodge. He was too painfully Christian for that. Yet Lodge's partisanship, obstinacy, and fundamental disagreement with the administration over foreign policy galled the president. Wilson's attitude seems to have taken the form of cold disdain, combined with attributions of evil. The two men's enmity simmered for the next two years, by which time Germany and the U.S. were on a collision course.

Desperate to win, Germany totally miscalculated that it could defeat Britain by launching unrestricted submarine warfare against every kind of shipping from all nations. The undersea blockade should bring transportation to and from the British Isles to a halt, even though the U.S., seeing its ships going to the bottom, would surely declare war. Berlin gambled that it could beat the Allies before American intervention made a difference. Germany even attempted to line up Mexico in a military coalition against the U.S.

Announcing that "the world must be made safe for democracy," in April, 1917, Wilson finally asked Congress for a declaration of war. But under Wilson's leadership, America could only wage a utopian war—a war to end war and reform the world. Then as now, fighting for ideals appealed to Americans, even to those reluctant to fight at all. Ever religious, Wilson described U.S. forces as "crusaders" bringing Europe "salvation." Lodge himself declared that in fighting beside Britain and France, the U.S. was engaged in a struggle for "freedom, democracy and modern civilization." Yet even Lodge's most expansive phrases fell deliberately short of Wilson's portrayal of World War I as "the culminating and final war for human liberty."

Another of Wilson's declarations, that politics was adjourned for the duration of the conflict, amounted to wishful thinking. Political tensions remained high. Recruiting a prominent Republican or two into his cabinet, as Franklin D. Roosevelt would do a generation later, might have helped, but Wilson apparently never seriously thought about reaching out to the Republicans. He also refused to take the Senate Foreign Relations Committee into his confidence. These were premonitions of political failures to come. On Capitol Hill, it was no mystery that as a matter of principle (and as an admirer of parliamentary systems), Wilson believed in permanently augmenting the power of the executive branch. Watching apprehensively as the president amassed tremendous wartime authority, many in Congress yearned to get their prerogatives back the minute the conflict ended.

During the spring of 1916, a year before America entered the war, Wilson had given a speech promoting his vision of the postwar world. Central to this vision was a League of Nations, through which a newly fledged community of democracies would cooperate in protecting one another (collective security). Rooted in centuries of thought, the idea of a world parliament had excited a good deal of discussion, notably in Britain, before the war. Wilson delivered his address to an organization called the League to Enforce Peace. After America declared war, Wilson's idea took form as the most vast and sweeping plan espoused by any leader. "What we seek," he declared, "is the reign of law, based upon the consent of the governed and sustained by the organized opinion of mankind." Laying out Fourteen Points early in 1918, Wilson called for the creation of "a general association of nations . . . affording mutual guarantees of political independence and territorial integrity to great and small states alike." Other points demanded international arms reductions, an end to covert diplomacy (secret treaties), free trade, free navigation of the seas, and national self-determination—the democratic right of peoples, including colonized peoples, to chart their own future.

Today these ideas have gained such wide acceptance, even becoming clichés, and the United Nations is such a familiar presence, that one must struggle to recapture just how radical the ideas seemed to the world of 1918. None was even remotely an established fact then. Democracies themselves remained rare. With the causes of World War I fresh in everyone's mind, Wilson expected that the Fourteen Points would permanently lead the world away from war. Wilson's plan, though, conflicted with the hallowed approach to foreign policy: the balance of power, in which coalitions of roughly equal strength supposedly prevented war by making it too risky for either side to start. To one degree or another, and certainly before World War I, the balance of power had dominated international relations throughout human history. Power always had a way of coming unbalanced, though, tempting one side to attack. Many Europeans shared the dark view that, rather than being a permanent condition, peace merely comprised the interval between wars. Wilson intended to consign such pessimistic fatalism to the past. His individual proposals as such were not original; yet the way he put them squarely before the world as a collective and coherent program for permanent peace was a true revelation. "There must be not a balance of power," he declared, "but a community of power; not organized rivalries, but an organized common peace."

In October, 1918, a collapsing Germany appealed for negotiations to end hostilities based on the Fourteen Points. At last, it seemed, a future of promise and hope could be salvaged from the muck of the trenches and 10 million deaths. By enunciating such a future, Wilson had made himself the preeminent statesman in the world.

✧   ✧   ✧

What failed now, incredibly, was the thing Wilson had studied and practiced his whole adult life—his political touch. It began to fail repeatedly. Wilson's historic task, as Richard Hofstadter put it, was to preach "a mission of world service" to the historically "insular and provincial" American people. In 1916 Wilson had won reelection by a hairbreadth, and by 1918, American voters had plenty of reason for dissatisfaction arising from inflation, repression of dissent, and other wartime disruptions at home. Wilson did not want to lose Democratic majorities in Congress, and then, with a political shadow over him, sit down at the peace table with the leaders of the Allies. So he made an appeal to the electorate for a vote of confidence in the November, 1918, congressional elections: "If you have approved of my leadership and wish me to be your unembarrassed spokesman in affairs at home and abroad, I earnestly beg that you will express yourselves unmistakably to that effect by returning a Democratic majority to both the Senate and the House of Representatives." Instead, the GOP swept both houses; and true to his fears, this political disaster undermined Wilson with the other victorious powers. Absent an international crisis or a state of war (World War I had all but ended), in voters' minds, foreign policy generally takes a backseat to more mundane economic and quality-of-life issues. As a historian and political scientist, Wilson surely knew this. When Wilson asked the public to elect Democratic majorities to help him in negotiating the peace, he took a huge gamble, and he lost.

Wilson's public appeal was raw meat for Lodge and Roosevelt. Along with other prominent Republicans including Taft, each man had flirted with the idea of an international organization, but hating Wilson as they did, a league with Wilson's (or the Democratic Party's) stamp on it aroused immediate suspicion. In any case, Lodge and Roosevelt fundamentally believed in the balance of power. Wilson's idealism struck both men as absurd. Wilson having thrown down the gauntlet, Roosevelt took it up by proclaiming that the president's "leadership has just been emphatically repudiated" and that "Mr. Wilson and his Fourteen Points . . . have ceased to have any shadow of right to be accepted as expressive of the will of the American people." Europe could not fail to understand the message, one that had particular force when delivered by such a towering figure as Roosevelt.

Now Wilson's political sensitivities failed him a second time. In choosing the U.S. peace delegation, Wilson appointed no Republican of stature and none at all from the Senate or its Foreign Relations Committee. To designate any Republican except Lodge would have amounted to snubbing Lodge—but Wilson could not bring himself to appoint Lodge. Wilson decided to lead the delegation himself. This made sense; each of the other victorious powers would also be represented in Paris by its leader. Yet blatantly snubbing the GOP-controlled Senate, which would have to approve the eventual treaty by a two-thirds vote, made no sense at all.

For the moment, Lodge remained quietly in the wings as the president basked in glory. During the latter months of 1918, Woodrow Wilson was undoubtedly the most popular person in the world. To all appearances, the hopes he raised exceeded those aroused by any other president in American history. In the European Allied capitals, he was mobbed; two million greeted him in Paris. The frantic cheering simply deepened his belief that his peace plan was what the world's peoples most wanted and that he alone truly spoke for them, even for the Europeans over and above their own elected leaders. He failed to see that while the Europeans on the winning side wanted peace, they also wanted revenge. In one of the classic cases of presidential hubris, Wilson lost his hold on reality, and not just political reality. Sigmund Freud, who despised him, concluded that Wilson had a Christ complex. Freud overstated. But it would have been hard for any mortal not to be swept away when greeted by banners in Rome proclaiming, "HAIL THE CRUSADER FOR HUMANITY" and "WELCOME TO THE GOD OF PEACE."

When Wilson actually engaged the other leaders of the Big Four—David Lloyd George of Britain, Georges Clemenceau of France, and Vittorio Orlando of Italy—he ran up against men whose countries had suffered vastly more than the United States and whose concerns ran to national security and revenge. To a degree, Lloyd George shared Wilson's broader goals. Clemenceau, a brilliant war leader nicknamed the Tiger, was overwhelmingly concerned with protecting France against Germany. Of Wilson's Fourteen Points Clemenceau reportedly remarked, "The good Lord made do with ten." "How can I talk to a fellow," Clemenceau once asked in exasperation, "who thinks himself the first man in two thousand years to know anything about peace on earth?"

Nevertheless, Wilsonian goals set the terms of debate in Paris, with Wilson the central leader. He was the only one of the Big Four who arrived at the table without a narrow national agenda, with no territorial or financial claims, and with the overriding goal of an equitable settlement. Wilson made creating the League his highest priority. But Wilson's lifelong inclination to think in terms of broad principles, not details, slammed into the very specific, concrete realities of European power politics. Though he was utterly certain that a harsh peace with Germany and future reliance on the old balance of power would open the door to another war, in order to secure a peace treaty at all, Wilson felt compelled to compromise his principles with the leaders of the Allies. Negotiated in secret, contrary to Wilsonian principles, the treaty did impose a brutal peace on Germany—open-ended reparations, disarmament, loss of European territory and foreign empire, acceptance of responsibility for the war. International free trade and free seas went by the wayside. Dramatic inequities occurred in breaking up the empires of the Central Powers.

The Allies compromised as well, though, and because Wilson influenced the course of events so strongly, a far better peace emerged—arguably even the best peace negotiable under the circumstances. Wilson thwarted some of the most extreme Allied demands. National boundaries were redrawn. And in Wilson's greatest victory, the conferees incorporated his League of Nations into the peace document itself. To Wilson, the most important final virtue of the Treaty of Versailles was the League.

Having had considerable success in Paris, Wilson now committed his third disastrous political error. He had made the necessary compromises (perhaps even more) with the leaders of the Allies; but he refused to make the necessary compromises with Henry Cabot Lodge. As always, the two men held much in common. Lodge agreed with Wilson that America had a unique moral mission in the world. Within the GOP, Lodge was not viewed as an extremist. A wide gulf separated the Republican Party's internationalist wing, to which Lodge belonged, from its powerful isolationist wing. Intensely suspicious of any entanglements in international power politics whatsoever, congressional Republican isolationists had voted against intervening in World War I while internationalists such as Lodge and Roosevelt insisted that American entry was overdue. Desiring a just peace, Lodge declared, in words that might have come from Wilson himself, "we have no territory to gain and seek no conquests." Lodge agreed with Wilson that, as Lodge put it, "to restore the [prewar] status quo . . . would simply be to give Germany a breathing space in which she may prepare to renew the war." Lodge went so far as to call Wilson's Fourteen Points speech "a good speech . . . as to terms."

Where, then, did Lodge and Wilson fall out? Over personal hostility, to begin with—and, as if more were needed, over party politics. In the 1920 presidential election, which Lodge desperately wanted his party to win, the Republicans could ill afford to let the Democrats secure their own version of an international organization on top of leading the country through a victorious war. Even more fundamentally, though, Wilson and Lodge had different views of how the world worked. Though each man's perspectives combined both elements, Wilson was basically an *idealist*. Lodge was fundamentally a *realist*.

The chief of British intelligence in the U.S. captured Wilson's intent with elegant brevity. Wilson, he said, "is not so much interested in the adjustment of this claim or that— the limitation of one power, and the strengthening of another—but his mind visualizes a new world in which there shall be no tyranny and no war." Through the League, Wilson expected, the United States would abandon the remnants of its nineteenth-century isolation and fully assume its role (which Lodge would not have protested) as the greatest of the great powers. This was this realistic side of Wilson talking; the U.S. had already become preeminent, whether it liked it or not, and must act as such. But, as always, Wilson took flight in the language of the pulpit. America's God-given destiny, he declared, was not mere power, but the "moral leadership" of the world: "It has come about by no plan of our conceiving, but by the hand of God who led us into this way. We cannot turn back. We can only go forward, with lifted eyes and freshened spirit, to follow the vision. It was of this that we dreamed at our birth. America shall in truth show the way. The light streams upon the path ahead, and nowhere else." Wilson preached "a new day . . . in which justice shall replace force and jealous intrigue among the nations." Calling the organization "the only hope for mankind," he predicted a "new order" thanks to the League. No more than Lodge did Wilson want the U.S. bogged down in international entanglements; but he believed that, through the League, America could somehow control world politics *without* such entanglements. In this he was remarkably naïve. He also proved naïve in his assumption that the other great powers would simply follow the American lead. When he discovered they would not, despite U.S. economic leverage over them, he became utterly dismayed. At a time when the British empire and commonwealth still controlled a quarter of the globe and the French empire spanned giant expanses of Africa and Asia, Wilson should never have expected them to.

Lodge disagreed with Wilson's central premise, that international relations could be fundamentally transformed. Wilsonian internationalism and appeals for universal benevolence went too far, and Wilson's sweeping rhetorical flights repelled Lodge. Convinced, like Wilson, that American national security was intimately tied to the nature of the peace settlement, Lodge's overriding concern involved finding the best means to contain Germany. He had wanted Allied armies to end the war by punching through to Berlin, forcing an unconditional surrender. When the Allies stopped far short, Lodge worried. "The first and controlling purpose of the peace," he declared, "must be to put Germany in such a position that it will be physically impossible for her to break out again upon other nations with a war for world conquest."

Containing Germany, Lodge expected, would require the closest collaboration between the victors. Just as Wilson was maintaining an arm's- length distance from the Allied governments and appealing directly to their peoples, Lodge actually wanted to tighten bonds with these governments. With his enduring faith in the balance of power, Lodge saw France as America's first line of defense. To Lodge, as Widenor puts it, "the future peace of the world depended, not on the universal prevalence of American ideals, but rather on the strength of France." Paris wanted the League to have an army for enforcing its decrees. Instead of an army, Wilson and Lloyd George pledged to encourage their own governments to provide guarantees of military aid should Germany attack again. Lodge would never have opposed such a treaty commitment to France, and Wilson knew it, but Wilson let the idea die.

In retrospect, while different in nature and narrower in scope, it seems clear that Lodge's commitment to postwar international engagement actually rivaled Wilson's. And if some sort of league had emerged that fit into his goals, especially a league disassociated from Wilson or the Democratic Party, Lodge would not have objected. Lodge's sort of league would have bound the victorious nations together to perpetuate the victory they had just won over Germany, if necessary through force of arms. In order to get the kind of peace he wanted, though, Lodge had to compel Wilson to compromise. Failing that, he had to block the Senate from ratifying the peace treaty at all.

The battle over the treaty, including the League, came down to specifics, and Wilson's failure to show how to implement his great dream with methods and resources galled Lodge. Lodge despised the idea of a league founded merely on an "assemblage of words, an exposition of vague ideals and encouraging hopes." No "practical and effective" league could possibly emerge, he asserted, "unless it has authority to issue decrees and force to sustain them." "Unlike Wilson, who always preferred ideals to application," writes Robert M. Crunden, "Lodge insisted on clear, limited, specific language that he and his country would then be willing to support with force. He preferred no treaty at all to a vague one." Lodge declared: "The details are vital."

The key detail had to do with Article 10 of the League Covenant (constitution), committing the League's member nations "to respect" but more than that to "preserve as against external aggression the territorial integrity and existing political independence of all Members of the League." What did these words mean? The Covenant left their meaning unclear— the League Council would "advise upon the means by which this obligation shall be fulfilled." Many Americans thought this meant that the League would sometimes have to use force of arms to ensure compliance with its edicts; yet many more, apparently, expected that the League's decrees would carry the day on the strength of their moral authority alone. Wilson himself set great store in moral suasion. Of the Covenant as a whole he declared, "throughout this instrument we are depending primarily and chiefly upon one great force, and that is the moral force of the public opinion of the world." Only if the "overwhelming light of the universal expression of the condemnation of the world" failed would military power come into play: "If the moral force of the world will not suffice, the physical force of the world shall." "The united power of free nations must put a stop to aggression."

Most fundamentally, the issue of Article 10 came down to what Lodge termed the relationship between "Force and Peace." Did Wilson intend for the League to possess an international military establishment—including American troops—with which to enforce its edicts? To Lodge the question seemed vital, but Wilson never clearly answered it. Any answer he might offer posed problems. Say the League Council ruled that one country had committed aggression against another. Wilson emphasized the role of peaceful means—binding arbitration and sanctions, including an economic boycott—as the next steps in bringing the rogue nation to heel. But what if these methods failed? As a last resort, would the League's member states together then have to use force? Wilson said yes. But if yes meant American troops too, how did this align with the Constitution, which reserved to Congress the power of declaring war? Might the League try unilaterally ordering U.S. armed forces into action, overriding Congress? The idea horrified Lodge. On the other hand, in a given case, the League Council might vote for war, Congress vote against it, the U.S. thus refuse to commit troops, and other countries do the same. Force would no longer be automatic but haphazard.

Lodge knew that the Senate would never approve of American participation in an international army, and that without an international army behind it, the League could never live up to expectations. But should America somehow become involved after all, where would U.S. obligations end? Lodge drew the line at a "general, indefinite, unlimited scheme of always being called upon to meddle in European, Asian and African questions," or "plunging the United States into every controversy and conflict on the face of the globe." He feared that Article 10 would obligate the U.S. to use its "military or economic force" to "guarantee the territorial integrity of the far-flung British Empire . . . , of China or Japan, or of the French, Italian and Portuguese colonies in Africa." Would membership eliminate or weaken the Monroe Doctrine, or American immigration or tariff policy? Lodge wanted to deny any league such authority over U.S. sovereignty. "There may be some vague declarations of the beauties of peace," he said, "but any practical league I do not think they can form." Human nature must be taken, Lodge the admirer of Puritans and Federalists remarked, "as it is and not as it ought to be."

The gauntlet that Lodge arrayed against the Wilsonian League of Nations, then, consisted of a methodical demonstration of logical inconsistencies, potential demands on American resources, and threats to U.S. sovereignty that would make the League impossible for the Senate or the American public to accept. Meanwhile, on key questions, Lodge actually encouraged the Allied leaders to resist Wilson. In the end, Lodge found that he had more confidence in the premier of France than in the president of the United States.

Early in 1919, Wilson and Lodge each made political plans to force the other to accept his version of the peace. Relying on moral suasion, Wilson wanted to override all quibbling over details by generating a politically irresistible public demand for the Senate to ratify the treaty at once. He utterly eschewed detailed explanations. The Republicans, though, controlled the Senate by two votes. As the new majority leader and chairman of the Foreign Relations Committee, Lodge spoke for his party. Thanks to Lodge, with his strong philosophical, personal, and partisan reasons for opposing the Wilsonian League, the treaty fight became utterly politicized. Grounded on the proposition that the American people would prove unwilling to meet their full international obligations under Article 10, Lodge's two-pronged strategy involved broadly publicizing the treaty's pitfalls while taking advantage of his own unique leverage over foreign policy. To the task he brought a mastery of parliamentary strategy.

Heady with his success in Paris, Wilson returned home in mid-February, 1919, the League covenant in his overcoat pocket. He ran straight into Lodge's elaborate minefield. Lodge's dual strategy of working on public opinion while simultaneously waging parliamentary warfare succeeded splendidly. All the negative publicity about the uncertainties and potential sacrifices that would accompany League membership eventually began to sour public opinion. Various ethnic groups (notably German-Americans) objected that the treaty was unfair to their particular people, while many Wilsonian perfectionists complained that the treaty fell far short of their leader's ideals. Wilson reluctantly met with the Foreign Relations Committee late in February. At the meeting, Lodge remained as silent as the paintings on the walls. A week later, Lodge introduced a so-called round robin resolution signed by over a third of the Senate, putting them on record against the League "in the form now proposed." The resolution recommended removing the League from the peace treaty so as to provide for separate consideration. Wilson responded that "you cannot dissect the covenant from the treaty without destroying the whole vital structure." But the round robin made it mathematically clear that Wilson did not have two-thirds of the Senate. Returning to Paris soon afterward, he got the other powers to recognize the Monroe Doctrine, seemingly resolving one big issue with Lodge; and additional changes were negotiated in order to satisfy objections on the Hill.

Nothing Wilson could do, though, would come close to satisfying the "irreconcilables," 16 senators (14 of them

Republicans) led by William Borah of Idaho. These men despised the very idea of a league. Another group, the "strong reservationists," Lodge himself led; they included most of the Senate Republicans and ranged from closet irreconcilables to moderates who would accept the treaty with the League of Nations included, but under clear conditions. Lodge packed the Foreign Relations Committee with strong reservationists and irreconcilables. In order to prevail, Wilson would have to unite his loyal followers in the Senate, who would take the treaty as it came, with a group of "mild reservationists" who could be appeased with limited alterations.

Here Wilson committed his fourth political sin. Convinced that overriding matters of principle were at issue, under the illusion that he was winning, and utterly sick of all the back-and-forth in Europe and at home, he absolutely refused to satisfy the mild reservationists. If the U.S. tried to modify the treaty in any way, he thought, other countries might reopen it too. His own hubris conspired in blinding him to political reality. Warned that he might not get two-thirds of the Senate, he declared, "Anyone who opposes me . . . I'll crush! *The Senate must take its medicine.*"

But Wilson's numerical disadvantage in Congress meant that he had to reach a compromise. To this day historians dispute how or even whether an agreement between Wilson and Lodge might have been fashioned. To begin with, was *Lodge* ever willing to compromise with *Wilson?* Did Lodge simply want to render membership in the League unthreatening to the United States—or was his public posture actually a ruse to deny Wilson his heart's desire by blocking U.S. membership? What portion of Lodge's behavior stemmed from political opportunism, and what portion from his often-stated commitment to the sanctity of treaty obligations and to informing the American public about them? On all these questions historians disagree. A narrow preponderance of evidence does suggest that Lodge was willing to compromise *if* Wilson agreed to strong reservations. But Lodge cared less whether or not the U.S. joined the League than about the terms under which it joined. He wanted strict guarantees that the U.S. "assumes no obligation" under Article 10 without congressional approval for every action. Wilson replied that while Article 10 was "a very grave and solemn obligation" it was "a moral, not a legal, obligation," and left Congress "absolutely free to put its own interpretation upon it in all cases that call for action. It is binding in conscience only, not in law."

In the end, the two men's inability to agree on Article 10 doomed the treaty. Today, their disagreement looks specious or irrelevant. As one historian has put it, "Wilson's interpretation of the obligation was clear to him but obscure to almost everyone else" including Lodge. Lodge declared that "there is to me no distinction whatever in a treaty between what some persons are pleased to call legal and moral obligations." Insisting that 10 would usurp the specific congressional prerogative to declare war, Lodge wanted Congress's responsibility reconfirmed. Technically this was not even a necessity; under the Constitution, that prerogative was a given. As for the League Council trying to override Congress, the Covenant provided that the council would have to vote unanimously, which gave the U.S. a veto before the issue of peace or war even got to Congress.

What Wilson actually wanted, however, was an American "moral" commitment *distinct* from the "legal" nuts and bolts of the Constitution or the Covenant. In Wilson's mind, a "moral obligation" was far "superior to a legal obligation, and, if I may say so, has a greater binding force." This may look like a distinction without a difference, but not to anyone with Wilson's religiously inspired cast of mind. A legal obligation simply amounted to a binding obligation, like driving with a license. A moral obligation, on the other hand, introduced "the right to exercise one's judgment," to make a deliberate ethical choice such as one does when deciding to tell the truth. Lodge viewed all treaties as binding in law, and he did not want to see America obligated by Article 10; the article should, he thought, go no farther than committing Congress to devote its attention to this particular crisis or that. Wilson genuinely believed that if adopted, Lodge's position would cancel out the element of moral obligation, and that to assume "no obligation" (as Lodge put it) would be to undermine America's commitment to collective security and ruin the League. America could not have it both ways—in order to meet its moral obligation and to achieve cooperation in collective security, it must relinquish some of its historic sovereignty and freedom of action. The remnants of isolationism must be uprooted. Only then could Article 10 truly become what Wilson called it, "the very backbone of the whole Covenant."

✧　　✧　　✧

Having fruitlessly tried to work things out with dozens of senators, Wilson committed his fifth great error. In late summer, 1919, after long contemplation, he decided to appeal over Congress directly to the American people, much as he had done in Europe. Now, it appears, Lodge's desire to humiliate Wilson did take over. From this point through the election of 1920, Lodge for all intents and purposes became an irreconcilable. Let Wilson just try to run for a third term, Lodge mused, with no peace settlement in sight. But these thoughts were carefully concealed. For public consumption, Lodge declared that all Wilson had to do to get his treaty through was agree to Lodge's reservations.

In September, 1919, Wilson launched his planned 10,000-mile trip, ignoring warnings from his wife and doctor that his health could not withstand the strain. "Even though, in my condition, it might mean the giving up of my life, I will gladly make the sacrifice to save the Treaty," he confided to his secretary. Some historians believe Wilson actually invited martyrdom. But Wilson, the former professor, spoke in terms of educating the American people about the treaty. Like other reformers of his time, Wilson had great faith in the power of rhetoric and the wisdom of an informed public. (Lodge regarded mass opinion with suspicion even as he worked to turn it his way.) Looked at objectively, Wilson's tour held out only a limited possibility of political success. Early on, public opinion had appeared to back the League enthusiastically, and 32 state legislatures had endorsed it. By now, though, Wilson would be making his appeal to voters who were turning their backs on him. Lodge, having reached an accommodation with the mild reservationists, remained absolutely in command of the Senate. Holding six-year terms, most senators did not face imminent reelection, so they could more or less safely ignore any public pressure that Wilson managed to whip up. And if Wilson's health *did* collapse, what then? The Democratic Party would resemble a football team seeing its star quarterback carried off the field, with no competent second-stringer to step in for him.

Over a span of three weeks, Wilson gave three dozen major speeches to audiences as large as 30,000. Only once did he even have one of the new loudspeakers to use. Blinding headaches constantly dogged him. No president before or since has ever matched what Wilson tried to do. Along with evoking the broader dream, he filled in details about the League, at last responding to the questions raised by his Senate opponents—some of whom followed him like bloodhounds, delivering speeches of their own. At first Wilson's audiences gave a mixed response; but then the people began to warm to the president, the crowds grew, and by the time he reached the West Coast, he was receiving thunderous acclaim. From all the evidence, public attitudes were turning his way again. He brought many of his listeners to tears. In Montana, a little boy ran up to give the president a dime. Stopping in Pueblo, Colorado, on his return eastward, Wilson got the biggest reception of all. That night, he collapsed. The rest of his speeches were called off and the train sped back to Washington. In the White House four days later, a massive paralytic stroke hit him. For all his eloquence and the upwelling public response, Wilson's trip had not changed the mind of one single senator.

For years, historians have tried to fathom Wilson's grim stubbornness over the peace settlement, contrasting as it does so vividly with his earlier finesse in driving through his landmark legislative program. Hubris explains part of it. So do underlying personality characteristics: Wilson had always tended toward stubbornness, for example, seeking refuge from facts in principles and generalities. Horse-trading had never appealed to him. Wilson clearly grew weary of endless dickering with the leaders of the Allies (studying maps on hands and knees on the floor of his suite at night, frequent 12- and 14-hour days). Exhaustion became his constant companion, degrading his ability to make sound decisions.

The biggest factor, though, was the stroke. Only during the past generation have medical specialists carefully examined the nature of Wilson's illness as a stroke victim, bringing to the task new knowledge lacking in Wilson's day. Meanwhile Wilson's medical records, long presumed destroyed, have reappeared. Wilson may have suffered his first stroke not in 1919 but as far back as 1896, with additional strokes occurring over the intervening years. Strokes can markedly exaggerate preexisting personality traits—for instance, self-righteousness, stubbornness, or intransigence—almost to the point of caricature. This clearly happened to Wilson; in a classic medical syndrome, the cardiovascular illness changed the nature of the man. In his wide swings between rage and tears, deepened tendency toward self-isolation, peevishness, irascibility, and denial of his disability—he even wanted to run again in 1920—Wilson manifested common forms of behavior that accompany stroke. More than ever (if that was possible), he now saw issues in religious terms, good-versus-evil. (The treaty represented God's will; one did not compromise over *that*.) He became utterly rigid. No one in his inner circle, not even his wife, Edith, could persuade him to compromise. New information about changing conditions was shrugged off. The remnants of Wilson's political logic fell away; the connection between his decisions and their results now escaped him. Half-paralyzed, partially blind, unable to stand, robbed of his former eloquence, unable even to concentrate for more than a short time or to deal with complexities, Wilson lived within an unrealistically comfortable cocoon spun by Edith, in collaboration with his doctor. No one got in to see him, no piece of paper crossed his line of sight without her say-so.

As it happened, the duration of the fight over the League of Nations was waged by an incapacitated president who, having hovered near death for a week, could not work for nearly three months and afterwards did so with radically diminished abilities. For more than seven months, Wilson did not meet with his cabinet, depending for information on the versions of the truth filtered through his wife. There was no disclosure of Wilson's full condition to the press, so, inevitably, wild rumors began to circulate. Wilson's physician urged that the president resign, and Wilson flirted with the notion; but Edith would not hear of it. (Contrary to legend, though, Mrs. Wilson's assumed powers did not quite reach so far as to make her the "first woman president.") Despite his missionary zeal, earlier political miscalculations, and hubris, had his health remained intact, Wilson might well have compromised even yet for the sake of the treaty. He had done this throughout the battles in Paris and following Lodge's round robin. Unless he really did regard the moral-legal aspect of Article 10 as utterly nonnegotiable, he might have fought stubbornly, then yielded just enough at the very last to get the treaty through. There is evidence that, before the stroke, he contemplated precisely this.

Truthfully if cruelly, it would have been far better for Wilson's historical reputation had the stroke of October, 1919, killed him outright. The vice president, Thomas R. Marshall, would then have succeeded him. Or the Constitution provided that the vice president could take over from a still-living but incapacitated president. None of this occurred. Speaking in Atlanta following Wilson's stroke, Marshall experienced what he later described as the worst moment of his life. In the midst of his speech, someone informed him that President Wilson had died. Having asked the crowd to pray for him, Marshall then learned that it was all a practical joke—"a most cruel hoax," Marshall called it. Marshall was a decent man but hardly presidential material. He is now remembered (when remembered at all) for his observation, "What this country needs is a really good five-cent cigar." Still, the nation might have fared better under Thomas R. Marshall, who thought the administration should accept Lodge's reservations.

In November, 1919, the Foreign Relations Committee sent the Versailles Treaty to the Senate floor. The 14 Lodge reservations (just as many as Wilson had points) were attached. Though some of these reservations had only the political value of tormenting Wilson, Lodge's "no obligation" provision was critical: the U.S. would not take action under Article 10 "unless in any particular case the Congress . . . shall by act or joint resolution so provide." Like Marshall, the Democrats in the Senate would willingly have voted for the treaty with the reservations. Wilson pulled them back, insisting the reservations amounted to a "knife thrust at the heart of the treaty" because no obligation meant no moral commitment. "Let Lodge compromise," he demanded. The version of the treaty with Lodge's reservations failed, 39–55. Then the treaty went down without reservations, 38–53. By the end of the year, both Wilson and Lodge were bucking the tide of public opinion, which favored some form of compromise. Though differing over the details, four-fifths of the Senate wanted U.S. membership in the League. Yet neither man would yield a yard. In March, 1920, yet another vote occurred. This time 21 Democrats broke ranks with Wilson and voted for the treaty with the Lodge reservations, which produced a margin of 49 for, 35 against—a clear majority, yet shy of two-thirds by seven votes. "The devil," Wilson afterwards remarked, "is a very busy man."

One historian has accused Wilson of "infanticide" in refusing to compromise. More commonly the blame falls on Lodge. Even Lodge, perhaps in recognition that he had succeeded too well, acknowledged that the League battle had not been "without its elements of tragedy." Before the 1920 vote, he had tried to strike a deal on reservations with Senate Democrats, but the irreconcilables pulled him back, accusing him of disloyalty and apparently threatening to oust him as Majority Leader.

On March 4, 1921, Wilson rode to the Capitol for the inauguration of his successor. Although he had recently received the Nobel Peace Prize, by now the stricken president's onetime popularity had all but evaporated. Wilson had called for the 1920 election to be a "great and solemn referendum" on the Covenant. Warren G. Harding, calling instead for a return to "normalcy," won in a huge landslide and went on to preside over one of the most scandal-plagued presidencies in American history. Albert Fall, who as a Senate irreconcilable had oiled his way into the presidential bedroom to ascertain Wilson's true condition, was a crony of Harding. Named interior secretary by the new president, Fall would distinguish himself as the first cabinet member ever sent to prison for corruption. In 1921, the United States signed a separate peace with Germany. America never entered the League of Nations. In November, 1923, in a radio address about Armistice Day heard by millions, Wilson decried America's current withdrawal "into a sullen and selfish isolation."

✧   ✧   ✧

"I am not one of those that have the least anxiety about the triumph of the principles I have stood for," Wilson told a crowd of veterans the day after his radio address. "That we shall prevail is as sure as that God reigns." Three months later, in February, 1924, he was dead. (Always Wilson's contemporary, Lodge died later that year.) In the end Wilson's failure was a *political* failure, but he knew that ideas in themselves have consequences. As he had predicted, his ideas eventually prevailed.

The costs of American isolationism became vividly clear after the rise of fascism in the 1920s and 1930s, followed by the Second World War. On his cross-country speaking tour Wilson had predicted that if the Senate hamstrung the League with reservations, there would arrive, "sometime, in the vengeful Providence of God, another struggle in which, not a few hundred thousand fine men from America will have to die, but as many millions as are necessary to accomplish the final freedom of the peoples of the world." For decades a debate has gone on as to whether an effective League of Nations, with the U.S. as a member, might have prevented the rise of Nazi Germany and the onset of World War II in Europe. Yes, Wilsonian internationalists have traditionally argued. Recently, though, historians have tended to answer No. Yet the fact is that had the League with American membership operated *as envisioned* by either Wilson (penalties backed as a last resort by military force) or Lodge (the French army spearheading the World War I Allies against Hitler's as yet unprepared military),

Hitler could have been ousted in the mid-1930s for his viola-tions of the Treaty of Versailles—probably with ease. Any American involvement would have required congressional authorization and the political support of the American peo-ple. This would have been a tall order, difficult to imagine even had the U.S. ratified the treaty.

As it was, during the Second World War, another Wilsonian, Franklin D. Roosevelt, would fashion a successor to the League, the United Nations. World War II and the early Cold War proved the decisive turning points away from isolationism. Wilson's historical reputation experienced a stun-ning revival. He achieved the stature of a prophet without honor in his own country, martyred, so many agreed, by a vil-lain from Massachusetts. The UN, declared President Harry Truman, was Wilson's final vindication. During the Truman and Dwight Eisenhower administrations, the United Nations enjoyed bipartisan support. The twentieth century became, as one scholar puts it, the Wilsonian century.

Yet Lodge's attitudes and anxieties have also persevered. Throughout the decades since World War II, America has relied on both a Wilsonian internationalist vision embodied in the United Nations *and* on the balance-of-power strate-gies that Lodge prescribed. The revival of great power strug-gles during the Cold War immediately compromised the UN as FDR had envisioned it; his model depended on coopera-tion among the big nations in the Security Council, which became all but impossible to achieve. After 1949 U.S. policy in Europe pivoted not on the UN but on the new North Atlantic Treaty Organization (NATO), perhaps the most suc-cessful military alliance in history. This and a plethora of lesser Cold War alliances vindicated Lodge. In direct contradiction to Wilson's fervent belief in arms control, America developed a mammoth military-industrial complex. Lodge had feared that a time would come when the League of Nations might seek to interfere with the prerogative of the U.S. to take independent military action against another country. Neither the United States nor other nations ever for a moment surrendered that right to the UN. In 1950, under American pressure and with preponderantly U.S. resources, the United Nations went to war to deter aggression on the Korean peninsula. Since then, America has intervened in other countries in behalf of and, at other times, in violation of the UN Charter.

One of Lodge's reservations declared that America "shall not [necessarily] be obligated to contribute to any of the expenses of the League." During the final decades of the twentieth century, the U.S. fell into deep arrears to the United Nations, a reflection of growing dissatisfaction in Washington with UN attitudes and performance. The Reagan administration (in an echo of Lodge) argued that the UN was acting contrary to American interests and hinted that the U.S. might cancel its membership. That never occurred, but since the Reagan era, the United States has remained strikingly aloof from the United Nations, in the spirit of Lodge. Today the UN accomplishes many things commendably, including humanitarian relief. But it cannot act militarily without adhering to FDR's proposition, agreement among the major powers on occasions of their choosing. The UN falls well short of reliably enforcing peace across the planet.

And so it remains an open question whose approach has seen the greater triumph, Wilson's or Lodge's. To the frequent bafflement of other nations, American foreign policy embodies both, speaking sometimes in the voice of one, sometimes in the other. Today the Democratic Party, the party of Wilson, still places more reliance on international agreements and the UN than does the conservative wing that dominates the GOP. This, as Nicholas Lemann has pointed out, "reflects fundamentally different views of human nature. Do you get people to behave the way you'd like them to through power and force, or by encouragement and friendship?" Nothing more clearly differentiates progressives (or liberals) from conservatives, whether in 1918 or the twenty-first century, than this clash over the essence of human nature. During recent years, the spiritual heirs of the irreconcilables have prevented the United States from signing numerous international agreements, such as those concerning global warming, biological warfare, or the rights of women and children.

The end of the Cold War ushered in an era after 1991 that astonished most foreign policy experts, because it left the United States utterly and increasingly supreme on the world stage. The multipolar world of eight or nine loosely equivalent great powers with which the twentieth century had opened, and the binary world of two superpowers that had characterized the Cold War from 1945 to 1991 had given way to a one-superpower world. The French foreign minister described the U.S. as a "hyperpower." How long this state of affairs would last could only be guessed at, but for the moment the facts spoke for themselves. By the early twenty-first century, American economic output exceeded that of the next three nations (Japan, Germany, Britain) combined. Unbelievably, U.S. military expenditures exceeded those of the next 15 powers combined. Most big world problems arrived at Washington's doorstep, precisely as Lodge had feared. Though Americans arguably remain, as in Wilson's day, the most self-absorbed of all the world's great peoples, and would gladly avoid the role, the sheer globe-straddling scale of American power drives the U.S. to play world policeman. The debates revolve around when and where.

In the meantime, as international terrorism threatens all reaches of the world, nuclear weapons spread from country to country, and environmental problems ignore international borders, the stakes of foreign policy grow only higher. Wilson's call for a new world order, which seemed so naïve to Lodge, arose again in the 1990s. The term "Wilsonian" came newly into fashion to describe those who espouse Wilson's constellation of ideas—peace, popular government, international law, collective security, arms control, human rights, the self-determination of isolated and colonized peoples, and free trade grounded on capitalism. America is viewed as a Wilsonian nation. The rhetoric of Wilsonianism, which Lodge thought so dreamy, has become the rhetoric of American foreign policy—even of a president as different from Woodrow Wilson as George W. Bush. More important, with the demise of their great antagonists, fascism and communism, the aspirations of Wilsonianism have become a consensus over the largest and most advanced portions of the globe. As Michael Mandelbaum observes, "although when Wilson unveiled his ideas at Paris they were utopian, eight decades later they had become pedestrian." Today they are unchallenged by any major systematic set of beliefs other than radical fundamentalist Islam.

In this broadest of ways, Wilson won his battle with Henry Cabot Lodge. As a schoolteacher in Muslim Kosovo—where today U.S. troops patrol the streets—has put it, "When Albanians think of Wilson, they think of him as the only diplomat who defended Kosovo at the Treaty of Versailles. . . . Wilson stood up for Kosovo's right to determine its own destiny. . . . Our love for America all started with Wilson." Only time can reveal to what final degree Wilson's ideas about peace and democracy will become realities, and against what obstacles. "I do not know any *absolute* guarantee," Wilson declared in his Pueblo speech, "against the errors of human judgment or the violence of human passion."

6

Ill-Housed, Ill-Clad, Ill-Nourished

Herbert Hoover, Franklin D. Roosevelt, and the Welfare State

W e are at the end of our string," the outgoing president confessed as the clock struck midnight. "There is nothing more we can do." When dawn came, clouds darkened Washington, spitting gusts of rain. On March 4, 1933, at the bottom of the Great Depression, the weather matched America's mood. By noon, 100,000 men and women had gathered in front of the Capitol, waiting for the inauguration of Franklin D. Roosevelt.

Protocol compelled the president, Herbert Hoover, to accompany Roosevelt from the White House to the Capitol in an open car. After losing to Roosevelt in a landslide four months earlier, Hoover had tried to persuade Roosevelt to commit himself to the same economic strategy that Hoover had doggedly pursued. Hoover's efforts simply heightened the tension between the two men. Now, as the car made its way through the crowds lining the route, Hoover sat rigidly with his head down, looking as though he was studying his knees. Roosevelt tried to trade pleasantries with him, to no avail. Eventually, Roosevelt turned outward to the people, waving a formal top hat and flashing his famous smile. It was something of a miracle that Roosevelt was alive at all. In Miami less than three weeks earlier, he had had a close brush with death. Sitting in a parked open car like the one he rode in today, Roosevelt was approached by the mayor of Chicago, Anton Cermak. Suddenly, from 35 feet away, an unemployed bricklayer with a grudge against everybody in power opened fire with a revolver. Aiming right at Roosevelt, he squeezed off five shots. Roosevelt, unflinching, stared him down. Five people were hit, including Cermak. Countermanding the Secret Service, Roosevelt ordered his chauffeur to stop the accelerating car and back up; then Roosevelt insisted that Cermak be lifted onto the seat alongside him. On the way to the hospital, Roosevelt cradled the bloody, dying mayor. Throughout the crisis, Roosevelt showed concern only for the injured, none whatever for himself. Afterwards he acted as though nothing had happened.

Reaching the Capitol with Hoover, Roosevelt rode part way to the speaker's stand in a wheelchair. Braced against the arm of one of his sons, he awkwardly struggled the rest of the distance on foot. He took the oath of office. Then, grim faced, he delivered one of the greatest speeches in American history. "Let me assert my firm belief," the new president declared, "that the only thing we have to fear is fear itself—nameless, unreasoning, unjustified terror. . . . This nation asks for action, and action now."

Hoover continued to sulk. He had reached the nadir of a life crowded with extraordinary achievements.

✦   ✦   ✦

Admittedly, nothing about Herbert Hoover's childhood in West Branch, Iowa, would have inspired anyone to predict that he would later become renowned. Born into a family of Quaker farmers in 1874, Herbert grew up reading the Bible every day.

His mother was an ordained minister. Orphaned at age nine, he found himself passed between relatives in Iowa and Oregon. He split logs, milked cows, and weeded onions one summer for 50 cents a day. As a boy, he was awkward, defensive, and shy. He spoke as if every single word he uttered cost him something. He would remain a loner all of his life.

Hoover's adulthood epitomized what his generation called pulling oneself up by one's own bootstraps. Spottily educated but very bright, he managed to squeak into the first entering class at Stanford. A geology student, he walked around campus head down, as if searching for ore. He joined with a coalition of other poor, self-supporting students to take control of campus governance away from the wealthy fraternity clans. Though not popular, Hoover was elected student body treasurer. He graduated from Stanford in 1895.

Starting out as a $2.50-a-day Nevada miner, he became a mining engineer in Australia, where he found a fantastically rich gold vein in the outback, and in China and Burma (now Myanmar). Beyond engineering, he proved enormously competent and competitive as an administrator, promoter, and financier. For 20 years, from 1897 to 1917, he rarely set foot in the United States at all, but he did establish lucrative consulting offices in New York and San Francisco as well as abroad. Known as the Great Engineer, he became a legend in his field. His wife, Lou, also a Stanford-trained mining engineer and a promoter of women's causes, followed him from place to place with their two sons. The older boy, Herbert Jr. (born 1903), had already circled the world twice when the family celebrated his second birthday. By 1914 Herbert Sr., had become a millionaire—an enviable status today but vastly more so then in dollar value. He was only 40.

Meanwhile Hoover had left much of his Quaker background behind. Eschewing the Friends' emphasis on personal moderation, he had aggressively amassed a fortune. He drank, smoked, fly fished on Sundays, and could swear like any hard-rock miner.

On the other hand, for the rest of his life, he continued to admire the Friends' belief in thrift, hard work, and voluntary cooperation. Iowa Quakers might scrape by and die relatively young, as his parents had, but they took care of themselves and their own. Hoover believed in individualism—but not in the tooth-and-fang Darwinian variety touted in the America of his youth. He believed in equal opportunity, notably for underprivileged children such as he had been. And he believed that "absolute equality of opportunity" combined with hard work inevitably bred prosperity. His own life seemed to prove the point.

As with many self-made men, wealth and success did not smooth the social awkwardness that clung to Hoover all his life. Being around anyone outside a tight circle of family and friends made him uneasy. When interviewed, he would pace back and forth. In a one-on-one conversation, he would habitually stare at the ground and, with one foot planted in front of him, jingle the keys or coins he carried in his pants pocket.

If Herbert Hoover powered his way to wealth without mastering the social graces, Franklin Roosevelt was born in 1882 into a world blessed with both. The only child of a lavishly devoted, domineering mother, he grew up on the family's Hudson River estate at Hyde Park. The Roosevelts lived on old, inherited money—not comparable to the stupendous fortunes then being made by Gilded Age tycoons, but sufficient to provide all the advantages. Roosevelt grew up with servants and sailboats and European vacations. Educated by Swiss tutors until age 14, he went to several of the schools one would expect of a cultivated young eastern gentleman: not a tiny Quaker academy or an upstart western university, but Groton, Harvard, and Columbia Law. Like Hoover at Stanford, Roosevelt was a middling scholar at Harvard, but unlike Hoover, he made friends, stood out as a leader, excelled at extracurricular activities, and ran the student newspaper. His biggest disappointment was being turned down for membership (for reasons that remain unclear) in Harvard's most exclusive student club. Otherwise, he resembled the privileged, self-assured fraternity men whom Hoover had helped oust at Stanford.

In 1905, now a 23-year-old law student at Columbia, Roosevelt married the favorite niece of his illustrious distant cousin. His cousin was President Theodore Roosevelt; the niece was Eleanor. Theodore himself gave the bride away, attracting a lot more attention than the newlyweds did at their own reception. Franklin and Eleanor, as she herself realized, made an odd match. He was blithely charming, gregarious, and handsome. Though born to wealth, Eleanor was a homely bundle of insecurities whose beautiful, remote mother, upset by Eleanor's looks and seriousness (even as a toddler), called her "Granny." Like Eleanor's mother, her father, a hopeless alcoholic, died young. Awkward and reserved, Eleanor grew up expecting others' love for her to fade. Early on she developed an intense desire to help the less fortunate—she had one of the biggest hearts in American history. This quality of compassion, along with her intelligence, certainly attracted Franklin Roosevelt to her. From the time of their marriage, though, Eleanor worried that Roosevelt would eventually stray.

As Eleanor, under her mother-in-law's dominating eye, raised the five children who came along, Roosevelt rose in the politics of the Empire State. Like Theodore, Franklin was drawn toward the life of stewardship, rather than financial striving, that often accompanies inherited money. Franklin fully shared his cousin's political drive as well. Unlike Theodore's branch of the clan, though, Franklin's was, in a lukewarm way, Democratic. Briefly diverging, Franklin entered Harvard as a Republican, then switched back. This was a career move: the GOP already had a complement of young, ambitious Roosevelts, including Teddy's sons. Within the Democratic Party, Franklin would have the field to himself. Adapting to his Democratic affiliation, Roosevelt dispensed with many of his aristocratic affectations, though not all; along with a folksy battered fedora, a jaunty up-tilted cigarette holder would remain one of his trademarks. He learned to rub political elbows with the tough, pragmatic immigrant-stock characters who ran New York City's Democratic political machine. From the state senate, in 1913 Roosevelt jumped into the new Wilson administration as assistant secretary of the navy, cousin Theodore's old job. While becoming one of the Democratic Party's rising young stars, he modeled his career on the Republican Teddy's.

✦   ✦   ✦

Meantime, inward and awkward as ever, Herbert Hoover hunted for something to do that would bring him greater satisfaction than merely making more money—"some job of public service." He believed that engineers trained in the practical dimensions of the industrial revolution could adapt their knowledge to the public good, lifting living standards and encouraging social justice. Perhaps his urge to serve carried over from his Quaker upbringing. In combination with service, Hoover also yearned for even greater, broader approval and prestige than he already enjoyed. He began reading heavily outside his own field—history, government, economics, sociology.

The arrival of World War I in 1914 produced the opportunities Hoover wanted, a perfect meeting of man and moment. At the request of U.S. diplomats, Hoover, then in London, coordinated the repatriation of 200,000 Americans stuck in Europe as war broke out. Next he organized a commission to supply food, fuel, clothing, and other necessities to 10 million civilians in Belgium, which had become a battleground. In the interest of feeding desperate people, he negotiated his way among the obstinate powers contesting Belgium the way he had once negotiated business deals. Then the Wilson administration recruited him as U.S. Food Administrator (1917–19). Hoover ushered in a landmark program for voluntary conservation at American dining tables, enabling the U.S. to triple food exports to its beleaguered allies. With slogans such as "Food Will Win the War" ringing in their ears, people called their cutbacks "Hooverizing." After 1919

Hoover directed the American Relief Administration (ARA) in Europe, which, astonishingly, fed *300 million* people in more than twenty countries. Hoover improvised a brilliant distribution strategy so that Europeans themselves transported and dispensed food under the supervision of a mere handful of Americans. A supporter of the League of Nations, at Versailles Hoover joined Woodrow Wilson in trying to persuade Europe to control its cannibalistic nationalism. The great British economist John Maynard Keynes called Hoover "the only man who emerged from the ordeal of Paris with an enhanced reputation." Decades later, Hoover would write *The Ordeal of Woodrow Wilson,* a sympathetic account of his illustrious Democratic predecessor's attempt to bring peace to Europe.

Out of the chaos of World War I emerged the Soviet Union, and with it mass starvation in Russia. By 1921 about a quarter of Russia's peasants went to bed at night with gnawing stomachs. In various places, they took to eating tree bark or horse manure, or human cadavers. Hoover could not turn his back on such misery. He had always conceived of the ARA as an institution with multiple purposes—fundamentally to feed starving people but also to unburden American farmers by shipping abroad the surpluses that depressed their crop prices and to stimulate postwar demand in the food-receiving countries for U.S. products of all sorts. In addition, Hoover viewed food distribution as a barrier to Bolshevism, which, like Woodrow Wilson, he despised. American and other troops inserted into Russia had failed to prevent the consolidation of the Soviet Union. Fair enough: once fed and no longer desperate, Hoover thought, the emboldened Russian people themselves would throw out the Bolsheviks. To Hoover's way of thinking, philanthropy equaled humanitarianism plus sound business practice, sound politics, and sound foreign policy.

Congress authorized $20 million for Russian relief. By 1922, a mere 199 Americans together with 120,000 Russians were distributing food to more than ten million people—the most ambitious single international relief program in history. Russians responded with awe to the businesslike efficiency of the ARA. Despite their desperate need for foreign aid, though, the Bolsheviks threw up constant barriers. Hoover's insistence on dispensing food independently, at arm's length from the new regime, enraged Lenin. Why should Lenin welcome food from a country whose troops had been battling his, distributed by an outspoken anticommunist who viewed food as a weapon? Knowing an enemy when he saw one, Lenin worried that Hoover might wind up with more influence among the Russian people than he had. "One must punish Hoover," Lenin insisted, "one must publicly slap his face so that the world sees." In spite of Lenin's barriers, Hoover's efforts may have saved ten million lives.

Outside Soviet leadership circles, as early as 1919 Hoover had become one of the most respected figures in the world, famous for both his idealistic humanitarianism and his remarkable efficiency. His conspicuous admirers included Franklin and Eleanor Roosevelt. As two of the Wilson administration's bright lights, Hoover and Roosevelt had dined together and socialized pleasantly. Within the Democratic Party, soundings began about a 1920 Hoover presidential nomination. When a friend raised the idea of running Hoover at the top of the ticket and Roosevelt for vice president, Roosevelt responded enthusiastically. "He is certainly a wonder," he wrote of Hoover, "and I wish we could make him President of the United States. There could not be a better one." It turned out, though, that while close to nonpartisan, when push came to shove Hoover was a Republican. His presidential race belonged to the more distant future. When Franklin Roosevelt did run for vice president in 1920, Ohio Governor James M. Cox occupied the top of the ticket, and they got trounced.

Newsreel footage shows Roosevelt striding about during the 1920 campaign, shaking hands and looking as if he hadn't a care. Behind the scenes, though, something had drastically changed. Late in 1918, Eleanor had discovered that Roosevelt was carrying on an affair—and had fallen in love—with her vivacious, attractive social secretary, Lucy Mercer. Eleanor offered a divorce. Roosevelt demurred, at least partly for political reasons. (As late as the 1960s, a divorce was the kiss of death for a presidential candidate; the first divorced president was Ronald Reagan.) Now all of Eleanor's earlier anxieties about herself and her husband seemed confirmed. "The bottom dropped out of my own particular world," she later acknowledged. Sex between Eleanor and her husband stopped altogether; instead of romantic love, what remained between them consisted of friendship, mutual respect, and shared values. Over the coming decades, they lived increasingly separate lives.

Another disaster followed. In 1921, Roosevelt, Eleanor, and their children visited the family's summer home at Campobello Island north of Maine. On August 10, they went sailing. Later in the day, Roosevelt challenged the children to a two-mile run followed by a swim. Then they ran some more. Roosevelt had been feeling odd, though, as if he were coming down with something. His legs ached. Two weeks later, after his condition had radically worsened, doctors finally made the diagnosis: infantile paralysis—polio—a viral affliction of the central nervous system.* By the time the illness had run its course, Roosevelt's legs, in the bleak assessment of one of his doctors, had withered into "flail legs." Despite shock and agonizing pain, Roosevelt acted cheerful and serene in front of others, as if nothing at all were wrong. From 1921 on, though, he depended on wheelchairs, heavy steel leg braces, crutches, canes, and friendly arms. Without them, sitting up, Roosevelt had to use his own arms to drag himself backward along the floor, his withered legs uselessly sliding along behind.

---

*Polio today is nearing worldwide extinction thanks to mass immunization techniques dating back to the 1950s, but in early twentieth-century America, it ranked among the most dreaded of all illnesses. Most whom it paralyzed quickly died of either the disease or its complications. There remains one question, though: was Roosevelt's 1921 polio diagnosis accurate? Recently, pediatrician Armond Goldman and a group of colleagues have raised the likelihood that Roosevelt instead suffered from Guillain-Barre syndrome, in which the body is attacked by its own immune system. Goldman acknowledges that a conclusive diagnosis is now impossible.

Polio transformed Roosevelt, at 39 years of age, into a more serious, resolute, and compassionate person. "Having been to the depths of trouble," observed future Labor Secretary Frances Perkins, "he understood the problems of people in trouble." The disease also knocked Roosevelt almost completely out of public life for seven years. Instead of politics, recovering an ability to walk became his overriding obsession. He underwent one type of therapy after another. None worked. While devoting herself to such causes as the League of Nations and ending child labor, Eleanor helped to keep Roosevelt's name afloat; she called herself his "legs and eyes." In 1924, almost midway through his seven years offstage, Roosevelt agreed to give the nominating speech for Al Smith at the Democratic national convention. It was an ordeal. Leaning on a crutch, supported by his 16-year-old son James, Roosevelt made it part way to the podium; then, using two crutches, he struggled the rest of the distance on his own. Looking up, he threw the breathless crowd of 12,000 a huge smile. As he trembled, they gave him a wild ovation.

For all that Roosevelt's storied triumph at this moment meant to him, Al Smith did not win the 1924 Democratic nomination, nor did a Democrat win the presidency. Calvin Coolidge did. No one in Coolidge's Republican administration commanded more respect than Herbert Hoover, who had served as secretary of commerce since 1921. Burnishing his reputation as a practical visionary, Hoover made Commerce one of the most effective departments of government. When Coolidge decided not to stand for reelection in 1928, Hoover was the obvious successor.

✧   ✧   ✧

Since college Hoover had excelled at everything he had attempted in an astonishing variety of fields—engineering, humanitarian relief, administration of wartime programs, and his cabinet career. Roosevelt, by contrast, had merely advanced as a professional politician before polio forced him into the political wilderness. Hoover had never run for public office and he still spoke in an uninspiring monotone, but in 1928 the small-town boy from Quaker Iowa defeated big city Catholic Al Smith by a landslide. At the campaign's outset, Hoover made a famous prediction: "We in America today are nearer to the final triumph over poverty than ever before in the history of any land. The poorhouse is vanishing from among us." By continuing the policies of the prior two Republican administrations, "we shall soon with the help of God be in sight of the day when poverty will be banished from this nation."

For all his personal awkwardness, Hoover was creative, politically progressive to a certain degree, and a far more capable man than his predecessors Harding and Coolidge. During the 1920s, he had laid out his personal philosophy with particular care. As Hoover defined it, rather than being purely selfish, "American individualism" (the title of a book he published in 1922) embraced a spirit of service in behalf of others. A "great spiritual force poured out by our people as never before in the history of the world," service made big government unnecessary in the United States. Government could act, so to speak, as cheerleader. It could play a limited regulatory role (over the new radio industry, for example). But only as a last resort should government step any further. If government fiat and bureaucracy ever replaced voluntary cooperation, only tyranny could result. Hoover's ideas were not merely theoretical; during World War I, he had applied this cooperative, voluntary strategy to Belgian relief and food conservation, and it had worked. As commerce secretary, he had demonstrated how such an approach could, through the formation of trade associations, improve the performance of American business, stabilize a national economic downturn (as it did early in the 1920s), and reduce the hours of labor.

Hoover opened his administration with some promising conservation initiatives and with overtures to African Americans and Indians. His worst enemy could not have planned the unprecedented economic disaster that began to wreck his presidency just eight months after his inauguration—though Hoover himself, despite his famous election prediction about ending poverty, had worried for years about the speculative boom called Coolidge Prosperity. In October–November, 1929, Coolidge prosperity came to a sickening end as stock prices plummeted.

Over the following four years, U.S. industrial production dropped by nearly fifty percent. A third of the country's banks collapsed. One out of four Americans wound up unemployed, countless more underemployed. By 1933, international joblessness stood at roughly thirty million—*half* of them Americans. The toll on individuals and families was catastrophic. Millions of middle-class Americans plunged through a trap door into poverty. Additional millions, already poor, became poorer. To keep up appearances, fired white-collar workers would leave home each day as though driving to work, sit on a park bench, then return in the evening at the usual time. Families that had had their utilities turned off for nonpayment built cooking fires in their back yards. Hunger marches snaked along the streets of New York and Chicago. Between one and two million Americans (including thousands of children) simply drifted, hitching rides or jumping freight cars. In the parks and vacant lots of cities across the United States, people who had lost their homes constructed shacks out of scrap wood, tarpaper, and cardboard. These bleak settlements were named after the president of the United States: Hoovervilles.

The term was ironic and cruel. A voter who had sensed in 1928 that the greatest depression in history lurked just around the corner might have felt even more inclined than otherwise to cast a ballot for Herbert Hoover. With his luminous record as a humanitarian, businessman, and public official, no person in the country seemed better prepared to confront it. According to widely (though not universally) accepted wisdom, government lacked any proper part to play in stemming an economic downturn. Hoover flatly disagreed. More than any prominent figure in Washington, he believed government *had* to take an active role. Previous presidents had intervened in the economy, but Hoover battled the Great Depression for nearly three and a half years using more weapons than any of them. He called conferences of business and labor leaders, extracting pledges from employers voluntarily to avoid layoffs and maintain wages, and from labor not to strike. He preached to bankers and farmers that they must cooperate to defend themselves. In his role as cheerleader, he issued a flood of optimistic statements aimed at inspiring business and public confidence. In June, 1930, he told a Catholic delegation that had come to request an expanded federal program to provide jobs for the unemployed by building public works that they had arrived "sixty days too late. The depression is over."

In keeping with his philosophy of decentralized, voluntary mutual support, Hoover relied on private charities such as the Red Cross and on local and state governments to aid the unemployed. Involving Washington, he feared, would further unbalance the federal budget, render aid recipients subject "to a remote bureaucracy," and undermine their character in a way that state or private charity somehow would not. Ultimately, under intense public pressure, Hoover did expand public works. He continued, though, to draw the line at federal "direct relief" (the dole, or straight welfare check). The new, reluctantly established Reconstruction Finance Corporation (1932) provided federal loans to shore up failing banks and corporations, as well as additional funding for public works—but did not give anything for direct relief or loans to ordinary people. The expectation was that eventually the benefits would find their way down to those at the bottom of the economic pyramid. For all its new initiatives, which clearly departed from pure voluntarism, the administration's approach remained tightly constricted by Hoover's philosophy of American individualism, along with his fear of red ink.

Ironically, by exploring every alternative to a mammoth federal role, Hoover actually whetted public demand for Washington to intervene. He became a vital transitional figure between an America in which the national government remained practically invisible to ordinary people except when they collected their mail, and a new America in which Washington became involved in nearly everything. The further his strategy for ending the Depression fell short, the more stubbornly Hoover defended it. Nothing, he believed, was basically wrong with the American economy; therefore nothing fundamental needed changing. People asked why the great humanitarian who had made a special point of feeding European children a decade before would not feed American children now. "No American," Hoover wrote, "should go hungry or cold if he is willing to work." The economy, he promised, would eventually turn right side up again. The problem, as Harry Hopkins, one of Franklin Roosevelt's key associates put it, was that "people don't eat in the long run—they eat every day."

By now Roosevelt, his health repaired as much as it would ever be, had become governor of New York, narrowly winning office just as Hoover won the presidency. At first Roosevelt did not differ strongly from Hoover over anti-Depression policy. In 1931, well into the Depression, Roosevelt became the first governor to set up a state relief agency. This fell in line with Hoover's belief in administering charity below the federal level. The personal relationship between the two men, though, was turning sour. During the 1928 campaign, Roosevelt urged voters to carry out Woodrow Wilson's legacy by electing Al Smith and charged that Hoover had surrounded himself with "materialistic and self-seeking advisors." In the spring of 1932, President Hoover kept Roosevelt and the other state governors waiting for an audience with him at the White House. Refusing to sit down, Roosevelt stood for half an hour locked in his leg braces before the president finally appeared. Rightly or wrongly, both FDR and Eleanor believed the delay was no accident. Potentially damaging rumors were then making the rounds that his disability rendered Roosevelt unfit for the presidency.

To be portrayed as a "cripple" would undoubtedly have destroyed Roosevelt's political career—even though polio actually strengthened his qualities of leadership. Early in the twentieth century, disability carried such a stigma that embarrassed families kept their disabled children or relatives out of sight. For a person with some significant visible disability even to appear in public, still less to run for office, was regarded as offensive, a matter of bad taste. Comedians cracked jokes about curved spines and seizures. All this helps to explain why Woodrow Wilson's entourage was so desperate to keep him out of public view. Except for Wilson, stricken while in office, no severe paralytic had ever played any conspicuous role in politics. Surely none had been elected president.

So Roosevelt made it a point always to appear healthy and "normal." As president, he would become the most filmed and photographed of Americans, but the images are remarkable for what they leave out. Although he was essentially confined to a wheelchair, apparently just three photos exist of him actually sitting in one. None was published during his lifetime. Less than a minute of movie footage—taken by an amateur and almost agonizing to watch—shows Roosevelt "walking." Twice, in public, he suffered major falls—in 1922, onto the glassy marble floor of an office building in New York (afterward he smiled and laughed); and at the 1936 Democratic national convention (he smiled and waved, then immediately gave one of the greatest speeches of his career). The White House wanted Roosevelt's infirmity played down, and the press willingly complied. The public vaguely knew he was lame and left it at that. Today, in an era when every inch of the presidential anatomy has become fair game, one can only imagine the images that would clog TV screens and wonder whether (even with more tolerance toward disability) Roosevelt would have been electable in the television-computer age.

Once he won the Democratic Party's presidential nomination in 1932, Roosevelt's campaign speeches generally addressed the Depression in the broadest generalities. Apart from their personalities, the big difference between the awkward, defensive, and now widely hated Hoover and his ebullient but opaque challenger was that Roosevelt sounded as though he *might* do something effective. The first nominee ever to appear before a convention to deliver his acceptance speech, Roosevelt pledged "a new deal for the American people." The term "New Deal," like Roosevelt's initials FDR, became a hallmark of the 1930s. During the campaign, some observers remained unimpressed. The celebrated pundit Walter Lippmann sniffishly dismissed Roosevelt as "a pleasant man who, without any important qualifications for the office, would very much like to be President."

Whatever "New Deal" meant, exactly, the very prospect alarmed Hoover. In pressuring Roosevelt—who had beaten him by 472 electoral votes to 59—to sign on to his own policies, Hoover was inviting FDR to join him in a political suicide pact. "He will have ratified the whole major program of the Republican Administration," Hoover wrote; "that is, it means the abandonment of 90% of the so-called 'new deal.'" Understandably, Roosevelt refused to commit himself, and their two postelection face-to-face meetings came to nothing. Roosevelt felt manipulated. Hoover's suspicions deepened. As they rode together to the Capitol on March 4, 1933, Roosevelt waving to the crowds, Hoover feared the worst.

✦　　✦　　✦

Roosevelt's brilliant inaugural address gave momentum to a freight train of legislation termed "the Hundred Days," unique in American history. Before the election, Roosevelt had called for "bold, persistent experimentation." During the next five years, his administration borrowed ideas from the Progressive Era (including Theodore Roosevelt) and World War I, combined them with some of Hoover's successful policies and a raft of entirely fresh ideas, and conducted the greatest series of experiments in the nation's history. "Take a method and try it," Roosevelt declared. "If it fails, admit it frankly and try another. But above all try something." The number and scale of federal programs exploded. Over three years a massive agriculture program drove up farm income almost fifty percent. In 1935 Congress passed the Social Security

Act. Workers, arguably the New Deal's biggest beneficiaries, gained the minimum wage as well as the right to unionize and bargain collectively. Roosevelt, declared one worker, "is the only man we ever had in the White House who would understand that my boss is a sonofabitch." Roosevelt agreed with Hoover that, as FDR put it, the dole (or welfare handout) was "a narcotic, a subtle destroyer of the human spirit." The notion of a "welfare class" spanning multiple generations, feeling entitled to taxpayer largesse, would have horrified either man. Roosevelt's solution: government-sponsored "work relief," which helped restore dignity for millions by providing jobs, with the dole left over for the remainder. The Works Progress Administration (WPA) gave 8.5 million people jobs at a cost of $11 billion—more than $144 billion in today's dollars, or about ten times the annual budget of the National Aeronautics and Space Administration. The Civilian Conservation Corps (CCC), primarily for young men, employed 2 million in reforestation and other projects. Hundreds of thousands more young people got new work-study jobs on high school and college campuses.

Roosevelt tirelessly sold his programs to the American people. He became the first president to master radio, scheduling folksy "fireside chats" to explain the New Deal and build support. Press conferences occurred continuously. Roosevelt's sunny, confident, reassuring manner made him the successful cheerleader Hoover had tried to be. The fact that the Depression bottomed out and the economy began a partial recovery, in tandem with the success of many New Deal programs, gave people something to cheer about. A greater contrast in styles can scarcely be imagined than between Herbert Hoover and FDR.

By the end of the 1930s, the essentials of the American welfare state were in place. In one way or another, to one degree or another, the federal government would furnish a safety net for nearly everyone and every major interest group, including labor, agriculture, and business. "There are usually two general schools of political belief," Roosevelt observed in 1941, "liberal and conservative." Liberals, on the one hand, believed that "as new conditions and problems arise beyond the power of men and women to meet as individuals, it becomes the duty of the government itself to find new remedies with which to meet them." Conservatives, on the other hand, believed "that there is no necessity for the government to step in." The Democratic Party, Roosevelt emphasized, was the vehicle for liberalism; he contentedly left conservatism to the GOP.

From the time the New Deal began, Herbert Hoover—once known as the Great Humanitarian, now regarded by millions as a man without a heart—dug in his heels. Contrary to Roosevelt's definition of a conservative, Hoover *had* used government to step in to a limited extent. Now, though, Hoover insisted that the New Deal had taken an errant course and that the country must turn back to the "right." "Most of Hoover's public and private statements" during the thirties, writes a biographer, "were devoted to attacking the New Deal." As early as 1934, just a year after FDR's inauguration, Hoover published *The Challenge to Liberty,* and for decades afterward, he elaborated on the book's themes.

Hoover loathed FDR's open experimentalism. He despised the way Roosevelt concentrated power in the presidency and FDR's instinct for centralized planning. He called the New Deal's regulation of business, banking, and agriculture "National Regimentation." New Dealers were "totalitarian liberals" bent on subverting the Bill of Rights. "There is no middle road between any breed of collectivist [i.e., socialist] economy and our American system," Hoover declared. He predicted that Roosevelt's approach would ring down the curtain on individual initiative and the free enterprise system as a whole. Hoover also predicted that despite its purported socialist impulses, in time the New Deal would actually spur the opposite of socialism—fascism. The New Deal, he claimed, was throwing up a "Fascist-Nazi state." Roosevelt's farm program reminded Hoover of Hitler's and Mussolini's. The young men of the CCC amounted to "potential mercenaries . . . under sinister military leadership." Looking back in his memoirs (1952), Hoover called the New Deal "an attempt to cross-breed Socialism, Fascism, and Free Enterprise." These were preposterous allegations. Behind them lay deep and legitimate anxieties about power and about government overstepping its bounds. But Hoover spun these anxieties into comparisons to some of the most demonic forms of government ever conceived. Fascism as practiced in Germany, Italy, or Japan was a dictatorial, racist, imperialist, and intensely militarized system that regimented the national economy behind wars of conquest culminating in World War II. Fascist regimes stamped out dissent with censorship, torture, and murder. Hoover's comparison of FDR's farm program to Hitler's or Mussolini's, or the CCC to some brutal fascist youth phalanx demonstrated how bitter he had become. Roosevelt utterly despised Hitler and Mussolini and would eventually make war against them. "The scars and humiliation of his presidency and defeat, the characterizations of him as the embodiment of selfish and arrogant wealth," writes a biographer, propelled Hoover "into a lasting hostility, a relentless effort to find quarrels with his triumphant opponents." A quiet, introverted man who always had trouble admitting his own failings, Hoover would summon the most flamboyant language to discredit his successor.

It is true that the New Deal marked a turning point, dramatically expanding the role of government in American life. The lightness of Washington's touch before 1933 would astonish today's citizen. Federal spending accounted for about three percent of gross national product in 1929; by 1936 this had grown to nine percent. (Today it is 20 percent of a vastly larger GNP.) By broadening the range of government, mainly in order to ease the plight of ordinary people, Roosevelt actually undermined anticapitalist movements *within* the United States. "What cut the ground out pretty completely from under us," remarked Socialist Party leader Norman Thomas, "was Roosevelt." At the end of the 1930s, the economy, though mixed, was still fundamentally private and still heavily dominated by large corporations.

When Hoover lamented the end of the nineteenth-century rural-small town America that had produced him, he stood on firmer ground than with his charges of extremism. The world of West Branch had given way to an intensely complex, increasingly urbanized society in which neighbors could not be counted on to feed or house the poor. In the big cities, people who lived side by side did not necessarily even know one another; nor could urbanites raise food to feed themselves. Welfare states emerged in Europe and under the New Deal in response to precisely these new realities, seeking to raise living standards and life expectancies above historic norms. The U.S. developed its welfare state very late, a generation or more behind Europe, and to this day, the U.S. version of the welfare state is much stingier than its foreign counterparts. America lacks, in particular, a national health care system, which has been proposed since Roosevelt's time but never adopted. American business learned to live with the welfare state and became one of its major beneficiaries. When government support goes to corporations or farmers, this is called a "subsidy"; only when it goes to the poor does the word "welfare" enter in.

Hoover also stood on entirely firm ground in pointing out, as he loved to do, that the New Deal failed to end the Depression. Four years into the New Deal, in his second inaugural address, Roosevelt acknowledged that even yet "I see one-third of a nation ill-housed, ill-clad, ill-nourished." In his memoirs, Hoover argued that "if the New Dealers had carried on our policies instead of deliberately wrecking them and then trying to make America over into a collectivist system, we should have made complete recovery in eighteen months after 1932." Maybe so; far more likely not. Economists disagreed in the thirties—they disagree today—about what the best route out of the Depression might have been. Under Hoover, businesses and banks had collapsed by the thousand. New Deal economic policy was a hash. First FDR encouraged massive business collusion in order to maintain prices and employment. After the Supreme Court unanimously ended this experiment, the New Deal turned around and embarked on the greatest antitrust crusade in American history. Business leaders reacted with wounded fury, referring to Roosevelt as "that man," or worse. Hoover was right: World War II, not the New Deal, ended the Depression. For millions, though, the New Deal made the wait far more bearable.

Beyond its policies and programs, a newfound sense of social openness marked the New Deal. Hoover's had distinctly been a so-called white Anglo-Saxon Protestant (WASP) administration. The FDR years marked the coming of age of a whole new America that had gotten off the ship during the last part of the nineteenth and the early part of the twentieth century. Urban-ethnic needs drew attention, and people from the newer ethnic groups found their way into government. The New Deal became, so to speak, the Polish Deal, the Greek Deal, or the Italian Deal. (Because many New Deal officials were Jewish, anti-Semites viciously branded it "the Jew Deal.") This sense of inclusion, and not just his programs, is why FDR was denounced as "a traitor to his class." As Joseph Alsop put it: "The vast majority of the really rich Americans in those days belonged, in one way or another, to one of the regional WASP in-groups; in varying degrees the positions of many depended on continuing the old WASP exclusive dominance; and Roosevelt's threat to this dominance . . . was what produced the Roosevelt-haters."

The New Deal's record for blacks, on the other hand, was, like Hoover's, mixed. Both personally and as president, Hoover had taken modest initiatives that ran counter to the widespread prevailing racism and benefited African Americans. He spoke out, for example, against lynching, though he failed to follow up with any legislation to help eradicate it. Nor did Roosevelt ever squarely attack the pattern of discrimination in the South. Wary of a rebellion against the administration's other programs, he supported not a single civil rights measure. Should he back a bill against lynching, he pointed out, southern senators and representatives would "block every bill I ask Congress to pass to keep America from collapsing." The administration's farm program actually hurt poor African Americans; some New Deal programs were segregated; and initially Social Security did not cover key occupations heavily populated by blacks (agricultural and household labor). At the same time, Roosevelt's administration had no peer except that of Abraham Lincoln 70 years earlier in bringing federal aid to the African American community. Roosevelt solicited advice from black leaders and appointed them to government posts. Among some New Deal programs (including the CCC), African Americans were significantly overrepresented. Most blacks clearly felt that FDR was going as far as he could. Many named sons for him.

The administration's greatest champion of civil rights was Eleanor Roosevelt. Lou Hoover had shown a commendable readiness to treat blacks with ordinary decency. Eleanor made racial justice a personal cause. In 1939, the Daughters of the American Revolution (DAR) denied the great black singer Marian Anderson an opportunity to perform in the organization's Constitution Hall because of her color. In protest, Eleanor resigned from the DAR. A Gallup poll showed that over two-thirds of the public approved. The administration provided a substitute concert site: the Lincoln Memorial, with Lincoln's famous statue poised over the 75,000 who attended free of charge.

Throughout the 1930s, Herbert Hoover found himself at war not just with FDR, but less directly with Eleanor too. Convinced that no matter how many measures her husband pushed through he could never achieve enough for the downtrodden, Eleanor became, quite simply, the conscience of the administration. Though her purity of motive was easily mistaken for mere naïveté, she lobbied effectively for people who might fall between the cracks. Along with African Americans, these included women, the poor, and the unemployed. While publicly playing down her influence, she pressured FDR endlessly. As she herself put it, "because I had this horrible sense of obligation which was bred in me, I couldn't help it." Eleanor would confront her husband, recounted one official, with "that devastatingly simple honest look," and say, "Franklin, I think you should. . . ." FDR actually *encouraged* this. While it made his life more difficult, he knew that her prodding and goading had policy benefits. What FDR and Eleanor's relationship lacked in personal intimacy, it vastly overmatched in political efficacy. The deficiencies of their marriage, and the peculiarities of their relationship, arguably strengthened them both as individuals and as a team. Eleanor comprised, so to speak, the New Deal's heart, and her husband its head. FDR's political genius combined charisma with cunning, a facility for manipulating people, and a measure of deviousness. The New Deal benefited from both the unsullied decency of the leader's wife and a leader who, to get measures through, had the ability to cajole or twist arms as the situation required.

As first lady, for 12 years Eleanor was continuously, astonishingly *visible*. She tirelessly traveled and spoke while publishing six books, nearly three hundred magazine articles, and 2,500 newspaper columns. She fervently backed workers and unions, once taking a mine train two miles down a coal shaft to look into labor conditions at the bottom. Even though New Deal programs rested on traditional assumptions about gender roles—seeking protection for women through social programs rather than outright equality between the sexes—unprecedented numbers of women achieved high positions under FDR, including the first female cabinet member, Secretary of Labor Frances Perkins. Eleanor's personal efforts led to the appointment of more than four thousand women to postal jobs. Her extraordinary display of energy and commitment violated the behavior code for first ladies, which resembled the code for Victorian children—that they be seen but not heard. There was a lot of snickering about the president's inability to "keep his missus at home." During the 1940 presidential campaign, FDR's antagonists wore buttons declaring, "We Don't Want Eleanor Either." Yet a Gallup poll in 1939—a time when traditional gender roles remained much stronger than today—showed that 67 percent of the American people and an even larger percentage of women approved of

Eleanor's performance as first lady. None of her predecessors in the role had even begun to accomplish what Eleanor Roosevelt did. No first lady who has followed her has come close either. It may take a woman president to make her match.

✧   ✧   ✧

The Great Depression and the New Deal utterly changed the way in which Americans thought about politics. For decades afterward, millions continued to blame their former president for what Democrats delightedly called the Hoover Depression. On one occasion in West Virginia, Hoover received a 21 gun salute. "By gum," groused an old man in the audience, "they missed him." To Hoover's enormous frustration, not just Democrats but numerous Republicans ignored his constant warnings about the menace of FDR. Some Republicans publicly shunned Hoover, and many wound up endorsing much or most of the New Deal. This gave rise to the sobriquet, "me-too Republican." Predictably, the GOP declined to renominate Hoover in 1936. The staff of presidential standard bearer Alfred M. Landon even spurned Hoover's offer of support.

With or without Hoover's help, Landon could not have fared much worse. Roosevelt got 60.8 percent of the popular vote. Landon carried two states, Maine and Vermont—8 electoral votes to Roosevelt's 523. No contested election had ever produced an electoral gulf that wide. As one journalist put it, "If Landon had given one more speech, Roosevelt would have carried Canada, too."

Roosevelt had crafted a voting majority that would dominate American politics for a generation. This New Deal coalition included (in often-overlapping categories) immigrants and their offspring, among them many immigrant women voting for the first time; Catholics and Jews; the northern cities; the South; organized labor; the poor and jobless; blacks in those portions of the country where they could actually vote; large numbers of farmers; and limited, nonconformist elements of the business community. This was largely a coalition of "outs" who wanted in, for whom the New Deal had provided both jobs and social inclusion. Nothing mattered so much in the 1936 campaign as social-economic class. Hating the rich had become a genuine fad. The "organized money" interests, Roosevelt told a cheering audience in Madison Square Garden, "are unanimous in their hate for me—and I welcome their hatred." Six million more people voted in 1936 than in 1932—five million of them for Roosevelt. In round figures, he won 40 percent of people with high incomes and 80 percent of unskilled workers, relief recipients, and union members. Most Roosevelt backers explained their vote this way: "He helped the working classes."

By 1939, though, the New Deal had practically jolted to a halt. Roosevelt had split his own party in 1937 by making war on a Supreme Court that had not only thrown out key New Deal legislation as unconstitutional but threatened to junk still more, including the just-enacted hallmark of the welfares state, the Social Security Act. In response, Roosevelt suddenly sprang a plan for "packing" the Court by adding up to six new justices, ostensibly to augment efficiency by supplementing the aging members but in fact to change the ideological makeup of the Court. This was FDR at his worst, for once losing his political touch, deceptive and coy; and it split the country and congressional Democrats alike.

If anyone wanted evidence to confirm Herbert Hoover's charges of looming presidential dictatorship, this, according to Hoover (and a lot of others) was it. Hoover accused FDR of plotting to alter the Constitution (actually, the Constitution does not specify the size of the Supreme Court). More to the point, Hoover warned of "President's judges" abetting chief executives' designs to acquire more and more power. "That is not judicial process," Hoover declared. "That is force." "Hands off the Supreme Court!" Hoover took to the radio waves against the plan, seeded nonpartisan groups to oppose it in nearly half the states, and fed information to antipacking Democrats. After

168 days of legislative fighting, Roosevelt lost the packing battle, though because the Court wheeled to the left, upholding what remained of the New Deal, he won the war.

The price of victory proved enormous. With Democrats, reformers, and the middle class at loggerheads among themselves over Court packing, a conservative coalition composed of Republicans and southern Democrats began to emerge in Congress that was determined to block the New Deal from going further. "For God sakes," pleaded a band of congressmen the following year, "don't send us any more controversial legislation." More and more, Roosevelt's attention was drawn to the fascist threat in Europe and Asia. After the U.S. plunged into World War II at the end of 1941, FDR transformed himself into one of the great war leaders of American history. Congressional Republicans and southern Democrats lost little time in tearing apart the New Deal's public employment programs. Elected to a fourth term in 1944, Roosevelt planned for a postwar liberal revival. On April 12, 1945, he died of a cerebral hemorrhage. That night Hoover attended a party in New York. With the nation at large shocked and in deep mourning, some of the partygoers expressed just the opposite mood. Hoover revealed no emotion at all.

✧   ✧   ✧

For the next 17 years, Eleanor kept the Roosevelt flame alight, continuing to call for social justice at home and abroad. In retrospect, she was the most important American woman of the twentieth century, linked by marriage to the most important American man. In 1958, the Gallup poll posed the question, "If you could invite any three famous persons in history—from the present or past—to your home for dinner, which three would you most like to have?" A representative sampling of Americans put Lincoln first, FDR second, and Eleanor sixth. Jesus placed eleventh.

Meanwhile, Herbert Hoover labored to debunk what he regarded as the Roosevelt myth. Once barely a Republican at all, he had become a perfectly avid one. From 1936 until 1952, he pleaded with his party to nominate candidates who would crusade against "New Deal radicalism." The ongoing tendency, as Hoover put it, to run "50% Republicans . . . against 100% Democrats" appalled him. He complained that his party was controlled by "pinheads." In 1952 the GOP scored its first presidential success in 20 years with the election of Dwight Eisenhower. A moderate of immense prestige, Eisenhower confounded the party's conservative wing by putting his implicit stamp of approval on the New Deal, signifying as nothing else could that by midcentury, the basic proposition of the welfare state had become a matter of bipartisan consensus.

As he aged, Hoover became more unbending and peevish. He insisted that the Hoover Institution, which he had launched at Stanford with a gift in 1919 to collect World War I documents, function as an intellectual capital of anticommunism and bar the door to anyone who disagreed. In 1960 he denounced John F. Kennedy for proposing what Hoover called an "evil" "new, New Deal," "socialism disguised as a welfare state." Kennedy's 1960 opponent, Richard Nixon, struck Hoover as just one more me-too Republican. As Lyndon Johnson's massive New Deal-inspired Great Society programs got underway, Hoover was privately urging Arizona Senator Barry Goldwater to run for the presidency in 1964. "Your success," Hoover told Goldwater after the senator seized the Republican nomination from the party's outraged moderate wing, "means the success of our country." Goldwater was about as far from Eisenhower-Nixon Republicanism as a candidate could get. He was a genuine reactionary: the federal government, he insisted, had no business at all running social programs or passing civil rights legislation. In foreign policy Goldwater was even more combatively anticommunist than Hoover. When Goldwater paid Hoover a visit that summer, Hoover yet again denounced the New Deal. But Hoover would not see election day. In mid-October, now 90 years old, he suffered internal hemorrhaging. Two hundred blood transfusions failed to save him. He died on October 20, and was buried where he had been born, in West Branch, Iowa.

Johnson took 61.2 percent of the popular vote in 1964 (just shy of FDR's 1936 landslide), and the Democrats ran up giant majorities in both houses of Congress. But had Hoover lived a bit longer, it would have delighted him to learn that Goldwater's seemingly disastrous campaign would provide the ash-bed from which conservative Republicanism would rise again. Beginning that year, as a consequence of Johnson's landmark civil rights legislation, the GOP steadily grew in the Old Confederacy. By the end of the twentieth century, the Republican base was no longer the Northeast, the heartland of moderate Republicanism. It had become the white South, animated by socially conservative Christian fundamentalist values, strong resistance to big government except for national defense, and heavy emphasis on cutting taxes. "Over the last generation," wrote political commentator Ronald Brownstein in 2003, "the GOP has conquered the South and the South has conquered the GOP."

By the beginning of the 1980s, it was becoming increasingly unfashionable to advocate new federal domestic programs of virtually any sort. "Government is not the solution to our problem," Ronald Reagan declared in his 1981 inaugural address. "Government *is* the problem." During the 1930s, federal programs had carried the personal imprint of FDR himself: "He gave me a job!" people exclaimed, or "He saved my home from foreclosure!" In later years, such programs turned faceless. Herbert Hoover had warned about "how bureaucracy . . . proceeds to fatten and enlarge its activities." In full agreement, Reagan set out to cut federal programs or at least limit their growth. Rollbacks in antipoverty programs went fairly smoothly (the poor no longer voted), but then an interesting discovery was made. The middle class fervently resisted curtailment of New Deal measures that benefited it. Social Security, the greatest middle class entitlement of all, was dubbed "the third rail of American politics"—touch it and you die.

How much of the New Deal survives today? The core of it does. Roosevelt permanently redefined the relationship between the American people and their government. He dramatically expanded Washington's role by providing a safety net for the poor, the elderly, the unemployed, farmers, and other groups. He also redefined the role and expectations of the presidency. He utterly reshaped the Democratic Party. The big surprise is how little the New Deal has been expanded upon. America now has the widest gap between rich and poor since the 1920s—the widest of any major Western democracy. And during the 1980s and 1990s, many of the business abuses and varieties of fraud that New Deal regulatory measures seemed to have ended once and for all made a reappearance, in part because Congress had recently weakened these very measures.

If the liberalism of Franklin and Eleanor Roosevelt still animates American political life, so does the conservatism of Herbert Hoover. While polls of historians place FDR with Lincoln and Washington among the unquestionably great presidents, Hoover is conventionally ranked average—that high, no doubt, because of the vital transitional role he played; that low despite all his extraordinary abilities. Between his college days and his presidency, Hoover displayed greatness in a wide range of fields. He was never as cold a man as he seemed, and at their best, his reflections about American individualism elaborated upon a great tradition. Today, many of Hoover's perspectives have returned to fashion so that he shares the last laugh with FDR. Over the past generation, the GOP has shown far more energy than the Democrats in generating fresh ideas, many of them devoted to abolishing, cutting back, or privatizing New Deal and 1960s-era federal programs. In doing so, Republicans rarely raise Hoover's name or use his language, but they certainly evoke his spirit, just as the Democratic Party still evokes the Roosevelts'.

7

All the Evil of the Times

J. Robert Oppenheimer, Edward Teller, and the Bombs

O f all the events of recorded history, it may be argued that the most important occurred on July 16, 1945, in a desolate southwestern desert that the early Spanish explorers called the Jornada del Muerte: The Journey of Death. For it was on that date, at 5:30 in the morning, just before dawn, that a team of scientists and technicians directed by J. Robert Oppenheimer exploded the first atomic bomb. Images captured on film of this and similar explosions have made the mushroom-shaped cloud a fixed point of mental reference for every literate human being on the planet since 1945. The immediate consequences of that scientific triumph were, of course, the destruction of Hiroshima and Nagasaki and the ending of the Second World War. The intermediate consequence was the United States' four-decade-long arms race with the Soviet Union that cost an estimated four trillion dollars. And the long-term consquences? They remain to be seen. At the least, continuing international instability, as a result

168

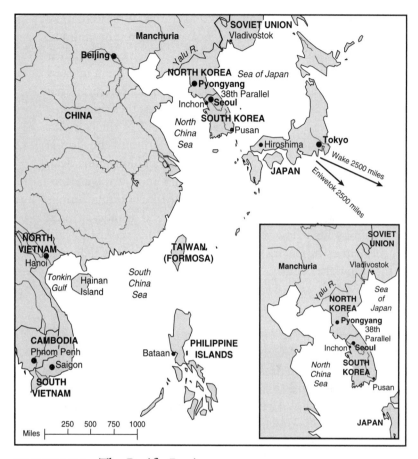

FIGURE 7.1 The Pacific Region.

of the threats posed by North Korea, Pakistan, and India, and in America, the constant fear of terrorists blowing up cities with suitcase-sized bombs. At the worst, a nuclear holocaust that would mean an end to civilization. Not for nothing has our time been called the Age of Anxiety.

Because this is the first moment in human history when men and women can make decisions and take actions of unimaginable consequence, the study of such people becomes more than merely a matter of interest in personalities and stories. Who were these people? How were they selected to take on these responsibilities? What did society demand of them in terms of their behavior, their morality, their beliefs? Who was entitled to judge them in these areas, and on what grounds? Most important of all, perhaps: What have the rest of us learned from trying to address these questions?

Some answers are provided through a look at the complex association of Robert Oppenheimer, the "father of the atomic bomb," and his colleague, sometime friend, and long-time rival, Edward Teller, the "father of the hydrogen bomb." It was an association that would end in 1954 in Oppenheimer's public humiliation and disgrace, partly because of Teller, and in Teller's virtual ostracism by his fellow scientists because of his actions toward Oppenheimer. It remains one of the compelling personal dramas of the twentieth century.

✧   ✧   ✧

On the morning of the Trinity test, as it was called, both Teller and Oppenheimer were present, though not as equals. Edward Teller was a respected theoretical physicist, but many others among the hundreds of scientists gathered at Los Alamos had contributed more significantly to the bomb than he had. The beetle-browed Hungarian with the artificial foot—the result of a childhood street-car accident—was regarded by not a few of his associates as a sore-head and a maverick, and on this morning, he "scared the hell" out of one onlooker when he lathered his face with protective cream and suited up with welder's goggles and heavy leather gauntlets— at a distance of more than ten miles from the bomb test site.

Much closer, in a sturdy wooden bunker less than six miles to the south of the blast, was Dr. J. Robert Oppenheimer. Always physically frail—six feet tall, he weighed only 130 pounds—the scientific director of the Manhattan Project had inspired, goaded, and cajoled his team for three years to reach this moment. He had also driven himself to the point of exhaustion, almost over-whelmed by the achievement he had wrought and by the tension of this first, critical test. If the bomb failed, not only would the war with Japan probably be prolonged but President Harry Truman's complicated negotiations with the Soviet Union concerning the postwar world would be jeopardized.

Objectively speaking, there was small likelihood that "the gadget"—the informal designation for the bomb that everyone from Oppenheimer on down used—would fail. And yet final ignition had already been postponed once, from July 4, due to a technical glitch; and an unusual electrical storm had swept across the desert earlier this morning, forcing a delay beyond the scheduled 4:00 ignition time. A darkly funny bit of doggerel circulated before the blast effectively described what was riding on its success, and how traumatic a failure would be:

> From this crude lab that spawned a dud,
> Their necks to Truman's ax uncurled
> Lo, the embattled savants stood,
> And fired the flop heard round the world.

As it turned out, the bomb was no flop. It was, in technical terms at least, an unqualified success, so extraordinary in its power that common measures of explanation fail to convey its meaning. Brighter than a dozen suns, the flash of light was visible throughout the state of New Mexico and as far away as Texas. The heat was greater than the surface of the sun—10,000 times hotter; observers with Teller ten miles away said it was like standing in front of a roaring fireplace. The mushroom cloud rose nearly eight miles within minutes. The shock wave from the blast moved across the desert like a living thing, pulling with it dust and debris, a yellow mass spreading outward, to the accompaniment of rolling thunder cracks that echoed back and forth from the surrounding hills. Windows were shattered in cities 100 miles away.

Enrico Fermi, the Italian immigrant who had unlocked the secrets of atomic fission in 1934, ingeniously gauged the intensity of the shock wave and the probable power of the bomb with half a dozen pieces of paper he had in his pocket. The air was perfectly still before the blast when he dropped the first scraps from a height of six feet. He repeated the process as the wave passed over him and again after it had gone. He thus was able, Fermi said, to "observe very distinctly and actually measure the displacement of the pieces of paper that were in the process of falling while the blast was passing. The shift was about 2½ meters, which, at the time, I estimated to correspond to the blast that would be produced by ten thousand tons of T.N.T."

In fact, the power of the bomb was twice Fermi's thumbnail estimate, the equivalent of 20,000 tons of T.N.T. For the past several months, B-29 Super Fortresses had been firebombing Japanese cities and wreaking incredible havoc. It would take 2,000 B-29 bombloads to match this single explosion in the New Mexico desert.

✧   ✧   ✧

"I am sure," one observer noted at the time, "that all who witnessed this test went away with a profound feeling that they had seen one of the great events of history." Others tried, with varying degrees of success, to describe what they saw and felt. A career army officer was particularly eloquent: "The whole country was lighted by a searing light with the intensity many times that of the midday sun. It was golden, purple, violet, gray, and blue. It lighted every peak, crevasse and ridge of the nearby mountain range with a clarity and beauty that cannot be described but must be seen to be imagined." Another officer speculated, perhaps in the context of setting off a demonstration explosion that would persuade the Japanese to surrender, that "an enemy observer stationed about twenty miles from the scene of delivery would be deeply impressed, to say the least." A third thought about the impossibility of defense against such a weapon and concluded that "henceforth" a large city was "not the best place in which to live."

But by far the most memorable impression was that of Robert Oppenheimer. A most unusual scientist, Oppenheimer had learned Italian in order to read Dante's *Inferno*, German for Karl Marx's *Das Kapital*, and Sanskrit for the Hindu scriptures.

He was a true Renaissance man in his wide-ranging intellectual curiosity, and a twentieth-century man of the left in his compassion for the poor, the powerless, the wretched of the earth. It was Oppenheimer, according to one account, who chose "Trinity" as the code name for the atom bomb test and its site, drawing upon his knowledge of the fourteenth Holy Sonnet by John Donne, the early seventeenth-century English poet and Protestant divine. Oppenheimer's use of the sonnet, which begins, "Batter my heart, three-person'd God; for you/ As yet but knock, breathe, shine, and seek to mend," implies that he was aware of the theological implications of what he was doing in building such a weapon. His reported utterance after the explosion of the now-famous lines from the Hindu *Bhagavad Gita* reveals a profound sense of transgression as well as spiritual awareness, of having gone too far in challenging nature: "If the radiance of a thousand suns were to burst into the sky, that would be like the splendor of the Mighty One," Oppenheimer murmured. "I am become Death, destroyer of worlds."

◆   ◆   ◆

In ordinary times, Oppenheimer would not have been called upon to make such a portentous observation. Born in 1904 in New York to a Jewish family with German roots, he was indulged and pampered as a child. He suffered the fate common to young people who are richer and smarter than those around them, especially when they are inclined, as Oppenheimer was, to solitude and disdainful of intellectual inferiors. When he was 14, playmates at a summer camp rewarded his arrogance by locking him in an icehouse overnight. Too slight for competitive contact sports, insufficiently coordinated for tennis, he took up sailing as a teenager and came to enjoy working with horses one summer in Colorado, where his parents sent him for the good air and physical demands of the outdoor life. In college, Oppenheimer crammed four years of demanding science courses into three. He was isolated and intense, making few friends and leaving no mark beyond the terse comment beside his name in the Harvard year-book for 1925: "finished in three years."

Only two years later, Oppenheimer had completed the work for his Ph.D. in physics at Cambridge, with additional work at Göttingen University in southern Germany. While his intellectual path was smooth and extremely fast—most candidates in such a difficult program took two or three times as long to complete it—Oppenheimer suffered from severe bouts of depression with potentially dangerous results not only for himself but for others. On a train trip to Paris in 1926, he encountered an old friend and tried to strangle him; a London psychiatrist then diagnosed a condition similar to schizophrenia. Not long afterward, he rushed to the home of a friend to retrieve the poisoned apple he claimed to have left for him. Near the end of that difficult year, some of his friends worried that he was suicidal, and he later said that "bumping myself off" had indeed been a possibility.

But these eruptions, not so unusual in highly strung artists and scientists, soon receded. In 1929, Oppenheimer won a prestigious double appointment to the University of California at Berkeley and the California Institute of Technology, 400 miles to the south. His special field of study was quantum mechanics, so rarefied and abstruse that few people without advanced scientific training could even begin to comprehend it. Its applications, however, were relatively simpler and, as the world drew closer to war in the 1930s, profoundly important. The atom was first split in 1931; the neutron was discovered in 1932. In 1934 artificial radioactivity was achieved through bombarding a target with alpha particles; that same year, Fermi produced radioactive elements by bombarding uranium with neutrons, a process that would come to be known as atomic fission. By the end of 1939, physicists understood that fission gave off energy and that it should be possible to achieve a chain reaction resulting in an explosion of unprecedented power.

At the center of this furious storm of intellectual energy was Robert Oppenheimer, confirming his early promise as a theoretician and gaining recognition as an outstanding teacher who drew gifted graduate students from around the world to his classroom and his lab. So intense and single-minded was Oppenheimer during his early career at Cal Tech and Berkeley that he blocked out events such as the stock market crash of 1929—it was only six months later that someone told him the country's economy had virtually dissolved—and avoided more than casual encounters with women, not marrying until 1939 when he was 35 years old. He later described his isolation from the world around him, saying his friends "were mostly faculty people, scientists, classicists, and artists." Although he read widely in science and in literature, he did not subscribe to a daily newspaper or read news magazines. He didn't even own a radio. "I was not interested in and did not read about economics or politics," he said later. "I was almost wholly divorced from the contemporary scene in this country. I was deeply interested in my science; but I had no understanding of the relations of man to his society."

The contemporary scene in America in the 1930s included not only the Great Depression, which suggested to many that the economic engines of capitalism were burned out, but the rising tide of fascism in Germany, Italy, and Japan. Jews were particularly alarmed at the virulent anti-Semitism that the Nazis had unleashed. The excessive violence and repression (and its own brand of anti-Semitism) already associated with Josef Stalin's regime in the Soviet Union discouraged many in the U.S. from joining the American Communist Party (CP); it was clearly out of line with most Americans' beliefs in democratic principles. However, to many intellectuals, especially in such vibrant academic centers as Berkeley, Cambridge, and New York, only the Soviet Union and communism seemed to offer an alternative between capitalism and fascism. Writers, artists, musicians, university professors, and scientists ranging from Edmund Wilson to Aaron Copeland to Albert Einstein were sympathetic to "the Russian experiment" and to the urgent need for radical change in the United States. The abrupt rise in American CP membership from fewer than twenty-six thousand in 1934 to nearly one hundred thousand in 1939 was clearly due to increased fears of the danger represented by Hitler's Germany as well as disillusionment in the capitalist system generated by the lingering economic depression. And for every card-carrying member of the American Communist Party, every "Red," there were dozens of "Pinks" and "fellow-travelers" who thought the American system of solving problems was irretrievably broken.

Inevitably, given the climate of the times, Oppenheimer became more involved with the "contemporary scene" than he intended—and perhaps more than he ever acknowledged. His younger brother, Frank, also a physicist, had joined the CP in 1936, as had Frank's bride of that same year. Though Frank was eight years younger than Robert, the two had always been close, and Robert had found him a position at the lab.

In 1937 Robert Oppenheimer met and befriended a Berkeley colleague named Haakon Chevalier, a professor of French literature and a CP member who was also active in organizing the local teachers' union. Through Chevalier, Oppenheimer met George Eltenton, a British chemical engineer employed by Shell Oil Company in Oakland. Eltenton belonged to the Communist Party and was a member of the local Federation of Architects, Engineers, Chemists, and Technicians (FAECT). He enlisted Oppenheimer's help in trying to enroll his colleagues and other staff members at Berkeley's Radiation Laboratory, where he was now spending much of his time, in the union. Oppenheimer threw himself into the membership campaign, even licking stamps for mailings after midnight. His friend and superior Ernest Lawrence, the director of the "Rad Lab," angered Oppenheimer when he complained, to no avail, about his "leftwandering."

In 1939 Oppenheimer married Kathryn Puening, whose first husband, Joe Dallet, had been a Communist Party organizer in the steel mills of Youngstown, Ohio. Dallet was killed in 1937 while fighting with the CP-sponsored Abraham Lincoln Brigade in Spain. Kathryn—or Kitty, as she was called—joined the CP after marrying Dallet in 1934, though she left both it and Dallet in 1936. When she met Oppenheimer, in 1939, Kitty was married to a British doctor who was interning in a Pasadena hospital. A brief affair followed their meeting. Kitty deserted her husband and married Oppenheimer after obtaining a quick divorce in Reno. None of this would ordinarily have wrinkled brows in distant Washington. The American Communist Party was not an outlawed organization, and bureaucrats thought academics were prone to messy personal lives and unconventional opinions. But Oppenheimer's conversion to political activism, even though he said he was not a CP member, would soon give military security and the Federal Bureau of Investigation considerable cause for alarm. In March, 1941, the FBI opened what would become its voluminous file on J. Robert Oppenheimer with a report of his attendance at a meeting in Chevalier's home the previous December at which two CP members had also been present.

✧   ✧   ✧

Edward Teller, four years younger than Oppenheimer, was also a precocious and indulged child of wealthy Jews. But his home was in Budapest, and he had witnessed the suffering caused by the brief communist reign of Béla Kun following the World War (as World War I was then known). Teller attributed the backlash that led to the extended rule of the right-wing Admiral Horthy to the ravages perpetrated by the communists, whom he viewed with the greatest distrust and contempt.

Nor did Teller see anything but grief coming out of Nazi Germany. After earning his Ph.D. in physics in 1930 at the University of Leipzig, under Werner Heisenberg, he took a research position at Göttingen—Oppenheimer's alma mater, and an indication of how small and closely knit the world of advanced physics then was. Forced out of his job when the Nazis came to power in 1933, Teller and his young wife, Mici, joined the exodus of talented Jews and others from Germany. In 1934 he joined the Institute for Theoretical Physics in Denmark, where Niels

Bohr, Heisenberg's friend and mentor, was working with a group of young scientists to unlock the secrets of the atom. In 1935 the Russian-born physicist George Gamow invited Teller to join him at George Washington University in Washington, D.C., to assist in devising rules for classifying subatomic particle behavior in radioactive decay.

By the end of the decade, it was clear to most of the scientific community that the Germans had as good a chance as the Americans or the British at developing an atomic weapon, if not better. If three of the greatest names in classical music were Bach, Beethoven, and Brahms, Teller later said, the three greatest names in nuclear physics were Einstein, Heisenberg, and Bohr. While Einstein was safe in the United States, Heisenberg remained at work in Germany, and Bohr and his team were in danger of being captured if Denmark was invaded by the Nazis, as it inevitably would be.

World War II began with the German invasion of Poland on September 1, 1939. That summer, Teller was teaching at Columbia University in New York with a fellow Hungarian émigré and distinguished physicist, Leo Szilard. Early in the evening of July 30, Szilard called Teller to ask a favor: would he drive him out to the far north fork of Long Island, 70 or 80 miles at least, to Peconic Bay? He had to talk to Einstein, who was vacationing there. Szilard did not drive, whereas Teller had a 1935 Plymouth of dubious reliability that would have to do. It was well after dark by the time the two Hungarians found the village of Peconic, where a little girl directed them to the house of "the man with the long, flowing white hair."

Einstein received his visitors cordially, serving them tea while Szilard explained that he had drafted a letter to President Roosevelt for Einstein to sign if he approved it. It was a warning that inasmuch as "the element uranium may be turned into a new and important source of energy in the immediate future," it was "conceivable" that "extremely powerful bombs of a new type may thus be constructed." As Teller later recalled, Einstein said that the prospect before them was truly revolutionary. It would be the first time that "we would get energy directly from the atomic nucleus, rather than from the sun which got it from the atomic nucleus." Einstein gave the signed letter back to Szilard, who then transmitted it to President Roosevelt. "The rest is known to everybody," Teller said years afterward. "I had played my essential role as Szilard's chauffeur."

✧　　✧　　✧

"The rest" to which Teller referred was the Manhattan Project, the then-secret code name for the three-year marathon race to produce an atomic bomb. The race began in June, 1942, and it covered the country, from Manhattan, where the Army Corps of Engineers had given the project its name, to the Chicago Metallurgical Laboratory and the University of Chicago, to the materials-production facilities at Oak Ridge, Tennessee, and Hanford, Washington, to Ernest Lawrence's Radiation Laboratory in Berkeley. All of these, and many lesser sites, were essential to this extraordinary effort, but by far the most important was the laboratory built from scratch on a lonely mesa called Los Alamos, high in the beautiful Sangre de Cristo mountains north of Santa Fe, New Mexico. And while the people involved in the successful completion of the Manhattan Project were also essential—Lawrence, Fermi, Teller, John von Neumann, Stanslav Ulam, Niels Bohr, Hans Bethe, all household names in the pantheon of physics, plus hundreds of others almost as gifted—the key figure among all of these men was indisputably Robert Oppenheimer. How he came to be so has been the subject of numerous popular plays, movies, novels, and TV documentaries.

The dramatic implications of the situation in which Oppenheimer came to be involved are clear. The army wanted the scientists to be commissioned as officers, but Oppenheimer argued successfully that they should keep their civilian status even while living on what came to be a military base with some six thousand people, including dependants, staff, construction personnel, and soldiers. The man in charge of the entire Manhattan Project was General Leslie Groves, an army engineer who had earlier supervised the construction of the Pentagon. Eight years older than Oppenheimer, and nearly twice his weight, Groves was capable, hard-driving, and charmless—"the biggest sonofabitch I've ever met in my life," one of his aides said later, with an ego to match: "I hated his guts." He was "absolutely ruthless" in identifying and solving problems and made life miserable for anyone who fell short of his demands. Nor was Groves inclined to defer to the geniuses he had been assigned to organize: during the early days of the Manhattan Project, a group of scientists vaguely estimated the size of the weapon, saying they might be off by a factor of ten. Unacceptable, Groves retorted; that was like telling a wedding caterer, "we don't know how many guests are coming—maybe somewhere between ten and a thousand—but see to it that you have the right amount of food for them."

Oppenheimer, of course, understood his colleagues' difficulty in defining the power of a weapon that had not even been imagined until recently. He was intimately involved with the intellectual problems associated with the bomb, originally stimulated by Lawrence, who asked his help with theoretical issues involved in using the cyclotron to separate out uranium. Shortly after Lawrence requested Oppenheimer's assistance, while attending a meeting in October, 1941, in Schenectady, New York, Oppenheimer provided a critical breakthrough when he accurately determined how much U-235 would be needed to make a workable weapon. Arthur Compton, the influential head of the Metallurgical Lab, was the director of the Bomb Project in Chicago. He wrote the final report that came out of the Schenectady meeting, which amounted to a blueprint for the bomb. Impressed by Oppenheimer's achievement, Compton asked him in January, 1942, to join the Bomb Project, and in May to take over as the director of that component of the Manhattan Project.

General Groves, when he first met Oppenheimer in October, 1942, was weary and discouraged because of his dealings with the scientists and the lack of visible progress in getting the Bomb Project moving. Surprisingly, the two men—one an overbearing general with no interest in art or literature or music, the other an intellectual humanist and theoretician—got along splendidly. Oppenheimer, puffing gently on his pipe, was able to explain without condescension to the impatient cigar-chewing engineer what the esoteric challenge in building the bomb entailed. He sympathized with Groves's frustration at getting researchers to work toward a common practical goal, particularly given the problems of keeping military secrets confidential. Scientists were not like assembly-line workers; they needed to know where their efforts fit into the big picture, which was difficult since the scientists were working at a number of separate facilities. Oppenheimer said the solution would be to bring them together in a secure laboratory where they could live and work together, exchanging ideas freely, for as long as was needed. But they would have to stay put for the duration, virtually interned, which presented huge problems in terms of maintaining morale, not to mention civility, among a disputatious lot.

Oppenheimer deeply impressed Groves as a fellow problem-solver. The general understood that only a scientist equal in stature to the best of those he was supervising would be able to run the novel experiment Oppenheimer had outlined. Within weeks, ruthlessly cutting administrative red tape, Groves recommended and secured interim approval of Robert Oppenheimer as head not merely of Compton's bomb project but of the new secure lab, meaning his responsibility was greatly expanded. Groves's certainty that he had the right man was confirmed by Oppenheimer's quick and practical solution to the problem of where to put the lab. For several years, Oppenheimer and Kitty had owned a vacation cabin in the mountains near Taos, and his familiarity with the region led directly to the selection of

Los Alamos. Within four months of Groves's first meeting with Oppenheimer, Los Alamos was up and running.

Nobody had a greater sense of the need for security at Los Alamos than General Groves; he even tried to keep the location of the lab a secret from the president of UC Berkeley, whose institution provided the academic support for the new lab, telling him only that it was "somewhere in the Rocky Mountains." Army officers as a class and according to their temperament are also disinclined to leftist sentiments. Groves was unhappy to learn that Oppenheimer joked to FBI investigators before his Los Alamos appointment that he had probably belonged to every communist-front organization on the West Coast. He was even more distressed during his first months at Los Alamos as disturbing reports kept trickling across his desk about the dangers to national security posed by his chief administrator. It says much about Oppenheimer's unique capabilities, not to mention the trust that this hard-bitten conservative Presbyterian soldier placed in him, that on July 20, 1943, Groves overrode all objections by his base security officer to granting Oppenheimer his final clearance. Do it now, immediately, Groves ordered, "without delay, irrespective of the information which you have concerning Mr. Oppenheimer. He is absolutely essential to the project."

In fact, Oppenheimer had quickly revealed an unusual gift for administration as well as intellectual leadership that did make him the indispensable man about the new town of Los Alamos. He was the expediter, the organizer, the cheerleader for the community, the de facto mayor with a finger in everything from garbage collection to evening musicales. He also provided a buffer between the army and the scientists. There was something of a summer camp atmosphere to living at Los Alamos. Everyone worked hard, and in their off-duty hours, they had to provide their own recreation. The married couples partied heartily, while many of the young single men were naturally drawn to the pretty secretaries. An officer frowned at such indiscretions and told Oppenheimer he had prepared an order to deal with them: "Male callers to the women's dormitories will be received only in the recreation rooms. Their presence in the sleeping rooms is prohibited." Don't bother with such silly rulings, Oppenheimer advised the officer: "I can assure you that they will not be obeyed." When Groves himself groused that if Oppenheimer's colleagues didn't stop having so many new babies, he was going to have to build on to the hospital's maternity ward, he got only an amused brush-off: preventing pregnancies, Oppenheimer said, "seemed hardly to be the responsibility of a scientific director."

Even more significant in terms of mission success was Oppenheimer's combination of charm and adaptable intelligence. He was now "Oppy" to everyone, a theatrical persona with his props and his presence: the pipe, the slouch hat, the lean figure, the closely cropped gray hair, the intense blue eyes, the quick, encouraging smile. And he was everywhere—in seminar rooms, in labs, in the field, pulling together experts in thermodynamics, shock waves, implosion triggers, and a dozen other fields, comprehending and interpreting all of these areas for his colleagues, insisting, against the wishes of the security officers, that all of them had to know what the others were doing in order to heighten their own effectiveness. Many of the men he directed were Nobel Prize winners, which Oppenheimer was not, but one of them, Hans Bethe, said later that it was clear that "he was intellectually superior to us." Another physicist asserted that nobody else could have handled "that mixture of international scientific prima donnas, engineers, and army officers, forging them into an enthusiastically productive" group.

✧   ✧   ✧

Among the most talented and difficult of Oppy's prima donnas was that intense amateur musician and lover of classical music, Edward Teller. In his later years, when he was famous as the main force behind the development of the hydrogen bomb and then as one of the chief architects and advocates of President Ronald

Reagan's antimissile system (nicknamed "Star Wars"), Teller's public persona was often seen as menacing. His dark, glowering stare, his pronounced limp, his Hungarian accent, and his frequently asserted conviction that the communists could not be trusted to live up to any arms control agreement led critics to malign him as a Dr. Strangelove, as mad as the title character of Stanley Kubrick's 1964 movie. Even his friends, most notably Fermi, joked about Teller's intense need to succeed on his own terms at everything he undertook—Fermi said he was the only monomaniac of his acquaintance who had several manias, not just one. Neighbors at Los Alamos who had to listen to Teller unwind by playing the piano late at night said he played all of Mozart *fortissimo*.

Teller was aware that he gave these impressions and sought to explain them to himself and others. He admitted that as a boy he had been overprotected by his adoring mother, reaching adolescence "still a serious child with no sense of humor." Drawing on the ancient notion of "humors," he acknowledged that Hungarians were said to be famously "melancholic," but thought his own temperament inclined more to the "choleric," or fiery, which accounted for his difficulties with some colleagues.

In fact, Teller had a wry, self-deprecating wit and a lively sense of humor; one of his favorite authors was Lewis Carroll, whose nonsense verse and parables of irrationality he loved to read to his children. He had a warm, congenial relationship with most of his colleagues, based partly on his ability to recognize and acknowledge their merits. He had been particularly impressed by Robert Oppenheimer, whose personality "overwhelmed" him after they met for the first time in 1937, when Teller was invited to give a lecture at Berkeley. He also respected Oppenheimer as a fellow "bricklayer," a theorist who laid down the foundations for future scientific developments.

The two became friendly, if not close, over the next several years, and Teller contributed significantly to developments that would result in Oppenheimer's successful completion of the Manhattan Project. But Teller was also persuasive and as articulate, in his accented English, as Oppenheimer was. Early in the summer of 1942, nearly a year before Los Alamos got off the ground, Teller startled a Berkeley gathering of physicists convened by Lawrence with a novel proposal. His idea derived from long talks the previous winter with Fermi, the man they all revered as a genius. Teller said that the physics of constructing the atomic bomb was already well understood. Finishing the project was now merely a problem of engineering. The real challenge was to move beyond the atomic bomb to what he called the "Super" bomb— that is, to design the atomic bomb to be the trigger for a much more powerful device that would fuse hydrogen into helium, a thermonuclear reaction like those that fueled the sun. The fuel for the Super would be liquid deuterium, more easily separated from heavy water than the usable portion of uranium U-235 was from its source, U-238.

One physicist who was present said that, at least for a short time, "Everyone forgot about the A-bomb as if it were old hat." Some were concerned, Oppenheimer among them, that such a super bomb might burn up the planet. He took a train to Arthur Compton's vacation cottage on Lake Michigan after the conference to ask for Compton's advice, and the two men reluctantly agreed that further research on the Teller/Fermi idea should be approved—in part because Hans Bethe said a few simple calculations served to prove such an accident was mathematically impossible—but that the atomic bomb as a weapon would remain their first priority.

Through the summer of 1942, Teller's relations with the Berkeley contingent were cordial—Ernest Lawrence took him sailing on San Francisco Bay, and Oppy and Kitty had the Tellers to stay with them as house guests. Teller enjoyed the visit but was disappointed that Oppenheimer seemed uninterested in his gift of a new recording of his favorite Mozart piece, the Piano Concerto in E-Flat Major. Later, Teller understood that the tension between himself and Oppenheimer was due to their conflicting certainties on the proper thrust of coming nuclear research. Teller continued to believe in the Super, while Oppenheimer had already determined that the technical problems that so enthralled Teller would take too long to solve. He was sure that the development of the atomic bomb as a useable weapon was essential to defeat Hitler and regarded Teller's fascination with the Super as a distraction from that goal.

✦   ✦   ✦

Oppenheimer apparently was right about the technical problems of developing the Super: not until 1952, after years of effort, would the first successful H-bomb be exploded. Therefore, if the Manhattan Project's efforts had been concentrated in the direction that Teller suggested, no useable weapon would have been developed in time for World War II. As it happened, the Germans surrendered in May, 1945, well before the gadget was ready to test. But Little Boy and Fat Man—the grotesquely jolly nicknames for the bombs that fell on Hiroshima and Nagasaki that August—did justify the enormous effort of the Manhattan Project by bringing the war with Japan to an abrupt end, though at costs that are still being reckoned.

It was Robert Oppenheimer who most eloquently captured the cost of the bomb, on July 16, 1945. As he saw the great fireball in the sky, he murmured the profoundly terrifying words of Vishnu from *The Bhagavad Gita:* "I am become Death, the destroyer of worlds." He is presumed to have experienced a kind of religious epiphany at this moment, a revelation of the powers of destruction he had helped to unleash, which may explain his subsequent opposition not only to Teller's Super bomb but to atomic weapons of any kind. He also felt a deep sense of guilt and thought that others in power should share it; he later startled and offended President Harry Truman by telling him to his face that both of them had blood on their hands, and he said repeatedly that "the physicists have known sin, and this is a knowledge which they cannot use."

In fact, Oppenheimer's utterance of the apocalyptic quotation from Vishnu apparently came sometime shortly after his first reaction. What he initially exclaimed, according to his brother Frank, was, "It works!" The split between Oppenheimer as philosopher/seer and Oppenheimer as scientist/administrator could not be clearer. He was divided in other ways as well. As a young man, he had been diagnosed with a schizophrenic condition. In the years to come, he would be charged with having conflicting views of his obligations as a government official and consultant. Oppenheimer's defenders then and later cited the deep humanity revealed by his recollection of the words of Vishnu; his detractors regarded it as contrived and self-serving, further evidence of his capacity for self-delusion.

Immediately following the war, however, Oppenheimer had no detractors, only admirers. His accomplishments at Los Alamos led to his appointment in 1947 as the director of Princeton's Institute for Advanced Studies. His talents as an administrator, unknown before Los Alamos, were now fully developed and helped him turn the Institute into one of the most influential intellectual centers in the world. But he remained well connected to his specialty in physics through a variety of appointments to ad hoc and standing committees; he was at the center of a network of influential policymakers in and out of government who were determining the direction of postwar nuclear policies and programs. The most important of his assignments was his position, beginning in 1947, as chairman of the Atomic Energy Commission's General Advisory Committee, what the press called the AEC's "atomic brain trust," its other members at the time being James Conant, the president of Harvard; Enrico Fermi; I.I. Rabi; and Glenn Seaborg.

One of this committee's concerns was how to resolve the controversy over the development of the H-Bomb. In September, 1945, just after the end of the war with Japan, Oppenheimer had joined with Arthur Compton in vigorously opposing the Super.

In language that anticipated the "better Red than dead" slogan of nuclear opponents in the coming Cold War, Compton and Oppenheimer said they did not oppose further development of the bomb because it was too difficult to make but "because we should prefer defeat in war to a victory obtained at the expense of the enormous human disaster" that its use would cause.

According to Herbert York, director of the Lawrence Livermore Laboratory during the 1950s when Teller was working there on the Super, the partisans of Oppenheimer and Teller wrangled for years in a "very acrimonious debate" concerning the effort expended between 1946 and 1949 on the H-Bomb. Teller himself blamed Oppenheimer in part for delays that cost the country critical years in the race with the Soviet Union, saying the Super could have been tested as early as 1947 instead of 1952. As anti-communists in both political parties would later note bitterly, these were precisely the years when the Soviet Union under Stalin and China under Mao were at their most aggressive and most ruthless, enslaving hundreds of millions of people in Europe and Asia—and a time when the threat of the H-Bomb might have deterred them.

✧   ✧   ✧

Opposing Mao and Stalin in this deadly high-stakes game of international diplomacy was a man many did not think up to the challenge. In July, 1945, Harry Truman was in the fourth month of his presidency. While vice president, he had been kept out of the information loop by FDR and was therefore at a disadvantage when he met with Churchill and Stalin, among others, in Potsdam to discuss postwar politics and policies. Thinking he would achieve some negotiating leverage, Truman, as he put it, "casually mentioned" to Stalin "that we had a new weapon of unusual destructive force." Stalin startled Truman by showing no surprise at this news, but then Truman did not yet know that Soviet spies had been stealing secrets out of Los Alamos and other facilities for years—this despite the security efforts of the FBI, of military intelligence, and especially of General Leslie Groves.

Debate continues on the degree to which stolen secrets were essential to the Soviet bomb program. The fact remains that a Soviet program that during the war included only 20 physicists, and a total staff of 50 at the main lab, somehow succeeded in exploding an atomic bomb on August 19, 1949. The political fallout in the United States was poisonous—Soviet spying had already been widely exposed, and the cases of Alger Hiss (see Chapter 9), Julius and Ethel Rosenberg, and scores of others were front-page news, month in and month out, from 1946 through the years of Senator Joseph McCarthy, finally winding down in 1954. Not yet public knowledge in 1949, but of increasing concern to the government, were revelations that the Soviets had operated two active espionage rings in Washington during the war—one had 27 members working in six different federal agencies, and included among its agents the assistant secretary of the teasury, Harry Dexter White, and a senior aide to FDR, Lauchlin Currie. Others included a congressman from New York, three state department officials, and the daughter of the American ambassador to Germany prior to World War II. Additionally, more than a dozen infiltrators had found their way into the OSS, the predecessor of the Central Intelligence Agency. A particular target for the Soviets was the Manhattan Project, which they code-named "Enormoz," and spies in Washington ("Carthage"), New York ("Tyre"), and San Francisco ("Babylon") were directed to concentrate their efforts on infiltrating it.

The frightening vulnerability of American secrets to being stolen was revealed in many ways, but none was more appalling, because of its banal simplicity, than the exposure of Soviet secret agent Klaus Fuchs in 1949. Fuchs, a German-born British citizen who worked at the heart of Oppenheimer's Los Alamos program, drove out the heavily guarded gate in his blue Buick every week for two years with top secret technical documents that he passed along to a Soviet agent in a Santa Fe park.

Fuchs's spying for the Soviets, which dated back to the mid-1930s, had been uncovered after a postwar review of everyone who had been given an emergency war-time security clearance, a category that included even such luminaries as Oppenheimer. FBI director J. Edgar Hoover was reportedly eager to challenge Oppenheimer on the basis of the earlier FBI reports that had stalled his first clearance until Groves pushed it through. But John Lansdale, the army officer in charge of security under Groves at Los Alamos, said then that he was "absolutely certain" of Oppenheimer's loyalty, even though he had been an "avid fellow-traveler" in the past. Oppenheimer received his renewed clearance in August, 1947, just weeks after his brother Frank was exposed by a Washington newspaper as "a card-carrying member of the Communist Party," a story whose details probably were leaked by Hoover in an effort to derail the clearance.

Oppenheimer thus continued to be influential in nuclear weapons policy matters and to oppose Teller's Super bomb. He had already mockingly dismissed the idea, saying he was "not sure the miserable thing will work, nor that it can be gotten to a target except by ox cart." More seriously, he worried in a letter to James Conant that "the thing appears to have caught the imagination, both of congressional and of military people, as *the answer* to the problem posed by the Russian advance." Conant agreed, saying the Super would proceed only over his dead body. The split between the two camps, Teller's and Oppenheimer's, grew wider and the language of the opponents more abusive. David Lilienthal, the former head of the Tennessee Valley Authority who assumed the leadership of the Atomic Energy Commission in 1946, said Teller's chief supporters, Ernest Lawrence and Luis Alvarez, were positively "bloodthirsty" and "drooling" over the prospect of the Super. Even Teller's old friend Fermi rebuked him, saying that "the use of such a weapon cannot be justified on any ethical ground."

Late in 1949, Lilienthal met with Admiral Lewis Strauss and the other three members of the AEC's policy commission that he chaired in order to consider recommending further work on the

Super. Strauss was not a scientist but a wealthy investment banker, well connected in Washington since serving as Herbert Hoover's personal secretary in the 1920s, and a recent political appointee of President Truman's to the AEC. He asked Oppenheimer if he would still recommend canceling work on the Super if the Russians said they would not reciprocate. Oppenheimer said he was sure they would follow America's example. Strauss was outraged by his answer. A few weeks earlier, after he had first learned about Fuchs, Strauss had called Groves to upbraid him about security. Groves wrote to Strauss and admitted that he should have acted on the information he had about Haakon Chevalier and Frank Oppenheimer before he insisted on pushing through Robert Oppenheimer's clearance in 1943. It was now clear to Groves that Oppenheimer had "sponsored, protected and otherwise looked out" for his brother, "knowing full well" that Frank and his wife had been communists.

✦   ✦   ✦

Lilienthal's committee voted four to one against further support for Teller's Super, largely on moral grounds that it was an inconceivably horrible weapon. Strauss, Teller's only supporter, resigned in protest. But Oppenheimer had won a battle only to lose the war. Truman had grave misgivings about the Super, saying "it is not an easy thing to order the development of a weapon that will kill ten million people." On the other hand, he had to recognize, as General Omar Bradley, Army Chief of Staff, pointed out, that the country "would be in an intolerable position if a possible enemy possessed the [Super] and the United States did not." In January, 1950, Truman authorized continued development of the Super. Teller, jubilant and full of energy, began to push for a new lab near Berkeley devoted to the bomb's development, and even invited his old colleague J. Robert Oppenheimer to work with him on it. Oppenheimer declined. The wheel had turned since their time together at Los Alamos, with Teller now on top.

Oppenheimer did not give up his opposition, however, and he remained influential in the political and scientific communities by virtue of his charismatic intelligence and especially through his governmental connections. By May, 1952, Lewis Strauss was telling an aide that he "had very good information to the effect that [Teller's] second laboratory was being sabotaged," clearly meaning sabotaged by Oppenheimer. Teller, like Strauss, wanted to prevent Oppenheimer's membership on the General Advisory Committee from being renewed by the president when his term expired in 1952. An FBI paraphrase of Teller's complaint to an agent said Teller felt Oppenheimer should be removed from the GAC because of "his poor advice and polices regarding national preparedness and because of his delaying of the development of H-bomb." Oppenheimer, sensing trouble, resigned on June 12, 1952, before Truman could announce his decision not to reappoint him.

On November 1, 1952, in the first successful Super explosion, the tiny coral island of Elugelab in the Pacific Ocean was vaporized by a ten-megaton bomb called Mike. Edward Teller's ambition was finally realized, as would be—for several decades, at least—Robert Oppenheimer's fears of an uncontrollable arms race with the Soviet Union. But Oppenheimer's ability to oppose Teller was about to be destroyed, in no small part because of his own actions a decade and more earlier.

✧   ✧   ✧

The Oppenheimer security-clearance hearings, which took place in a nondescript government building in Washington from April 12 to May 6, 1954, were a genteel affair compared with Senator McCarthy's long-running Roman circus in his open Senate hearings. They were behind closed doors, they were supposed to be private, and the issue was deceptively undramatic: should Dr. Oppenheimer's security clearance be revoked? Unlike some of McCarthy's victims, he was not threatened with imprisonment, he would not lose his job, and he was treated with deference and respect by four of the five current AEC committee members who had to decide what to do about his clearance. The fifth member was Lewis Strauss, recently reappointed to the AEC and made its head by the new president, Dwight D. Eisenhower. He was not as polite as his colleagues.

It is little short of amazing, and a testament to Oppenheimer's continuing stature during the postwar period of fear concerning communist subversion at home and aggression abroad, that he retained his influence as long as he did. His undeniable contribution to the making of the atomic bomb, his place in the scientific community, even his candor about his prewar communist associations, had made him untouchable up to now. His integrity was his shield. But on December 23, 1953, Strauss called Oppenheimer into his office at the AEC and told him that the FBI had determined that he was a security risk on several grounds, including moral and ethical questions about his personal character. Strauss offered to let him resign without prejudice from the several committees and commissions on which he still served and that required the highest "Q" clearance. When he left Strauss's office, Oppenheimer took with him the bill of particulars that a Strauss aide had drawn up. He replied to it the following day, requesting the hearing that Strauss had said was the alternative to accepting his decision to revoke the clearance.

Five years after the Oppenheimer hearings, in 1959, Lewis Strauss would be denied Senate confirmation as President Eisenhower's commerce secretary. Conservatives said he was a victim of political persecution; liberals said he was paying the price for destroying Oppenheimer. At the very least, Strauss lacked a sense of fair play, perhaps because he was miffed at being called by Oppenheimer's supporters "the tugboat admiral" for his reserve commission, which had not led to service beyond cruises on the Hudson River. In his zeal to oust Oppenheimer, Strauss resorted to tactics he had learned in 1930, when his old friend and boss President Hoover was worried that the Democrats had information damaging to his administration. Hoover, in what must be seen as a striking anticipation of Richard Nixon's Watergate misadventure, authorized Strauss to "utilize the services of any one of our various government secret services" to find out what the Democrats possessed. Nothing particular came of that forgotten episode, but Strauss now revived his interest in clandestine surveillance and directed that wiretaps be placed on Oppenheimer's home, allowing his team to listen in on Oppenheimer's discussion of his defense with his lawyers. In one of those conversations, Oppenheimer said bitterly that he was a victim of "all the evil of the times." There is no record of Strauss's reaction to this remark.

Sadly, though, the revelations that came out of the hearing would confirm, for Edward Teller, and for others as well, that Strauss had cause for his fears concerning Oppenheimer's integrity. For it was now revealed that not only had Oppenheimer lied about an important security matter in 1943 to the FBI and to General Groves but he had lied to his old and dear friend, Haakon Chevalier. The origins of the story lay in a conversation in Berkeley shortly before Oppenheimer went to Los Alamos in March, 1943. Chevalier told Oppenheimer that George Eltenton, the Shell engineer and CP member, had asked him to find out if Oppenheimer could be persuaded to pass useful details concerning his research at Berkeley to the Soviets. Chevalier later claimed that he simply thought Oppenheimer should be "forewarned" about this attempted approach, and that it was trivial, a "molehill" out of which a mountain was later constructed.

The mountain, it turned out, consisted of Oppenheimer giving conflicting stories about this incident to investigators at different times, the first time to army intelligence officers before he left for Los Alamos. Initially, he said three different persons had been approached by an unnamed intermediary; later that there were three intermediaries, each of whom approached a different scientist; and finally, to General Groves, that Chevalier was a potential spy. Some of Oppenheimer's conflicting stories had been caught on audio tape, a devastating surprise to him when he was confronted with transcripts of them during the hearing. Roger Robb, the AEC counsel, later described Oppenheimer's demeanor during the questioning. He was "hunched over, wringing his hands, white as a sheet." He admitted that he had deliberately fed the investigators "a cock-and-bull story." Why had he lied? "I was an idiot," was all Oppenheimer could say. Later, it was assumed by sympathizers that he was defending his old friend Chevalier. But as Chevalier knew to his sorrow, his old friend had actually implicated, not defended, him.

Before the hearing, when Edward Teller learned that he would be asked to testify, he assured Oppenheimer that he did not believe he had done anything "sinister." He said elsewhere that all scientific advances depended on free and open exchange of ideas, and that he thought Oppenheimer's problems were due mostly to Strauss's excessive concern for secrecy. He intended to say that it was not disloyal of anyone to have opposing ideas, as Oppenheimer did about the Super, and to express concern that a clearance might be lifted "for a mere mistake in judgment." He said he anticipated being asked, "Do I consider Oppenheimer a security risk? And I was prepared to answer 'no' to that question." But Teller was shocked when, a few minutes before his testimony, Robb showed him the transcript in which Oppenheimer admitted lying and revealed that he had betrayed Chevalier. Teller said "with some heat," according to Robb, that he too had been "deceived and misled" by Oppenheimer. If there was one thing he knew for sure, it was that Oppenheimer was not an idiot.

Now that he was on the witness stand, Teller told Robb that he did not believe Oppenheimer was disloyal, and did "not want to suggest anything of the kind." However, "in a great number of cases I have seen Dr. Oppenheimer act—I understand that Dr. Oppenheimer acted—in a way which for me was exceedingly hard to understand. I thoroughly disagreed with him in numerous issues and his actions frankly appeared to me confused and complicated. To this extent I feel that I would like to see the vital interests of this country in hands which I understand better, and therefore trust more." Teller added, under cross-examination, that he did not believe that Oppenheimer would "knowingly and willingly do anything that is designed to endanger the safety of this country." Insofar as "intent" was concerned, he did "not see any reason to deny clearance." However, he continued, "if it is a question of wisdom and judgment, as demonstrated by actions since 1945, then I would say one would be wiser not to grant clearance."

When Teller left the witness stand, he turned to Oppenheimer, who was seated on a leather couch at the back of the room, and the two men shook hands. "I'm sorry," Teller said. "After what you've just said," Oppenheimer responded, "I don't know what you mean."

✧   ✧   ✧

On June 28, 1954, Lewis Strauss announced that Oppenheimer would lose his security clearance "because of the proof of fundamental defects in his 'character.'" Outwardly, little changed for Oppenheimer, who returned to Princeton and lived quietly, revered by those who regarded him as a victim of McCarthyite witch hunters. In 1967, at the age of 63, he died of cancer. Across the continent, at the Lawrence Livermore Lab, Teller continued his work on the Super, which would become the most potent weapon in the American arsenal—though, unlike the atomic bomb developed by Oppenheimer, one that has not yet been used in battle. In 2001, two years before his death at 95, Teller published his memoirs, which were widely and favorably reviewed.

The 1954 Strauss ruling meant that in political terms, Teller had won his long contest for dominance with Oppenheimer: "Teller's is now the featured face (instead of Oppenheimer's) in the role of Scientific Statesman," David Lilienthal confided to his diary in the late summer of 1954. In moral terms, however, Oppenheimer has long been viewed by most in the academic community as a martyred saint, and Teller, at least for a time, as a traitor to his colleague and to his kind. Teller was still troubled by the controversy nearly half a century later, as his comments on it in his memoirs indicate. But he continued to dispute the essential premise behind Oppenheimer's assertion that as a result of their endeavors, physicists now "knew sin." No, Teller said: they "knew power."

The thorny issues of nuclear weapons—their use, their ownership, their very existence—remain very much with us. Surprisingly, given all that has been written about him, so do questions about the puzzle of Oppenheimer's character and his fate. While he had long admitted to sympathizing with communist causes before he joined the Manhattan Project, he had steadfastly denied ever belonging to the American Communist Party. Even Lewis Strauss never seriously questioned this denial. But in September, 2002, Gregg Herken's *Brotherhood of the Bomb* was published. In it Herken suggested, on the basis of newly discovered letters by Haakon Chevalier and others in San Francisco, that Oppenheimer had indeed been a member—a card-carrying member, in the phrase made notorious by Joe McCarthy—of the American Communist Party. Herken, a historian at the Smithsonian Institution, is widely respected; he admires all three members of the brotherhood he writes about—Ernest Lawrence, Teller, and Oppenheimer—and does not suggest that Oppenheimer betrayed American secrets. But his persuasive findings do tarnish the legend of Robert Oppenheimer as a blameless victim of "all the evil of the times."

8

No Substitute for Victory

Harry S. Truman,
Douglas MacArthur,
and the Korean War

In April, 2001, a Chinese jet fighter clipped the propeller of an American reconnaissance plane flying in international air space off the island of Hainan, in the South China Sea. The American pilot managed to land his crippled plane on Hainan, but the Chinese pilot whose reckless harassing maneuver had caused the collision was killed. The Chinese military held the American crew as prisoners for 11 days, claiming that their lumbering plane had deliberately struck the Chinese fighter jet and demanding an official American apology from President George W. Bush.

As was noted at the time, the truculent hostility of the Chinese during this incident was not what would be expected from a country with which the United States has diplomatic and trade relations—as compared, say, with Cuba or North Korea. Public reaction in the United States while the 24 servicemen and -women were in Chinese hands was muted, but after they were released, it was clear that most Americans regarded the Chinese government, not entirely fairly, as a repugnant totalitarian regime little changed in character from what it had been under Chairman Mao half a century before.

Imagine, then, what Americans must have felt about China in 1950–1953, when the Cold War turned hot in Korea. China was then an international outlaw with which the United States had no diplomatic relations at all. Mao was at the terrible peak of his power, actively encouraging the North Koreans who had invaded the South, which prompted the United States to come to the South's defense. The United States had the means, including the atomic bomb, to annihilate China as a military power, and many Americans thought it should do so. Their hero and spokesman was Douglas MacArthur, one of the greatest generals of the twentieth century, who threatened that America would bomb China's mainland, blockade its coasts, and destroy its cities if it did not withdraw its troops from Korea. His opponent, President Harry Truman, was often disparaged as a political hack, not up to the demands of his office. Truman first rebuked MacArthur for overstepping his authority as commander of allied forces in Korea, then relieved him of command and ordered him to retire from the army. The political firestorm that followed remains one of the most intense in American history.

✦   ✦   ✦

The story began on a quiet summer weekend, at 9:20 on the evening of June 24, 1950.* Harry Truman was in Independence, Missouri, visiting with his wife, Bess, who preferred their modest Victorian farmhouse and the quiet pace of midwestern life to the White House and its demands. With them was their daughter, Margaret. The telephone rang. It was Dean Acheson, the secretary of state, sounding shaken: "Mr. President, I have very serious news. The North Koreans have invaded South Korea."

---

*June 25 in Korea because of the International Date Line.

Though Truman did not ordinarily respond emotionally to crises, Margaret remembered how shocked he was by Acheson's call: "My father made it clear, from the moment he heard the news, that he feared this was the opening of World War III." He was also determined to resist, telling Margaret, even before he returned to Washington and before the United Nations convened, "We are going to fight."

Korea in 1950 was not only remote to most Americans but a place to which they were supremely indifferent. A 500-mile long peninsula appended to the belly of the Asian continent, its 27 million people had been under Japanese rule since shortly after the turn of the century. As World War II ended, Korea was arbitrarily split into two halves, north and south, by American and Soviet negotiators to facilitate the surrender of Japanese troops stationed there. The Soviets, who shared with Korea a 12-mile border in its far northeastern corner, near Vladivostok, had control of the peninsula south to the thirty-eighth parallel (roughly the same latitude as Philadelphia, on the other side of the world); the Americans controlled everything south of that line.

The line—which still exists today as the DMZ, or demilitarized zone—was supposed to be a temporary division. The World War II allies, including the Soviet Union, had agreed that Korea would be a free and independent nation after the defeat of Japan. With the dropping of the Iron Curtain in 1946—the phrase that Winston Churchill coined in that year to describe the closed and isolated communist regimes in Europe and Asia—agreement between the U.S.S.R. and the United States over how Korea should be governed proved impossible. Efforts by the United Nations, supported by the U.S., to hold free nationwide elections throughout Korea were frustrated by the Soviets. In 1947 Seoul became the capital of the newly formed Republic of Korea. The communists in the North denied the legality of the Seoul government and asserted their own sovereignty as the Democratic People's Republic of Korea, with Pyongyang as its capital. By mid-1949 most American troops had left South Korea, except for a handful of military advisors. Soviet troops were supposedly withdrawn from the North by December, 1948, though in fact large numbers remained there or just across the border in the Soviet Union.

The South was led by Syngman Rhee, a crotchety old tyrant beloved by American conservatives because he was a Christian and he hated communism. In the North, the hard-line communists, led by Kim Il Sung, established the most repressive dictatorship in the world, outdoing even China and the Soviet Union. (It remains so today, under Kim's son and designated heir to power, Kim Jong Il.) Encouraged and supported by the neighboring Chinese, Kim built a military machine that dwarfed that of the South. From 1946 through the rest of the decade, as the Cold War intensified in Europe, Mao Zedong routed the Nationalist forces of Chiang Kai-shek and established complete control over mainland China. Chiang retreated to the large island of Formosa, or Taiwan, in 1949 and formed the competing government in exile that continues today to be the major thorn in the side of Beijing. In 1950 the North Koreans felt certain that the South, which they correctly saw as weak and corrupt, was ready for the taking. They were encouraged by a speech in which Dean Acheson seemed to suggest that Korea was not included with Japan as beneath the umbrella of American defense. Soviet military strategists helped the North Koreans out with advisers and attack plans, the Chinese gave their approval, and Kim attacked with an initial assault by 90,000 men on the night of June 25, 1950 (Korean time).

Little of this background and motivation was known in the West at the time of the attack. Some officials worried that the Korean incursion was merely a feint—that there was a larger attack in the works, perhaps on Taiwan by the Chinese communists or on Yugoslavia or Berlin by the Soviet Union. Suspicion and distrust filled the air. The political right assumed that everything bad anywhere in the world was the result of an international communist conspiracy led by the Soviet Union, while the left argued the contrary—that ongoing troubles in central Europe, in Greece, and in Korea stemmed from internecine quarrels between "progressive" and "reactionary" forces in which the West seemed always to take the wrong side (i.e., the reactionary.) But most Americans agreed that if the attack in Korea was not a clear and flagrant case of communist aggression, whatever its cause, then nothing was. They understood that this would be the first major test of the new United Nations, the successor to Woodrow Wilson's failed dream of the League of Nations (see Chapter 5).

On Sunday afternoon, June 25, the UN Security Council met and approved the American resolution that the North Koreans cease hostilities and withdraw their forces to the thirty-eighth parallel. The council approved the vote 9–0—the Soviets lost their chance to veto the UN participation because the Soviet representative, Jacob Malik, had boycotted its proceedings since earlier that year when the council refused to unseat Chiang Kai-shek's Nationalist China to make room for the People's Republic of China. On June 30 the American public learned that U.S. troops were going to fight as part—by far the major part—of a United Nations force in Korea. It was not a war that they were going to fight, the Truman administration told the country; it was a "police action," with America as the chief cop. This was the first instance of the now-familiar international peacekeeping missions, such as those recently in Kuwait and Kosovo, but at the time, "police action" was regarded as Orwellian doublespeak.

Nevertheless, widespread approval greeted Truman's declaration of not-war: the *New York Times* applauded it on its editorial pages, as did Walter Reuther of the United Auto Workers union, former Republican candidate for president Thomas E. Dewey, and George Kennan, the author of the "containment" philosophy. Even more important, perhaps, Truman had the enthusiastic support of the average citizen, such as the midwestern Republican who wrote him: "You may be a whiskey guzzling poker playing old buzzard as some say, by damn, for the first time since old Teddy left there in March of 1909, the United States has a grass roots *American* in the White House."

Harry Truman's career as a military man was a good deal less dramatic than Theodore Roosevelt's. Turned down by West Point and Annapolis because of poor vision, Truman passed the physical for the Missouri National Guard in 1916 by memorizing the eye chart and was sent to France as an artillery officer (lieutenant, later promoted to captain). Short and a bit thick around the middle, Truman would not have served as a model for a recruiting poster, and the closest he came to injury was when his horse fell on him during an artillery barrage. In his later years, Truman would become a student of military history, seeing confirmation in his reading of his personal conviction that most generals were "dumb," "like horses with blinders on." His experience as a captain in France also left him, as David McCullough writes, "with an abiding dislike of the military caste system and its West Point stuffed shirts in particular."

The man on whom President Truman now depended to carry out his military rescue operation in Korea was Douglas MacArthur, the personification of West Point in its best and some of its less attractive aspects: the best in terms of giving one's all for Duty, Honor, and Country, the less attractive in terms of aristocratic assumptions that struck the ordinary citizen as unacceptable in a democracy—precisely the caste mentality that Truman hated. Born in 1880, four years before Truman, MacArthur had also aspired to West Point and served in France. But while Truman, denied entry to the Academy, never did go to college, MacArthur had graduated first in his class of 1903—his worst enemies would never call him "dumb"—and been voted most likely to succeed by his classmates. Harry Truman was "utterly lacking" in charisma, according to Alonzo Hamby in his scholarly biography. MacArthur was six feet tall; as handsome as the actor Gregory Peck, who portrayed him later in a film biography; dashing and brave; eloquent and dramatic. His first assignment was to the Philippines, where, in 1904, he mapped the peninsula of Bataan (40 years later he still remembered every detail of it, including the tide tables) and killed two bandits who had ambushed him. In 1916 he was a colonel serving as chief of staff of the Forty-second Division, the Rainbow Division. Promoted to brigadier general in 1917, commanding the Eighty-fourth brigade of the Rainbow Division in France, MacArthur won a reputation as a fighting general whose flamboyant, romantic style was matched by real feats of courage on the battlefield—he became the most decorated American soldier of the war, winning five Silver Stars. By the end of the war, he was promoted to major general and named the commander of the Rainbow Division.

After the war ended in 1918, Harry Truman returned home and slowly climbed the political ladder, reaching what he considered his peak in the 1930s as a New Deal senator from Missouri. Following Pearl Harbor, he won respect for his outstanding work on overseeing military expenditures, which saved the country billions of dollars. In 1944 he was nominated for vice president under Roosevelt.

MacArthur, frustrated by American failure to recognize the growing threat posed by Japan in the 1930s, resigned his commission in 1935 to direct the defense of the Philippines, with the grand title of Field Marshal, for President Manuel Quezon. Recalled to U.S. duty after Pearl Harbor, he was designated commander in chief of the Southwest Pacific Area and later of all Allied air and ground forces in the Pacific theater, with the exception of the Marines and naval air forces, which were part of Admiral Chester W. Nimitz's Central Pacific Fleet. Making up for early errors, including a botched defense of Bataan, MacArthur capped a series of brilliant military successes by accepting the Japanese surrender on the battleship *Missouri* on

September 2, 1945. It was a moment of high drama and great dignity that won him deserved acclaim. His final assignment, as it was generally understood, was to serve as the de facto leader of Japan during the years of its reconstruction after the war. He was the Dai Ichi, the number one man, who oversaw a series of extraordinary restructurings of Japanese politics and government that would result in transforming the country within 20 years into a functioning democracy and an economic powerhouse.

By any measure, Douglas MacArthur in 1950, as the Korean War began, was at the zenith of his career. He challenged Eisenhower for preeminence as, if not the most revered American general still on active duty, the most picturesque. But he was much more than that. William Manchester was criticized for overstating his case for MacArthur in calling him an "American Caesar," but the military historians Ernest Dupuy and Trevor N. Dupuy agree that among all the military leaders of World War II just "one man—Douglas MacArthur—may have risen to join the thin ranks of the great captains of history."

By 1950, however, at 70, MacArthur was also the oldest American general still on active duty. During World War II Army Chief of Staff General George Marshall had wisely exempted MacArthur from the rule that field grade officers past the age of 60 were too old for active command. Now he was a decade older, an aging general who had been asked to direct a sadly depleted American army that was nearly beyond help. For the past five years, following the demobilization of the military after World War II ended in 1945, the Truman administration had chosen to rely on a policy of nuclear deterrence that would make large standing armies redundant. It allowed the army and the Marines in particular to deteriorate during the late 1940s to a shameful condition—"a monument," in the words of Geoffrey Perret, "to the theory of defense on the cheap." Divisions had been stripped of their tank battalions, and field artillery battalions had been cut back from three batteries of guns to two. The Eighth Army in

Japan, the one that would bear the brunt of the early fighting in Korea, consisted of just four divisions instead of six; it had been one of the most seriously affected by the crippling economies of the Truman administration.

Even more serious was the deplorable condition of the American soldier. Five years of peacetime occupation in Japan had made even the career soldiers—the "lifers"—soft and complacent. The draftees—garage mechanics, bank clerks, and farmers back in the States who had thought themselves lucky to serve out their two years in a country with a relaxed attitude toward sex and drink—were even worse off. In a week they were pulled out of their comfortable billets and thrown into the rice paddies of South Korea, fetid with the odor of human waste used as fertilizer. The North Korean troops who opposed the GIs had been training for this assault for years, and they believed they were fighting to unify their own land. Within a few weeks, the UN forces—mostly the Americans and their South Korean allies—had been nearly pushed off the peninsula at its southern tip, near Pusan. The U.S. commanding general Walton Walker issued a "stand-or-die" order that linked what was happening to the worst disasters of World War II: "There will be no Dunkirk, there will be no Bataan."

At home Truman's initial public support was fast disappearing. Letters and telegrams soon began running 20 to 1 against pursuing the war: "In heaven's name, what are you doing? The blood hasn't dried from World War 2. . . . We have nothing to do with Korea. These people are capable of settling their own affairs." MacArthur, for his part, was pleading with the Joint Chiefs for approval to approach Chiang Kai-shek on Taiwan for help. He said the big island was an unsinkable aircraft carrier from which the UN could hold off China and support the effort in Korea, and noted that Chiang had nearly a million men available to take on the North Koreans. In August, 1950, Truman sent Averell Harriman to Tokyo to warn MacArthur to "stay clear" of

Chiang; he feared that allowing the Nationalists to get involved would guarantee an incursion by the Chinese communists on the side of the North Koreans. Walker's men continued to hold on to the Pusan perimeter, but barely.

Then, in mid-September, MacArthur pulled off one of the most audacious maneuvers of his long career. He landed the First Marine Division 200 miles behind enemy lines at Inchon, 40 miles west of the South Korean capital of Seoul. The attack was risky because of high tides at Inchon but went off flawlessly. The Marines took Seoul and drove south as Walker's forces broke out to the north from the Pusan cordon, and the North Korean army barely escaped with their lives back across the thirty-eighth parallel. It was one of the greatest comebacks in American military history, and MacArthur was not shy about taking credit for it. Only three months after it began, the war now appeared to be in hand.

✦   ✦   ✦

Harry Truman's most popular biographer, David McCullough, argues that he deserves praise for having the courage to let MacArthur undertake the Inchon operation: "He took the chance, made the decision for which he was neither to ask nor receive anything like the credit he deserved." Clay Blair, who has written the most detailed account of the military operations of the Korean War, regards MacArthur's achievement at Inchon as admirable but overpraised: "Contrary to later descriptions, Inchon was neither a 'brilliant' nor an extraordinary concept"; it was "standard Army doctrine for peninsular warfare." Truman may or may not have sought the credit for approving the operation, as some charged, and it may or may not have been the stroke of original genius by MacArthur that it was supposed to be. But the president and perhaps the general knew that a personal meeting between them now would be good public relations. Truman in particular must have hoped (though his advisers sternly denied it) that some of the Republican MacArthur's glory would rub off on Democratic candidates running for office that November. A meeting was set for October 15 on Wake Island. MacArthur griped to his staff about taking time for a trip but must have been flattered that the president would literally go more than half way to meet him, and, presumably, to resolve their growing differences.

It was a peculiar encounter that ensued, far, far out in the Pacific Ocean, on the tiny island of Wake—the site of heroic but futile American resistance against the Japanese army in the early days of World War II. The precise purpose of the meeting was never clear. Dean Acheson thought it would look as if the president was going to pay homage to the general, and he declined to tag along, explaining later that "while General MacArthur had many of the attributes of a foreign sovereign . . . and was quite as difficult as any, it did not seem wise to recognize him as one." The navy's chief of staff, Admiral Arthur W. Radford, was more than willing to go, feeling that it was important that the two leaders should meet for the very first time: "Two men can sometimes learn more of each other's minds in two hours, face to face, than in years of correct correspondence."

The event was high on drama: the president's party flew 14,000 miles on three planes, an entourage that included Radford, Army Chief of Staff General Omar Bradley, and Dean Rusk, who was later the secretary of state under John F. Kennedy and Lyndon B. Johnson. There were also 35 correspondents and photographers. MacArthur had a much shorter flight, only 4,000 miles from Tokyo, and he came without his usual platoon of admiring reporters and photographers (security concerns, the White House staff said). Truman had promised MacArthur he did not want to keep him away for long from his important duties in Korea, apparently not realizing the implied message he was sending about his own dispensability from affairs in Washington. As Truman stepped from the plane into the blistering tropical heat of Wake Island, MacArthur gripped his right arm with his left hand, shook his hand vigorously and said warmly, "Mr. President." Truman flashed his famous grin and said, "I've been waiting a long time" for this meeting. "I hope it won't be so long next time, Mr. President," MacArthur replied. Unspoken at the time was the suspicion by some of Truman's supporters that MacArthur's eager double handclasp had been his way of finessing the salute that he should have given his commander-in-chief; and Truman later recalled his silent disapproval of MacArthur's familiar open-necked khaki shirt and "greasy ham and eggs cap," the gold-braided officer's cap with the wire grommet removed, as much a part of the general's signature as his sunglasses and corncob pipe.

But all was apparent amity as the two men climbed into the backseat of the best car on the island, a black two-door Chevrolet, and drove to a quonset hut a few miles away for a half hour of private talk. Truman later recalled in his *Memoirs* that MacArthur assured him that victory was at hand in Korea. MacArthur apologized for his recent statement to the Veterans of Foreign Wars on the need for help from Chiang, for which Washington had rebuked him. Think no more of it, Truman told the general—a gracious response, MacArthur later told Averell Harriman, that had impressed him very favorably.

After their brief private chat, the two leaders and their staffs engaged in a discussion about the progress of the war in Korea. Truman was an avid poker player, and he had recently allowed the stakes to be raised in the game with the Chinese: not content with merely driving the KPA (Korean People's Army) across the thirty-eighth parallel and then resting in place, the UN command had sent its forces rolling almost unopposed into North Korea. It was intent on pursuing the North Korean army to its destruction—or driving it across the Yalu River into Manchuria. MacArthur, the Joint Chiefs, the other important members of the UN command such as the British and the French, Dean Acheson, George

Marshall, and Harry Truman were all agreed on this course—a military juggernaut on the attack was almost as hard to hold back as an army in panicked retreat. Americans at home were eager to see the North Koreans punished, and there was no political support for a timid halt when the job was only half done; they had the opportunity to unify Korea and make it a bastion against communism and they should take it. But Truman and his advisers worried about Chinese intervention. He pressed MacArthur on this point and was assured by him that the chances of Chinese involvement were minimal. He'd have the American boys home for Christmas, MacArthur promised.

A second, inconsequential meeting on Wake was concluded after only 60 minutes. This meant that the total time that Truman and MacArthur spent together—the first and last time they would ever meet—after combined travel distances of 18,000 miles, 4 days, and considerable expense, was exactly 91 minutes. MacArthur declined Truman's invitation to lunch, saying he had work to do in Tokyo. They chatted informally about politics while a joint communiqué was drawn up for their signatures. MacArthur said the emperor of Japan had asked him to inquire whether Truman planned to run for reelection—which may or may not have been true—and Truman asked MacArthur what his own plans were in terms of political office. "None whatever," was the smiling response: "If you have a general running against you, his name will be Eisenhower, not MacArthur."

Each man seemed to leave the island with better impressions of the other than he had expected. MacArthur had always had the gift of turning on his vivid charm like a lamp, and his physical presence, even for a man of 70, was one of great vitality and grace. Truman was gratified that MacArthur "seemed genuinely pleased at this opportunity to talk with me, and I found him a most stimulating and interesting person." MacArthur, in his *Reminiscences*—written long after his dismissal—said he "had been warned about Mr. Truman's quick and violent temper and prejudices, but he radiated nothing but courtesy and good humor during our meeting. He has an engaging personality, a quick and witty tongue, and I liked him from the start."

Stopping in San Francisco on his way home, Truman gave a speech in which he said the general had written a "glorious new page" in military history with his Inchon operation, and that "it is fortunate for the world that we had the right man for this purpose—a man who is a very great soldier—General Douglas MacArthur."

✧   ✧   ✧

On November 24, 1950, barely six weeks after MacArthur said the boys would be home by Christmas, more than a quarter million Chinese soldiers attacked American forces well south of the Yalu. They had been pouring across the border for weeks, as military intelligence had accurately reported to MacArthur's headquarters. Several hundred thousand more were soon to follow. MacArthur had split his forces on opposite sides of the peninsula in their march northward, hoping to catch the enemy in a pincers movement. It was a risky maneuver that undoubtedly would have worked had the Chinese not intervened when forward units of UN forces approached the Yalu River. Within days, the UN forces were reeling backward, in even more danger than they had been the previous July—not simply of being pushed into the sea, as the British had been at Dunkirk, but of being overwhelmed and forced to surrender, as at Bataan, the worst defeat by a foreign power in American history until this time—and one over which General MacArthur had also presided.

On November 28, Harry Truman met with his National Security Council to determine how the U.S. forces should respond to the Chinese intervention. Bitter reproaches by Truman's team were directed at the absent MacArthur, who was said to be denying that he had ever promised to have the boys home by Christmas, but Truman said the council members should not cast doubt on their field commander. Marshall warned that the U.S. must avoid getting "sewed up" in Korea; it had to "get out with honor." Above all, the U. S. must not go to war with China; "to do so would be to fall into a carefully laid Russian trap. We should use all available political, economic and psychological action to limit the war."

But the administration was nearing a state of panic. On November 30, Truman spoke to the press about the situation in Korea. His prepared statement said simply but emphatically that UN forces and the U.S. "shall rapidly increase our military strength." Then, in response to questions, Truman implied that dropping the atomic bomb against China was under consideration. Moreover, he said, UN authorization would not be required to do so: "The military commander in the field will have charge of the use of the weapons, as he always has." There was no other way to read this except as a statement that General MacArthur could bomb China at his own discretion. The White House staff hurried desperately to amend Truman's remarks, saying "the use of any weapon is always implicit in the very possession of that weapon," but only the president could authorize the use of the atomic bomb and no such authorization had been given. But the world press reacted with alarm approaching hysteria, and the Soviets were reported to be taking steps with their army in Siberia that "deserved watching," according to the Central Intelligence Agency. The press conference was, McCullough notes, a "fiasco," and Truman's remarks were "devastatingly foolish."

MacArthur, in the meantime, had been warning that the UN forces were in danger again of being pushed out of Korea, as they had been the previous summer before his Inchon landing had saved them. He had gone well beyond merely complaining to his superiors—his *nominal* superiors, as he thought of them— at the Pentagon, voicing his concerns to sympathetic congressmen and reporters who he knew would make them public. At a meeting on December 3, the Joint Chiefs, Secretary of Defense

George Marshall, and Dean Acheson all groped for a course of action with regard to MacArthur's intransigence, his military missteps, and his refusal to keep his reservations about administration and UN policy to himself. Only Lieutenant General Matthew Ridgway, the tough paratrooper who had pioneered airborne operations in Europe during World War II and was now vice chief of staff of the army, had the courage to say that the situation with MacArthur was intolerable. Acheson would later write that finally "someone had expressed what everyone thought—that the Emperor had no clothes on"—but neither he nor anyone else followed up then on Ridgway's comment.

In January, 1951, MacArthur again told Washington that Chiang's Nationalist troops had to be unleashed, that China must be blockaded—and that he wanted to drop 30 to 50 atomic bombs on Manchuria and mainland cities in China. Outlandish though this sounds today, MacArthur was not entirely alone in thinking about using the ultimate weapon, for the Joint Chiefs agreed that "mass destruction of Chinese cities with nuclear weapons was the only way to affect the situation in Korea." Truman had not hesitated to drop atomic bombs on Japan in order to end World War II, but he did not agree with the Chiefs in this matter now. He wired MacArthur that "great prudence" was essential: the United States must do nothing that might involve "Japan or Western Europe in large-scale hostilities."

As it happened, the Chinese would be driven back, not by atomic weapons but by the man who had questioned MacArthur's ability to carry on the war, Matthew Ridgway. Two days before Christmas, the routed Eighth Army's ineffective commander, Walton Walker, was killed in a jeep accident, and Marshall sent Ridgway to replace him. MacArthur knew Ridgway's extraordinary competence and said to him, "The Eighth Army is yours, Matt. Do what you think best." As tough and colorful as George Patton when he chose to be, Ridgway wore live grenades strapped to his chest. A few days after his arrival in Korea, he stood in the road with his .45 raised to stop fleeing soldiers, and he frequently commandeered light planes to fly him over dangerous terrain for personal reconnaissance. He fired half of his high command within weeks, flooding Washington with ranking officers for whom it had no assignments, and promoted younger men who reflected his own aggressive image. By the end of January, 1951, he had arrested the Eighth Army's flight south, and by spring, he had the Chinese and the PKA fleeing northwards. Omar Bradley, a sober judge of character and of events, said that he and the other planners in Washington had to "look beyond" MacArthur to Matt Ridgway insofar as military operations were concerned—the old general was now only a "figurehead who had to be tolerated."

MacArthur was pleased with Ridgway's performance but outraged at the limitations placed on UN prosecution of the war. He complained in early March, 1951, to the American ambassador in Tokyo, William Sebald, that Washington was suffering from a "policy void." He wanted to launch massive attacks into Manchuria and to "sever" Korea from Manchuria with a huge field of radioactive waste along the Yalu River, 300 miles long and 10 miles wide. On March 7 he complained to American journalists that the "savage slaughter" of American soldiers was the result of the current battle of attrition.

On March 21 the Truman administration, equally concerned to end the battle of attrition, submitted a proposal for peace talks with the Chinese to the other 17 UN participants in the war. MacArthur saw the proposal the day before its intended release and sabotaged it by sending his own proposal to the Chinese two days later (March 23 Washington time), before Truman's could reach them. It was an insulting message, deriding the Chinese as incompetent to carry on an extended war and asserting that only the heretofore "tolerant effort" of the United States to keep the war from spreading beyond Korea had allowed the Chinese to escape disaster. The Chinese should be aware, MacArthur said, that "an expansion of our military operations" to its "coastal areas and interior bases would doom Red China to the risk of imminent military collapse." He stood "ready at any time" to meet with the Chinese to determine a settlement of the war.

"I couldn't send a message to the Chinese after that," Truman complained; "I was ready to kick him [MacArthur] into the North China Sea . . . I was never so put out in my life. . . . MacArthur thought he was the proconsul for the government of the United States and could do as he damned pleased." Somewhat more formally, in his *Memoirs,* Truman said MacArthur had acted "in open defiance of my orders. . . . This was a challenge to the President under the Constitution. It also flouted the policy of the United Nations. . . . By this act MacArthur left me no choice—I could no longer tolerate his insubordination." Still, the president hesitated to recall the general. Truman had virtually no public support—a Gallup Poll on March 14 showed his popularity level at only 26 percent (as low as Richard Nixon's after Watergate). A great many Americans agreed with Courtney Whitney, MacArthur's aide, that the general had done no more than make "a bold effort to stop one of the most disgraceful plots in American history, meaning the administration's plan to appease China."

MacArthur intensified the pressure. On April 5 House Minority Leader Joe Martin made public a personal letter that MacArthur sent him. Martin had made a speech accusing the administration of defeatism, and MacArthur agreed, adding that he believed the Nationalist Chinese should be loosed upon the communists. Employing the logic of what would become known as the domino theory (see Chapter 9), MacArthur said the real war against communism was here in Asia, because "if we lose the war to Communism in Asia the fall of Europe is inevitable." Win it, he said, "and Europe most probably would avoid war and yet preserve freedom." He concluded with the ringing phrase that would become (after "I shall return" to the Philippines) the most famous of his career: "There is no substitute for victory." This was the last straw for Truman: MacArthur had now allied himself with his most rabid right-wing enemies. Even so, he hesitated long enough to provoke a scornful *Washington Post* cartoon by the liberal Herblock that depicted "Captain Harry Truman" trembling in fear on his World War I army cot at the prospect of taking on the five-star general.

Finally, though, at one o'clock in the morning of April 11, 1951, Harry Truman's press secretary read this statement to a group of hastily assembled and sleepy reporters:

> With deep regret I have concluded that General of the Army Douglas MacArthur is unable to give his wholehearted support to the policies of the United States Government and of the United Nations in matters pertaining to his official duties. In view of the specific responsibilities imposed upon me by the Constitution of the United States and the added responsibility which has been entrusted to me by the United Nations, I have decided that I must make a change of command in the Far East. . . . It is fundamental . . . that military commanders must be governed by the policies and directives issued to them in the manner provided by our laws and Constitution. In times of crisis, this consideration is particularly compelling.

Delayed longer than it should have been, when the announcement finally came, it appeared to be the end result of a hurried and disorganized damage-control effort on the part of the White House. Elaborate plans to inform MacArthur in private before Truman's decision was announced to the public had been frustrated by a probable leak to the conservative *Chicago Tribune*. The dire possibility now was that the general might learn about his dismissal before he received it and one-up the president with a dramatic and publicly announced resignation. Furious when he learned about the leak and its possible effects, Truman said, "The son of a bitch isn't going to resign on me, *I want him fired.*"

MacArthur would finally get the news, not through proper channels but from an aide who heard it on the radio. He took the report with dignity and composure, though he said later that "No servant would have been dismissed with such a callous disregard of the ordinary decencies." A great many Americans, even those who thought MacArthur should go, agreed that the manner of his dismissal was a grievous blunder, typical of the Truman administration and the all-too-common man who was its leader. It was a bad beginning for what would turn out to be a public relations disaster for Harry Truman and a godsend for MacArthur, allowing the general to take the moral high ground, at least in his opinion. The next few weeks would never be forgotten by either man.

The public and political reactions to MacArthur's recall were more than enough to justify Truman's hesitation in issuing it. The Republicans demanded and got promises of a congressional investigation and invited MacArthur to address a joint session of Congress. Edging close to the lunatic fringe, Indiana Senator William E. Jenner charged that the country was "in the hands of a secret coterie," and said, on the Senate floor, "Our only choice is to impeach President Truman and find out who is the secret invisible government which has so cleverly led our country down the road to destruction." Other critics charged that Truman's action constituted "another Pearl Harbor"; it was "a great day for the Russian Communists"; MacArthur was fired "because he told the truth." On April 12 the *Chicago Tribune* called for impeachment and said, "The American nation has never been in a greater danger. It is led by a fool who is surrounded by knaves." Forty thousand telegrams were received in 48 hours by the Republicans in Congress, all but a few hundred along the lines of "IMPEACH THE IMBECILE."

One Republican leader said joyfully that "this is the biggest windfall that has ever come to the Republican Party." Richard Nixon, the young Republican senator from California, was one of Truman's most articulate critics. Later, as president himself, Nixon would be harried by his own war in Asia; and, after Watergate, he would learn how public opinion could force a president out of office. (See Chapter 9.) Now, having won election as a crusader against communism, he said MacArthur had been fired "simply because he had the good sense and patriotism to ask that the hands of our fighting men in Korea be untied." The "happiest group" in the country, he said, "will be the Communists and their stooges" because Truman "has given them what they have always wanted—MacArthur's scalp."

Thanks to Matt Ridgway, the war in Korea was going better by now, but at home the Truman administration was almost submerged by the tide of disapproval following his dismissal of MacArthur. The corresponding high-water mark for MacArthur was soon to be reached, as he gave his final address to the Congress on April 19, 1951. Americans in the following decades would experience many dramatic events through radio and especially live television—the murder of President Kennedy's assassin, Lee Harvey Oswald in 1963; the first landing on the moon in 1969; Richard Nixon's departure by helicopter from the White House after his resignation in 1974; the space shuttle explosions in 1986 and 2003; the World Trade Center destruction in 2001. MacArthur's farewell address was an event of comparable magnitude, improbable though that may seem today. His enemies dismissed MacArthur's speech as a garrulous gripe by an old man who had lost his job. But it was a moment of the highest personal and national drama, one that revealed as nothing else could have the powerful personality and character of the man—and also one that explained why it had taken so long for Truman to do what he had to do.

The scene and the speech and the aftermath have since become the stuff of American legend, told and retold in countless books and television documentaries. All of its elements had been carefully orchestrated during the eight days after the general's dismissal was announced. MacArthur's departure from Tokyo, his arrival in San Francisco, his landing at Washington's National Airport the night before, were emotional extravaganzas, involving thousands of people declaring their admiration and love for him. The American Caesar was home from Gaul for the first time in 14 years. He was the very "personification of the big man," as *Time* magazine put it, who had been done in at the hands of Harry Truman, who was "almost a professional little man."

"I address you with neither rancor nor bitterness in the fading twilight of life," MacArthur began his address to Congress, "with but one purpose in mind: to serve my country." For the next 34 minutes, he explained—pausing 30 times for resounding cheers and applause—what his goals had been and why those who had opposed him (i.e., Harry Truman and his administration, the liberal press at home and abroad, and, of course, the communists in Russia and China) were wrong. It had been clear to him that he had to destroy Chinese bases north of the Yalu, to use Chiang Kai-shek's 800,000 men on Taiwan, to blockade the coast of China. Failure to do these things "forbade victory," and the "very object" of war was victory. He repeated himself, wishing to emphasize his point: "there can be no substitute for victory."

Those who opposed him, who wanted to appease China, "were blind to history's clear lesson, for history teaches, with unmistakable emphasis, that appeasement begets new and bloodier war." Failure to win in Korea would lead to other failures in Asia and in Europe: "You cannot appease or otherwise surrender to Communism in Asia without simultaneously undermining our efforts to halt its advance in Europe." We had the means at hand to do what had to be done, but we were not using them: "Why, my soldiers asked of me, surrender military advantages to an enemy in the field?" He paused, allowing his voice to drop dramatically to a hushed near-whisper, and said, "I could not answer."

An estimated thirty million Americans were watching on television as MacArthur spoke; perhaps twice that number listened on the radio. Schoolchildren were ushered into auditoriums across the country for the speech; there was no squirming in seats, no adolescent horseplay as they listened to what would become perhaps the most famous conclusion to a speech, a career, and an era that they would ever know.

"When I joined the Army, even before the turn of the century, it was the fulfillment of all my boyish hopes and dreams," MacArthur said, his voice rich with emotion but controlled:

> The hopes and dreams have long since vanished. But I still remember the refrain of one of the most popular barracks ballads of that day which proclaimed most proudly that, 'Old soldiers never die. They just fade away.' And like the old soldier of the ballad, I now close my military career and just fade away—an old soldier who tried to do his duty as God gave him the light to see that duty.
>
> Goodbye.

✧   ✧   ✧

Americans are idealistic, even sentimental; they are also pragmatic and inclined to cynicism, especially about their leaders. On this day, and for many days to come, sentiment prevailed. In the words of a senator from Pennsylvania, the whole country went on "a great emotional binge." Personality, religion, and patriotism all came together for a congressman from Missouri, Dewey Short, who was transported into an ethereal realm by the general's speech: "We heard God speak here today, God in the flesh, the voice of God!" Some ordinary citizens agreed that the general had "the attributes of God; he is kind and merciful and firm and just. That is my idea of God." Former President Herbert Hoover, who was still bitter over losing his job in 1932 to Franklin D. Roosevelt, did not miss this chance to attack Truman and to praise MacArthur as "a reincarnation of St. Paul into a great General of the Army who came out of the East."

The emotional frenzy went on for days, peaking with a ticker-tape parade in New York. It took MacArthur's motorcade nearly seven hours to travel 19 miles through a crowd of several million people that "roared and shrilled itself to near-exhaustion," according to the *New York Times;* "the metropolis formed a gigantic cheering section rocketing its shouts of approval for the 71-year-old soldier-statesman."

Harry Truman's support declined even further as the wave of emotion for MacArthur reached its crest. Although Democratic and especially liberal leaders defended Truman, a Gallup Poll indicated that 69 percent of the population supported MacArthur, a number that meant many Democrats thought Truman was wrong. When Truman tossed out the first ball to open the 1951 baseball season, he was booed by the crowd; the last president to receive such treatment was Herbert Hoover in 1931.

✧   ✧   ✧

But more pragmatic, not to say cynical, responses to MacArthur's positions and his personality were emerging even in the midst of the emotional firestorm he had ignited. One observer of the speech had worried, he said later, that if it "had gone on much longer there might have been a march on the White House." The incendiary combination of personality, patriotism, and religion had toppled countless regimes in the past in other countries. But though MacArthur may have hoped to win the Republican nomination for president, he never suggested that he would countenance, much less lead, an insurrection. His three days of unpersuasive testimony later that spring before joint hearings of the Senate Foreign Relations and Armed Services committees, though dramatic, also tended to undercut his appeal.

To begin with, he did not admit that he was wrong in discounting the possible entry of the Chinese into the war, blaming faulty intelligence information. He did admit that he was "not familiar" with Pentagon and other studies concerning the danger of a wider war. Most important of all was the unified front put up by George Marshall and the Joint Chiefs. MacArthur had wrongly claimed in his speech before Congress and elsewhere that his views on how to deal with China were "fully shared" by the Chiefs—he had also omitted his advocacy of using nuclear weapons in his speech, but since this position was well known, he implied the Chiefs' approval of this policy as well. Now "Marshall, Bradley, and the Joint Chiefs . . . refuted absolutely MacArthur's claim that they agreed with his strategy," as David McCullough explains—though in fact they had been on record earlier as thinking seriously about allowing nuclear weapons to be used, they had pulled back from that position, leaving MacArthur out on a limb.

A counterreaction to the unrestrained adulation for MacArthur set in by late spring. He was never an unambiguous hero, even in his best days. Before Pearl Harbor, he had refused to implement Plan Orange, which called for stockpiling supplies on Bataan, because he thought planning for retreat was defeatist; the result was the immediate loss of the Philippines and his own flight to Australia. In Korea, his triumph at Inchon must be balanced against his perverse misreading of Chinese military capabilities.

MacArthur also paid the price for his aristocratic aloofness. He had a genuine concern for the lives of his men as their leader during World War II, and his strategy of leaving Japanese strongholds to "wither on the vine," isolating rather than attacking them when possible, had led to fewer casualties in his command than in any other during the war. Moreover, there was never any serious question that he had in abundance the absolute prerequisite for the soldier, personal courage. But his self-aggrandizing histrionics, his courting of a sycophantic press, his regal quarters far distant from the front lines, and his departure in 1942 from the doomed Corregidor for the safety of Australia (as ordered by Roosevelt) all served to distance him from the average GI, who called him "Dugout Doug." Even at the height of his public appeal, just before his address to the Congress, some sardonic minion in the lower reaches of the White House put his finger on the general's vulnerability to satire with a mock "Schedule for Welcoming General MacArthur" to Washington that included these "events":

12:30	Wades ashore from Snorkel submarine
12:40	Parade to the Capitol with General MacArthur riding an elephant
1:00	General MacArthur addresses members of Congress
1:30–1:49	Applause for General MacArthur
1:50	Burning of the Constitution
1:55	Lynching of Secretary Acheson
2:00	21-atomic bomb salute
2:30	300 nude D. A. R.s leap from Washington Monument

Harry Truman himself did not watch or listen to MacArthur's speech or the "carrying-on" and the "damn fool Congressmen crying like a bunch of women" that followed it. But he had read it beforehand—after sending his reluctant secretary of the army to get a copy from the general's staff—and he had an opinion: it was "a hundred percent bullshit."

✧   ✧   ✧

Perhaps to his own surprise, General MacArthur did indeed fade away, his place in the spotlight taken by another war hero, Dwight David Eisenhower. The two famous generals had served together in the Philippines before World War II, when Ike was a lieutenant colonel on MacArthur's staff—he studied drama under MacArthur, he later joked, while MacArthur mockingly recalled that Eisenhower was the "best secretary" he had ever had. Ike had the last laugh, winning the presidency in 1952 and ending the shooting war in Korea the following year. MacArthur became—unlikely though it might have seemed—a business-man, a figurehead executive with Sperry Rand Corporation. His corporate income, along with generous fees from his many speaking engagements, allowed him to live out his years in a luxury suite in the Waldorf-Astoria—the famous New York hotel whose other illustrious occupant was Herbert Hoover. Both men would die in 1964. MacArthur's widow, Jean, continued to live there until her death in 2000.

Harry Truman's standing with the public was never high while he was in office, except briefly in 1948 when he came from behind to defeat Dewey and at the outset of the war in Korea. But his true decline, his "downward spiral," as Alonzo Hamby in his biography of Truman terms it, began with Korea and did not end until long after he left office in 1952, certain that he would never win reelection. Happily, he lived another 22 years, until 1974, back home in Independence—long enough to see his reputation change dramatically for the better. When he left Washington, Harry Truman was widely seen as a time-punching ward-heeler who became an accidental president, who tolerated the most corrupt administration since Warren G. Harding's, and who dragged the country into a no-win war on the other side of the world. Now he is celebrated as the feisty common man who grew in his job, a paragon of common sense and democratic decency. His cashiering of General MacArthur, which may well have cost him another term in office, is seen as a profile in courage. Historians rank him now among the near-great presidents.

But the personalities of MacArthur, the aristocratic intellectual as warrior, versus Harry Truman, the common man, have to some degree obscured the meaning of their quarrel. Very few Americans seriously doubted that Truman had the right to fire MacArthur; the general himself never questioned that right. The real issues remain and may not be solvable. They turn around this question: how much of its irresistible force does the United States dare use in pursuit of its international policy? With nuclear weapons, America could easily have bombed Vietnam back to the Stone Age, as Air Force General Curtis LeMay suggested (perhaps in jest), just as it could have pursued the Iraqi army to Baghdad in 1991 and destroyed the regime of Saddam Hussein. Instead, America allowed the communists to prevail in Vietnam and left Saddam in place until returning to finish the job in 2003. The U.S. often hesitates and falters in its course and refrains from using its full power even when it does go to war, for the same inherently frustrating reasons that it chose not to attack the Chinese in Korea—because ultimately a great military empire that is also the world's greatest democracy has to accept the hard truth that there *are* substitutes for total victory. Korea was the first instance of that hard truth—a truth to which the thousands of American soldiers who are still stationed there today can attest. Iraq, as of this writing, may well prove to be another.

9

What in the Name of God Have We Come To?

Richard M. Nixon, Daniel Ellsberg, and the Pentagon Papers

"A feeling is widely and strongly held," wrote John T. McNaughton in May, 1967, "that 'the Establishment' is out of its mind. The feeling is that we are trying to impose some U.S. image on distant peoples we cannot understand (any more than we can the younger generation here at home), and that we are carrying the thing to absurd lengths. Related to this feeling is the increased polarization that is taking place in the United States with seeds of the worst split in our people in more than a century."

What is remarkable about this observation is not so much its pertinence—a great many people were making similar observations about the American involvement in Vietnam by 1967—but the nature of its author and his audience. Both were key members of the very "Establishment" that was supposedly "out of its mind." McNaughton was a former law professor at Harvard now serving as assistant secretary of defense, writing a memo to his boss, Secretary of Defense Robert McNamara, a principal architect of the plan that had brought the country to the sorry condition so effectively described by his assistant.

McNamara did not take offense at McNaughton's candid memo; he lived by facts, not emotions. As a young man during World War II, McNamara had developed management systems for the air force, winning a reputation as one of the organizational "whiz kids" who would go on to revolutionize American industry and technology after the war. In 1960 he left his remunerative post as president of Ford Motor Company to become President John F. Kennedy's secretary of defense. The dashing young president had promised that the United States would "pay any price, bear any burden," in the pursuit of American ideals, notably the defeat of world communism.

By 1967 Kennedy had been dead for nearly four years and the burden of the war in Vietnam had grown intolerably. A few weeks after receiving McNaughton's memo, on June 17, 1967, McNamara commissioned an "encyclopedic and objective" study of the Vietnam War. It would cover the three decades from the end of World War II, when the United States agreed to help the French keep their colonies in Indo-China, to the present. By the time the report was distributed, in November, 1968, the American political landscape had been transformed: McNamara had resigned his post at Defense, President Lyndon B. Johnson had declared that he would not stand for reelection and was limiting future American military commitments in Vietnam, and peace talks were under way in Paris. Richard M. Nixon was the Republican president-elect, having defeated Johnson's vice president, Hubert Humphrey, partly on the basis of his promise to end the war in Vietnam.

Nixon's staff of course received a copy of the report, an unwieldy collage of 47 volumes of materials, totaling 7,000 pages, assembled by a team of 36 anonymous researchers and midlevel bureaucrats. Its official title was *The History of U. S. Decision-Making Process on Vietnam Policy.*

For all its bulk, this was anything but a complete history, or even a history in the usual sense of the word. The primary sources were the files and records of McNamara and McNaughton and of William P. Bundy, former assistant secretary of state for Far Eastern affairs. But White House archives were unavailable, as were oral discussions of the National Security Council or intimate meetings of different presidents with their closest advisors, such as Secretary of State Dean Rusk. There was virtually no discussion of military or political responsibility for civilian casualties or for violating various rules of war set down by international conventions. Finally, the report lacked a coherent narrative and a clear unified summary of its various threads. It was really little more than what Hedrick Smith, a reporter for the *New York Times,* called an "extended internal critique . . . a middle-echelon and office view of the war." Small wonder, then, that its director, Leslie Gelb, cautioned his readers against expecting too much: "Writing history, especially where it blends into current events, especially where the current event is Vietnam, is a treacherous exercise."

The report was classified top secret, though President Nixon's secretary of defense would say in 1971 that 98 percent of it did not require any sort of classification, much less a top secret one. Its intended use remains obscure. Though valuable to future historians as archival material, it hardly fulfilled McNamara's original directive for a complete record of American involvement in Vietnam. Furthermore, its unwieldy bulk and its restricted distribution meant that it could have little influence on future policy. Only 15 copies were authorized, fewer in number than the squads of researchers who had labored on it "with ant-like diligence," in the words of Leslie Gelb. Three copies would be hand delivered to McNamara at the World Bank, which he was now heading; other copies would go to the state and defense departments, to President Lyndon B. Johnson, and to Nixon's staff. Given its bureaucratic origins, style, and bulk, Gelb's massive report was probably destined, like most such endeavors, to be filed and forgotten.

But there was one more copy to go out, to the Rand Corporation, a private "think tank," or research organization, in Santa Monica, California, with major clients in the defense industry and the federal government. (Rand is an acronym for Research and Development.) The Rand official charged with its safe delivery would be a former Marine officer and Ph.D. in economics, the only one of the thirty-odd authors of the report permitted to have read it all the way through. His name was Daniel Ellsberg. Little known outside the circle of "defense intellectuals" in the government, the military, and the major universities, Ellsberg would achieve worldwide notoriety as the man who leaked the top-secret documents he was charged to protect to the *New York Times.* The *Pentagon Papers,* as the report became known to millions, were transformed through Ellsberg from a four-foot shelf's worth of dry prose into a time bomb that would eventually blow President Richard M. Nixon out of the White House.

The odd pairing of Richard Nixon, the only president in nearly two hundred years of America's history as a nation to resign his office, and Daniel Ellsberg, former Cold War hawk who exposed national secrets and was tried for espionage, highlights perhaps the most important issue that confronts anybody in a position of influence. That is, what does one do when faced with a conflict between personal obligations—including the dictates of conscience—and duty to one's country? And, as a consequence of that question, what means are legitimate toward achieving an end that is regarded as essential? Both Nixon and Ellsberg wrestled with these questions—and with each other.

✧   ✧   ✧

What did Ellsberg see in the report he worked on that alarmed him so much he felt he had to leak it to the press? The answer to that key question lay several years in the future. For the moment, it is sufficient to note that most nonspecialists who looked at it were overwhelmed by the sheer magnitude and complexity of the material: there were over two and a half million words worth of position papers, cables, instructions, correspondence, memos, charts, tables, maps, summaries, and analysis and interpretation. It was the raw material of saga and legend, of stirring tragedy, of villainy and heroism—those elements that still draw us to Homer's *Iliad* and Tolstoi's *War and Peace*—but crucially lacking the vivid characterization and driving narrative of epic poetry and fiction that make events come to life for the average reader.

Daniel Ellsberg was, to be sure, hardly the average reader. But in his early years, he was an average American in that he did not doubt the essential malice and folly of communism, Soviet-style or Chinese. Nor did he question the necessity of fighting it as vigorously as President Kennedy had pledged to do in 1960. Born in 1931, Ellsberg distinguished himself while attending Cranbrook, an elite prep school near Detroit, as a talented pianist, good enough to have considered a career as a performer. He was a brilliant student—his college board scores in 1947 were a perfect 800 for the verbal portion and 783 for the math, the highest for that year in Michigan. He won a scholarship to Harvard, graduating in 1952 with honors and a prestigious Woodrow Wilson fellowship to study advanced economics in England at Cambridge University, where he continued to shine; one fellow student marveled that Ellsberg had "as good a mind as anybody . . . ever." His oral examination for his Master's exam at Harvard two years later was given the unusually high grade of "Excellent Plus."

Marked for academic stardom, Ellsberg then confounded his teachers and friends by joining the Marines in 1954, passing up a certain draft deferment to subject himself to the rigors of officer training school in the toughest branch of the military. His tour fell between wars—after Korea and before Vietnam—but he volunteered to extend it by a year in hope of seeing action during the crisis-ridden year of 1956, when the Russians crushed the Hungarian Revolution and the Egyptians took control over the Suez Canal from the British. He saw no action, but he was fascinated by the interplay of politics and force that clearly shapes the world. By the time he returned to the Harvard Ph.D. program in 1957, he was well on his way to becoming a defense intellectual.

Ellsberg's particular area of expertise was game theory, still an exotic concept today to the general public—as seen in audience reaction to *A Beautiful Mind,* the popular 2001 film biography of John Nash, who won a Nobel Prize in economics for his work in game theory. Ellsberg's imaginative early work in "risk analysis" as it related to military and diplomatic policy won him a temporary consultancy in 1958 with Rand in Santa Monica and a full-time appointment in 1960. In 1959, still a Ph.D. candidate at Harvard, Ellsberg was invited to give two lectures at the Lowell Institute on "The Art of Coercion: A Study of Threats in Economic Conflict and War," their focus being patterns in "the art of influencing the behavior of others by threats." In the first lecture, "The Theory and Practice of Blackmail," Ellsberg argued that aggression can be deterred by the judicious use of threats. President Dwight D. Eisenhower's secretary of state at the time was John Foster Dulles, who was responsible for adding the word "brinksmanship" to the lexicon of international diplomacy, and Ellsberg quoted Dulles with admiration: "The ability to get to the verge without getting into the war is the necessary art." Ellsberg also provocatively cited Hitler as an example of the effective use of blackmail in his second lecture, "The Political Uses of Madness." Because Hitler was so erratic and unpredictable, Ellsberg said, he conveyed the unsettling but useful impression of being irrational, even insane, throwing his opponents off balance.

The "madman theory" that Ellsberg described would later be adopted by Richard Nixon. Henry Kissinger, a Harvard professor who became Nixon's national security advisor and then his secretary of state, had not been one of Ellsberg's instructors, but the two were acquainted. Tom Wells, Ellsberg's biographer, says Ellsberg "believes Nixon probably got the madman idea from Kissinger, 'who, in turn, almost surely got it from me, as a phrase to describe a concept.'" Thomas Schelling, Ellsberg's mentor at Harvard, doubts any direct influence, noting that by the time Nixon became president, "the idea that a madman might be more credible than a fully rational person" was no longer a novel idea, and that "he as well as others besides Ellsberg had already made the same point." Nixon himself nowhere acknowledged in so many words a belief in the "madman" theory; but the evidence is strong that the idea of frightening your opponents into thinking you're crazy was one that intrigued him as much as it did Ellsberg, his possible source for it.

✧　　　✧　　　✧

Well into the mid-1960s, Nixon and Ellsberg also shared, along with almost everyone else, a belief in the domino theory. The theory provides a useful if misleading tool for connecting world events whose links may otherwise seem obscure. Vietnam, for example, was a French colony, part of what was French Indo-China, until World War II, and America had traditionally opposed colonialism of any kind. But the U.S. chose to help France financially in its fight after the war against Ho Chi Minh, the leader of the communist insurgency in Vietnam, rather than see it and the region "go communist," as China had under Mao Zedong. The French military effort came to an end in April, 1954, when their most vital garrison, at Dienbienphu, fell to the communists.

The defeat of the French in Vietnam, remote though it may have seemed to most Americans, was a matter of vital concern, President Eisenhower explained at a press conference: "You have a row of dominoes set up, you knock over the first one, and what will happen to the last one is the certainty that it will go over very quickly. So you could have a beginning of a disintegration that would have the most profound influences," including not just military positions but people and resources. Richard Nixon, as vice president, had said a few months earlier that if Indo-China, as it was then known, became communist, then Japan, which "trades and must trade with this area in order to exist, must inevitably be oriented toward the Communist regime." Other metaphors commonly used to signify the idea of inevitable spread and disintegration of the West as a result of communist victories anywhere in the world were related to physics ("chain reaction"), natural disaster ("leaky dikes" leading to flooding), agriculture (one "rotten apple" in a barrel spoiling them all), and even to women's fashions ("a silk stocking with a run in it"). Significantly, the communists themselves liked to view themselves as the inevitable "wave of the future," while Americans thought they were like vermin, rats "burrowing from within."

The domino theory was persuasive because its roots lay in the recent past, in the violent acquisition of other countries by the Axis powers of Germany, Japan, and Italy that culminated in World War II. Its adherents included not only conservative and middle-of-the-road Republicans such as Dulles and Eisenhower but the Democratic nominee for president in 1952 and 1956, Adlai Stevenson, who warned in 1953 that all of Asia "would slide behind the Iron Curtain" if Vietnam were "absorbed into the Moscow–Peking empire." By the time Daniel Ellsberg began his career, it was widely agreed that the United States simply had to win the struggle in Vietnam—not for any tangible benefit to America but because failure would encourage our opponents to believe that the West was weak and that communism was indeed the wave of the future.

Some in the intellectual community, however, especially at the elite universities such as Harvard, denied the validity of the domino theory and the justification or need for American involvement in Vietnam. Opposition on the campuses was subdued until the growing expansion of the war by the Johnson administration required the huge step-up in the draft in 1965. Now that the question of fighting and perhaps dying in Vietnam was no longer academic for many young men, campus protests, including "teach-ins" condemning the war, proliferated across the nation. Daniel Ellsberg, on leave from Rand in 1965 to work for McNaughton in the Pentagon, became an administration point man on the campuses. Still a true believer, and no less articulate than when he had won his "Excellent Plus" grade for his Master's thesis defense, Ellsberg entered many of the academic lions' dens, including the one at his alma mater, Harvard, and made the administration's case. Then he requested reassignment to Vietnam, in order to see for himself what was happening in the war. He would test the theory against the facts, not as a Marine but as a civilian observer and planner.

Ellsberg stayed in Vietnam from mid-1965 through mid-1967, a period of enormous expansion of American involvement in the war. In mid-July, 1965, when he left the U. S., there were only 75,000 American "advisers," as they were then called, in Vietnam. General William Westmoreland, commander of U.S. forces in Vietnam, wanted 175,000 more men by year's end; it was anticipated that 275,000 would be needed by mid-1966, just to let us "stop losing"; ultimately, several key administration figures speculated, "500,000 in five years" would be necessary—or still more. The Chinese might come in on the side of the North Vietnamese, as they had in Korea in 1951, to Douglas MacArthur's surprise. If they did, another 300,000 American men would have to go to Vietnam, and the ultimate total figure of one million seemed possible. President Johnson wondered if the Americans were not about to go "off the diving board."

Far from these Washington debates, deep in the heart of the conflict, Ellsberg at first retained his enthusiasm for the war. He was assigned at his request to Edward Lansdale's counterinsurgency team of operatives. Lansdale was a legendary master of operations against the communist guerillas in South Vietnam, the Vietcong, and was the developer of the "strategic hamlet" program that was supposed to protect the South Vietnamese farm and fishing villages. Ellsberg, the ex-Marine who had never seen combat, gloried in the danger of behind-the-lines exploits. Though most of these simply involved getting from one place to another, Tom Wells describes Ellsberg as brave to the point of recklessness. Wandering through enemy territory as though he was seeking death, he was remembered by Rand counterinsurgency associates as a would-be "shoot-them-dead superhawk," if the occasion should arise.

Gradually, however, Ellsberg began to conclude that the U.S. had indeed gone off the high board. He grew increasingly uneasy as the focus shifted from protecting the South Vietnamese, a defensive mission, to active "search and destroy" offensive missions designed for American forces to kill all the enemy soldiers they could find. The higher command's demands for what Ellsberg called "optimistically false reporting at every level, for describing 'progress' rather than problems or failure" became notorious, as did such phrases as "body counts," "winning hearts and minds," and "the light at the end of the tunnel." Ellsberg was also troubled by our failure to learn from experience: a South Vietnamese officer told him, in 1968, "You Americans feel you have been fighting this war for seven years. You have not. You have been fighting it for one year, seven times."

The more he saw, the more convinced Ellsberg became, he later claimed, that the American effort in Vietnam was doomed. If there was one single incident that "changed me," he said, a "summary of what I had learned" there, it was in 1967, when he saw what happened to a South Vietnamese village. No Americans were involved in this incident, but that did not matter to Ellsberg in terms of assigning guilt: the village was under the nominal protection of a South Vietnamese ranger unit, and therefore under American protection as well, in theory. But the South Vietnamese soldiers exploited the village, plundering its meager resources and even raping some of its women. The farmers were driven into the arms of the enemy for protection from their protectors, who then torched the village in retribution. Ellsberg walked through it immediately afterwards and never forgot "the smoke rising from the burned sleeping mats, the blackened hearths, [and an] old woman picking up a pink teacup from the ashes."

✧   ✧   ✧

Ill with hepatitis, depressed enough to start seeing a psychiatrist, Ellsberg moved into a Malibu beach cottage upon his return from Vietnam in July, 1967. He was still on the Rand payroll, but the intellectual super hawk ex-Marine now flirted with the fringes of the late 1960s counterculture. He let his hair grow long and became known as a "swinger," living with several different women while separated from his wife and children and frequenting a seedy enclave in the mountains known as Sandstone that was notorious for loose sex and drugs—with the emphasis on sex. His colleagues thought Ellsberg, then 36 years old and nowhere near the academic or scholarly eminence that had been anticipated for him, was going through an early midlife crisis. In fact, if Ellsberg's unsympathetic but assiduous biographer is to be believed, these tendencies had long been part of his personality, and Ellsberg's negative qualities stand out as much as his intelligence: extensive entries in Wells's index under these traits—from "boasting and arrogance" through "dishonesties, exaggerations, and untruths" and "grandiose sense of self" to "self-centeredness" and "strangeness"— add up to a man who throughout his life some might admire but few could like.

But for all his odd behavior, his difficult personality, and his increasingly outspoken misgivings about the war, Ellsberg was still sufficiently on board with Rand and the defense department to accept the call to work on the McNamara research project in September, 1967. Though he later claimed to have made valuable contributions as a member of Leslie Gelb's team, his performance, according to Gelb, was poor (he "just didn't do his work") and not only because of his recent adventures with the counterculture. Ellsberg had a reputation dating back to his graduate school days as a procrastinator who promised more than he delivered and as an egomaniac whose claims to influence—as for instance with his madman theory and its supposed direct effect on Nixon—often seemed overblown even to his admirers.

Because he was considered too indiscreet and emotionally high-strung to be entrusted with top-secret materials, Ellsberg was assigned to work on the supposedly less critical early years of the Kennedy administration's involvement with Vietnam. In October, 1967, Ellsberg participated in an antiwar demonstration in front of the Pentagon because, he said, he was "totally sympathetic" to the goal of ending the war. In one of his more memorable vignettes, Ellsberg claimed that after dropping in on the demonstration, he went back inside the Pentagon and "wandered into McNamara's office," where the secretary was standing by the window, looking down grimly on the noisy crowd. Ellsberg stood silently beside the secretary, hoping, he said later, that what McNamara saw was "making a strong impression on him."

✧   ✧   ✧

The English novelist Graham Greene described one of his characters as "a burnt-out case," which is what Daniel Ellsberg looked like in 1968 and 1969. Professionally, he was still an influential defense intellectual, entrusted to deliver sections of the report when they were completed to Rand as he shuttled between Washington and Santa Monica. Personally, though, he was wracked by problems with his family, his health, and his behavior, all of these compounded by his apparently sincere anguish over the continuing war in Vietnam.

Richard Nixon, by way of contrast, was now the king of the hill. If Daniel Ellsberg was the perfect image of a conflicted intellectual, Nixon was the model not merely of a shrewd and accomplished politician but of a resilient fighter who was incapable of accepting defeat. He had been a star from his earliest days in politics, first in 1947 as a California congressman, next as a senator, and finally as President Eisenhower's vice president for eight years, from 1953 to 1961. Then, in 1962, Nixon leaped to his political death—or so it was said—with a grotesquely bitter postelection farewell to the reporters who had covered his losing race for governor of California against Edmund "Pat" Brown, during which he said that the press "wouldn't have Dick Nixon to kick around any more." Eight years later, he had risen from the rubble of a destroyed career to win the presidency he had coveted for so many years.

Richard Nixon fascinated both his enemies and his admirers. His origins are reminiscent of Herbert Hoover's, as are some aspects of his temperament and his character. He was born in 1913 to a lower-middle-class Quaker family in southern California. Money was tight and Nixon had to work to put himself through college and law school. An outsider and a loner by nature, he was the antithesis of the stereotype of a gregarious, back-slapping politician. He was also an unlikely Quaker, scrappy and unforgiving of an offense. Smart, single-minded, and ambitious, he graduated third in his class at Duke Law School in 1937 and worked in President Franklin D. Roosevelt's Office of Price Administration before joining the navy during World War II. After four years in the Pacific as a supply officer, he won his initial political campaigns for the House of Representatives and the Senate by suggesting that his opponents were communist dupes. From the beginning of his political career, Nixon had operated on the assumption that communism was a mortal threat to the United States. Anyone who disagreed was also a threat to be eliminated, by fair means if possible, foul if necessary.

Nixon was by no means alone in his detestation of communism and his fear of subversion. It was the Democratic President Harry Truman who signed Executive Order 9835 in 1947, requiring the screening of all federal employees for security purposes. Scrutiny of those who worked for the government was intensified when 11 Communist Party leaders were convicted of sedition and sentenced to prison terms, and the country would soon learn that the practical effects of espionage included the leaking of atomic secrets to the Soviets. A newly invigorated House Committee on Un-American Activities (HUAC) proceeded to hunt out communists as a result of these and other disclosures, and the young congressman from California, Richard Nixon, became one of its junior members. The committee was widely disparaged as a collection of intellectual midgets—one of its members thought a hair tonic known as "Kreml" was part of a red plot, clearly suggesting as it did "Kremlin"—and Nixon feared that his appointment to it was a mixed blessing, a possible political kiss of death. But it was the making of him: as Herbert Parmet explains, Nixon was immeasurably brighter and cooler-headed that his peers on the committee; "more than any other single person, [he] . . . restrained HUAC from some of its excesses, enhanced its credibility, and helped to establish its validity as a legislative arm."

The most striking example of Nixon's intellectual independence, his strength of purpose, and his ruthless pragmatism was his handling of the strange case of Alger Hiss—a man whose name Nixon would later link directly to Daniel Ellsberg. Hiss was a Harvard Law graduate who apparently personified the ideal of public service during his years with the Roosevelt and Truman administrations. In 1948, he sued an admitted ex-Soviet agent named Whittaker Chambers for libel—Chambers had charged that Hiss was also a Soviet agent. Hiss was shown to be a liar during two different trials and sent to prison for perjury, not espionage, but his treason is now generally acknowledged.

Hiss himself never admitted committing espionage or lying, and his cause became something of a holy war during the 1940s for the American left. At the age of 80, in a 1984 interview with

Herbert Parmet, he retained the elegant, patrician bearing, along with the unmistakable impression of moral rectitude, that had persuaded almost everyone of his innocence in 1947. Hiss intimidated the HUAC panel members—all except Nixon, who saw Hiss for the liar he was and pursued him relentlessly. Hiss complained to Parmet about Nixon's "crudity and lack of sensitivity," while conceding that his own evident "snobbishness" might have excited the young congressman's antagonism—but this concession in itself seems to be Hiss's wily way of deflecting the original charges against him.

The significance of the Hiss case in the later context of Daniel Ellsberg and the leaking of the *Pentagon Papers* is this: Nixon achieved his goal of sending Hiss to jail by extra-legal means—that is, leaking confidential material to the press. He was frustrated both by Hiss's persuasive appearance of probity and by the inexplicable reluctance of the director of the FBI, J. Edgar Hoover, to use his power to convict Hiss. Nixon's solution to this two-fold problem was to sidestep it by manipulating the press, leaking damaging confidential committee material "all over the place." In fact, he said, "we won the Hiss case in the papers." For the rest of his life, Hiss's name and his own "were ever to be linked."

As Hiss's telling comment about snobbishness reveals, there were elements of class warfare in the battles over Richard Nixon that would surface again in the *Pentagon Papers* affair. To the right, he was the defender of the faith, the handsome young navy veteran who had pulled himself up from poverty through hard work and strong moral values. To the left, he was "tricky Dick," the deviously exploitive witch-hunter, an American incarnation of Shakespeare's villainous Richard III. As the 1960 vote count would indicate, very close to half the electorate wanted Nixon to be president even then, but his supporters could never match his detractors for their eloquence and their influence in intellectual and artistic circles. Nixon despised his enemies, the chattering classes, as they are called in Britain—the columnists and pundits and intellectuals who shape public opinion. He thought they were moved by pique and by upper-class disdain for hard-working, patriotic middle-class achievers such as himself and his supporters. For Nixon, Hiss was the enemy personified, just as Ellsberg would be later; he was "the darling of the elitists. The worst thing you could do to the intellectuals [was] to prove them wrong."

In fact, it took a certain amount of courage in the 1950s for those who thought of themselves as intellectuals to say Nixon had proved his case. One such man was Leslie Fiedler, the literary critic. Another, ironically, was Daniel Ellsberg, still a Harvard undergraduate, who had been "shocked" by the case and "really made a study of it. I read everything I could read. . . . And I became convinced that Hiss was guilty." But most of "the elitists," as Nixon called them, demonized him. Thanks to political cartoonists like Herblock of the *Washington Post,* Nixon became a serio-comic villain, famous for his ski-slope nose, distinctive widow's peak hairline, five o'clock shadow, and, as he grew older, heavy dark jowls. It helped his enemies that Nixon was physically maladroit, as suggested in photos and television shots of his awkwardly upthrust hands signaling double V for victory, his black suit jacket bunched around his neck, and his visible unease with small talk or affectionate gestures, even among family and friends. Intensely self-conscious, he worried about his image. White House Chief of Staff Bob Haldeman recalled how Nixon spoke revealingly of himself, typically in the third person, during one of their conversations: "All people think the P's doing an excellent job, but no one loves him, fears him, or hates him, and he needs to have all three."

More positively, by the time he became president, in 1969, it was clear that Nixon was much less doctrinaire and conservative than the right wing of his own Republican Party. This faction, led by Arizona Senator Barry Goldwater but outdistancing even him in its zealotry, particularly despised Henry Kissinger for his influence on Nixon and attacked both of them for policies of détente with the Soviet Union and, of course, for the famous "opening" to China. Indeed, it was this reputation for pragmatic problem solving, with the biggest problem being the termination of the war in Vietnam, that had propelled Nixon into the White House (along with voters' disillusionment with the Democrats and the George Wallace third-party insurgency). The war was widely viewed as a Frankenstein's monster unleashed by Lyndon Johnson, and Nixon had nothing to gain by perpetuating it. He intended to pursue a program called Vietnamization, which involved gradual withdrawal of remaining American forces but continued financial support for the U.S.-backed South as well as military training and equipment to enable it to fight on its own.

But he had been dealt a bad hand. The North Vietnamese, with nothing to gain by letting the Americans so easily off the hook, insisted on conditions that would lead to the destruction of the South. At the same time, they ratcheted up the pressure with incursions into the South through adjoining Cambodia and Laos. Nixon was in a bind. He could not simply condemn an ally to destruction by deserting it (although that would eventually be what happened, in 1975). He was prohibited by international law from pursuing the enemy into his privileged though flagrantly illegal sanctuaries in Cambodia. And the route of total war advocated by air force General Curtis LeMay, bombing North Vietnam "back to the Stone Age," was simply not possible, leading as it probably would to war with China and the Soviet Union.

Nixon took what he thought was the only step open to him. Two months into his first term, in March, 1969, he directed the Air Force to begin secretly bombing North Vietnamese positions in Cambodia. When Nixon ordered a joint United States-South Vietnamese ground incursion into Cambodia late in April, 1970, violent antiwar protests spread throughout the country. On May 4, on the campus of Ohio's Kent State University, panicky National Guard troops killed several protesting students, including some who were merely bystanders, fueling rage and calls for a huge antiwar rally in Washington later that month. Certain that the North Vietnamese were stalling the peace talks in Paris and would only respond to force, Nixon persisted, increasing the bombing of both North Vietnam and Cambodia in November, 1970. Protests continued at home throughout the winter and into the spring of 1971, with increasingly desperate and vituperative confrontations between those who supported the war and those who opposed it. The terrible national sundering that John McNaughton had envisioned two years earlier in his memo to McNamara was coming to pass—though McNaughton at least was spared from having to see it, having died in a plane crash the previous year.

✧   ✧   ✧

Saturday, September 12, 1971, was one of the happiest days of Richard Nixon's life. A doting father, for all of his natural reserve, he had witnessed the marriage of his daughter Tricia to Edward Cox in a beautiful ceremony at the White House. The picture of the beaming president and Mrs. Nixon appeared on the front page of the next morning's *New York Times*.

But it was Nixon's fate to have his best moments tarnished, then and for years to come, by the Vietnam War he had promised to end. On the same page as the wedding photo appeared another prominent story, with an understated but intriguing headline: "Vietnam Archive: Pentagon Study Traces 3 Decades of Growing U.S. Involvement." For the next three days, until publication was temporarily enjoined by an order of the U.S. Supreme Court, some of the key parts of the McNamara-commissioned report on which Daniel Ellsberg and many others had worked would become public knowledge. Months earlier, Ellsberg had secretly copied and transmitted large sections of the 47 volumes to Neil Sheehan, a *Times* correspondent he had first met in Vietnam. Now, finally, the revelations that Ellsberg was certain would make the American public demand an end to the war had seen the light of day.

Ellsberg's decision to leak the documents to the *Times* was not impetuous or precipitous. In October, 1969, more than a year and a half before the *Times* series began, he had tried unsuccessfully to get the prominent antiwar Democratic Senator J. William Fulbright to release the documents as part of hearings before the Senate Foreign Relations Committee, which Fulbright chaired. When that effort failed, he negotiated with members of the left-leaning Institute for Policy Studies (IPS) to turn at least some of the documents over to them, again to no avail, due to questions of control. The IPS, frustrated with Ellsberg's reluctance to part with the documents, turned to Neil Sheehan of the *Times*. Sheehan met with Ellsberg in late December, 1970, barely a month after Nixon had initiated the heavy bombing campaign in North Vietnam that had, as Wells says, "intensified Ellsberg's desire to get the *Pentagon Papers* out." By March, 1971, he had turned over the documents to Sheehan, and the *New York Times* management, after considerable internal debate, had agreed to publish them.

For all they left out, the *Pentagon Papers,* as the McNamara report would henceforth be known, were undoubtedly significant. They confirmed some of the worst suspicions of the war's critics. The single most spectacular revelation concerned the Gulf of Tonkin incident in the summer of 1964, when North Vietnamese gunboats had purportedly attacked American warships in international waters off the coast of North Vietnam and provoked Congress into giving Johnson the emergency war-making powers he wanted and needed to have in order to expand the American presence in Vietnam. Though there were two closely coinciding incidents that seemed to suggest an unprovoked attack at the time, the *Pentagon Papers* revealed that these were exaggerated, or "spun," by Johnson's White House, the Pentagon, and the CIA into something more serious than the facts warranted.

Less dramatic but even more powerfully disturbing were the larger elements of original intent and continuing confusion over U.S. goals in Vietnam, all of which suggested bad faith not only with the American people but with our allies, not to mention our antagonists. The United States had approved the Geneva Accords of 1954, agreeing to the temporary partition of Vietnam into North and South, pending elections in 1956 that would bring about unification. But Eisenhower's National Security Council viewed the agreement from the first as a "disaster" and urged a program of economic and military aid for the South Vietnamese and their new government. The later refrain of the U.S. that the North Vietnamese were solely to blame for the collapse of the Geneva Accords was clearly not just inaccurate but deliberately misleading.

The *Papers* also revealed how the Kennedy administration broadened the limited commitment it had inherited from Eisenhower, increasing forces from 1,600 in 1961 to 16,000 by November, 1963. But the real sea change came with Lyndon Johnson, and the *Papers* showed that Johnson was expanding plans for both covert warfare against North Vietnam and for overt war in the spring of 1964—just as he was tarring Barry Goldwater as a warmonger, a successful tactic that figured significantly in Johnson's overwhelming election to a full term as president that November.

The *Papers* also confounded the argument that American involvement in Vietnam was the result of a series of gradual, incremental steps, each based on overly optimistic advice by the intelligence community. We may have made a terrible mistake, but it's not our fault, was the plea of Kennedy apologists as eminent as the historian Arthur M. Schlesinger, Jr. The *Papers* confirmed Ellsberg's charge at an American Political Science Association meeting in Los Angeles in September, 1969, that American intelligence officers had been persistently and accurately pessimistic about prospects for victory in Vietnam, and that they had warned their superiors repeatedly, particularly in 1964 and 1965, that the bombing of North Vietnam would not result in a lessening of support for the Vietcong insurgents in the south.

Finally, the *Papers* revealed the frustration and growing despondency felt by those like McNamara who were charged with pressing the war effort. If McNamara now sees, as he has said repeatedly through his long years of remorseful reminiscing, that the effort should have been cut short as far back as 1961, then what did his failure to see the truth, to act on it, and to persuade others to do likewise cost this country, Vietnam, Cambodia, and Laos—indeed, the world—in the years after 1961?

All of this is presumably what made Ellsberg so confident that the *Papers* would bring the war to a sudden halt once the American public knew their contents. In fact, though, by June, 1971, attitudes for and against the war had solidified: the *Papers* were preaching to the choir of those convinced the war simply had to end. For most readers, the material was too dense. One member of Ellsberg's legal defense team said he "couldn't believe anybody would have read" the *Papers* as printed in the *Times* because they were hardly "fascinating"—indeed, if the Nixon administration had ignored them, they "would have sunk like a brick." Another member of the defense team thought the "nearly universal judgment" among those who knew beforehand (and there were many in the antiwar community who did know) about the forthcoming release of the *Papers* was that they would have little impact on public opinion.

These lawyers for Ellsberg and his Rand associate Anthony Russo, who had helped him copy and distribute the documents, naturally had a vested interest in minimizing the damage their clients had caused. But even in the White House, the initial reaction to the damage caused by the *Papers* was cautious. Public opinion polls indicated more disapproval of the prior Democratic administrations for their complicity in the war and of the motives and circumstances surrounding the release of the *Papers* than of Nixon. Soon, however, panic and fury swept through the White

House. One key aide, Charles Colson, later claimed that Henry Kissinger was particularly outraged—and worried about his own skin because Nixon had noted that "virtually every one of these people" involved with Ellsberg was either a student or an associate of Kissinger's. Kissinger also said Ellsberg was more than annoying, he was dangerous because he was smart and he had access to information—both Kissinger and Nixon were undoubtedly concerned that Ellsberg might have the capability of revealing details of the continuing illegal bombing of Cambodia, which was to go on for another two years. Bob Haldeman thought Ellsberg was suffering from "psychiatric imbalance"—that he had "flipped" from drug use. Kissinger even suggested to Nixon, according to Colson, that they ought to "kill" Ellsberg, presumably in the sense of destroying his reputation and his credibility. It did not take long for Nixon to agree that Ellsberg was a dangerous menace who had to be destroyed.

✧   ✧   ✧

Daniel Ellsberg survived and even prospered because Richard Nixon shared his obsession with recent history. In Nixon's case, this took the form of a late-blooming need to have a complete record of everything he said as president. In February, 1971, he directed that a voice-activated taping system be installed in his office in the White House, with similar devices later put in place in other offices in the Executive Office Building, Camp David, and the cabinet room. He intended the tapes to be his personal property, not the government's; they were to assist him in writing his memoirs and other books. Nobody else knew about the system, aside from Nixon's chief of staff Bob Haldeman and one of his aides. Perhaps this explains why Nixon felt free to be so unguarded in his remarks—that, and the natural tendency to forget about something that is invisible and quiet.

The tapes only came to light because of the strange series of events known as "Watergate," which is the name of an apartment and office complex in Washington, D.C. In 1970 Nixon authorized surveillance of antiwar groups, including those Ellsberg had associated with, by the FBI, which was legal. But similar snooping by the CIA (which was supposed to be limited to overseas functions), as well as the Internal Revenue Service and the National Security Agency, was clearly illegal. The most flagrant violation of the law came after the *Pentagon Papers* were released, when Nixon staffers organized a surreptitious group called "the plumbers" because they were to find and fix such leaks as Ellsberg's. In June, 1972, during the height of the presidential reelection campaign, the plumbers were caught trying to plant wiretaps in the Watergate office of the Democratic National Committee. The incident was virtually ignored at the time and Nixon easily won reelection, but a series of inquiries by *Washington Post* reporters and others resulted in Senate hearings, beginning in January, 1973, into the break-in and related illegal activities by Nixon's operatives. The tapes, and what Nixon said on them, eventually forced him to resign his office on August 9, 1974. Pardoned by his successor as president, Gerald Ford, for whatever crimes he might have committed while in office, Nixon was never convicted of committing or authorizing any illegal activities. He was not even charged.

Daniel Ellsberg would not be so lucky. Insofar as his limited but critical role in the Watergate saga is concerned, the key dates are as follows: June 28, 1971, when he was first indicated for the theft of secret documents and espionage; September 3, 1971, when the office of his psychiatrist, Dr. Lewis Fielding, was broken into by the plumbers; June 23, 1972, when Nixon's remarks concerning one of the plumbers provided the "smoking gun" of culpability to the Watergate investigators; and May 11, 1973, when the case against Ellsberg was dismissed in Los Angeles because of revelations about the White House involvement in the Fielding break-in. A brief look at some of the White House tapes and other materials from this busy two-year period confirms Nixon's obsessive interest in Ellsberg. It also shows why most impartial observers today think Nixon broke the law in his efforts to discredit Ellsberg. Among the most striking revelations on the tapes are those that link Nixon's past success with sending Alger Hiss to jail two decades earlier and his current plans for Ellsberg.

Indeed, the frequency and intensity of these references suggest that Hiss and Ellsberg had coalesced for Nixon. Consider the following sequence of his remarks on June 30 and July 1, 1971:

"Don't worry about his [Ellsberg's] trial. Just get everything out and try him in the press. . . . Leak it out. We want to destroy him in the press. Press. Is that clear?"

". . . we won the Hiss case in the papers. We did. I had to leak stuff all over the place. Because the Justice Department would not prosecute it."

"I have a project that want [sic] somebody to take it just like I took the Hiss case. . . . You probably don't know what I meant when I said yesterday that we won the Hiss case in the papers. We did. I had to leak stuff all over the place. . . . It was won in the papers. . . . Now do you see what we need? . . . I really need a son of a bitch . . . who will work his butt off and do it dishonorably."

"I leaked everything. I mean, everything that I could. I leaked out the testimony. I had Hiss convicted before he ever got to the grand jury. . . . Now, how do you fight this [Ellsberg case]? You can't fight this with gentlemanly gloves."

"I played it [the Hiss case] in the press like a mask [sic: master?]. I leaked out the papers. I leaked everything . . . I had Hiss convicted before he ever got to the grand jury."

". . . convict the son of a bitch in the press. That's the way it's done."

Still referring to Ellsberg as well as Hiss, but in the larger context of his enemies generally, Nixon says he is not "worried about all the legal niceties. Those sons of bitches are killing me. I mean, thank God I leaked to the press [during the Hiss controversy]." "We're up against an enemy, a conspiracy. They're using any means. We are going to use any means. Is that clear? Did they get the Brookings Institute raided last night? No. Get it done.

I want it done. I want the Brookings Institute's safe cleaned out and have it cleaned out in a way that it makes somebody else [responsible?]."

The Brookings Institution was a liberal think tank not directly related to the Ellsberg case, except insofar as these remarks suggest the president's willingness to order a break-and-enter operation. On July 7, John Ehrlichman, the president's chief assistant after Haldeman, assigned two of his aides to work with the plumbers. The lead plumber was a sometime-CIA operative and writer of spy thrillers named E. Howard Hunt, who was supposedly "tough as nails." Assisting him was the colorfully macho G. Gordon Liddy, who once held a flame to his hand in a restaurant to impress his date. Hunt was given carte blanche, Ehrlichman said, to find out everything he could about Ellsberg and to do what he could to impugn his credibility. The plumbers got most of their information legally from the FBI, whose agents questioned virtually everyone who had ever known Ellsberg, combed through his financial records and his credit card histories, and obtained authorization for wiretaps. The plumbers did not even try to tap Ellsberg's phones without authorization, which upset Nixon—"What the hell did they do then? What did we pay them [for]?"—until he recalled that the FBI could handle the "bugging once it got into the case."

Legal (or mostly legal) means having availed them nothing, the plumbers commenced to burglarize the office of Ellsberg's psychiatrist. Following a time-honored way of discrediting an opponent, they hoped to show that Ellsberg, the famous explainer of the madman theory, was himself crazy. The effort failed, through comic ineptitude on the part of the plumbers. The next day, September 8, 1971, Ehrlichman told Nixon, "We had one little operation. It's been aborted out in Los Angeles which, I think, is better that you don't know about. But we've got some dirty tricks underway. . . . We've planted a bunch of stuff with columnists . . . about Ellsberg's lawyer."

Bizarre in the extreme, some of the material on the tapes dismayed even Nixon's presumed allies when it was released in response to a Supreme Court order on July 24, 1974. One respected moderate, Pennsylvania Senator Hugh Scott, said that what he heard was "shabby, disgusting, and immoral." It is disconcerting even decades later to read the tapes in the widely available versions edited by Stanley Kutler, and more so to listen to them in the portions now released. As far as Ellsberg is concerned, Nixon's defenders still argue that nothing in the passages cited here (or many others not cited) shows the president's prior or current knowledge of the break-in. But as was the case with what Nixon showed concerning Alger Hiss, it takes a prodigious leap of faith to insist that the president was innocent and not much more than common sense to agree that he knew about as much as his many aides did—dozens of men who, from Haldeman and Ehrlichman on down to Hunt and Liddy, did time in prison for their crimes.

Daniel Ellsberg, for his part, ultimately escaped a prison term because of Nixon's bumbling plumbers. His trial did not get underway until well after Nixon handily won reelection in November, 1972; it was in the administration's interest, Nixon said, to drag out the affair as long as possible, to keep the *Pentagon Papers* case before the public as a "running sore" for the Democrats. The crucial conversation, the so-called smoking gun, when Nixon agreed to the scheme to tell the CIA to instruct the FBI to stop its investigation of Watergate, occurred on June 23, 1972: Nixon says the FBI director has to have his investigators "lay off" Hunt, the chief plumber: "Hunt . . . knows too damn much and he was involved, we have to know that. And that it gets out . . . it's going to make Hunt look bad . . . and he's just gotta tell 'em, 'lay off.'" A year later, on June 25, 1973, Nixon's young lawyer John Dean testified that when Hunt threatened to expose the "seamy things he had done for the White House," Nixon authorized hush money for Hunt to keep him quiet. The

Watergate investigators, as well as reluctant Republican Nixon defenders, agreed that the references to Hunt's activities on the tapes confirmed Dean's statement and proved White House involvement in the Fielding break-in, among other events.

On April 25, 1973, Attorney General Richard Kleindienst and President Nixon spoke about denying any knowledge on the president's part of the Fielding break-in. (By this time Nixon knew that the investigators were aware of his taping system, though Kleindienst did not and therefore did not know that their conversation was on the record.) Nixon says the plumbers were "crazy fools" who had gone off on their own with no authorization, other than perhaps that of John Dean—which clearly sounds implausible to Kleindienst, who worries that taking this tack will suggest "another Goddamn cover-up." Kleindienst suggests the government's prosecuting attorney in the Ellsberg case should tell the presiding judge that the new knowledge of the circumstances of the Fielding break-in has so tainted the case that it should be dismissed.

And dismissed it was, on May 11, to Nixon's evident distress—"the sonofabitching thief [Ellsberg] is made a national hero and is going to get off on a mistrial. And the *New York Times* gets a Pulitzer Prize for stealing documents. . . . They're trying to get at us with thieves. What in the name of God have we come to?"

✧   ✧   ✧

Daniel Ellsberg, who has prospered as a speaker and writer about his role with the *Pentagon Papers,* presumes to answer Nixon's anguished query in his 2002 memoir, *Secrets.* It was not what we had "come to" but what the country had "come back from" that mattered, Ellsberg says—back from being an "elected monarchy" under Nixon to a "democratic republic." He regards his decision to release the *Pentagon Papers* not as betrayal but as an act of higher loyalty: "Like so many, I put personal loyalty to the president . . . above all else. Above loyalty to the Constitution.

Above obligation to truth, to fellow Americans, and to other human lives." It was the courageous commitment of the antiwar protesters, he says, that "awakened" him to these "higher loyalties." He feels that he ended the Vietnam War earlier than it would have otherwise ended by provoking Nixon into sending the plumbers after him. He also argues that, more than the better-known Watergate burglary, the ensuing cover-up of the Fielding break-in was what brought the president down. Most of those who have reviewed Ellsberg's book agree that he makes a reasonably strong—though unpleasantly self-congratulatory—case for this interpretation.

Most historians judge Richard Nixon harshly, which is probably appropriate. He came from a Protestant tradition that holds individuals responsible for their own fates. His story is replete with elements of treachery, achievement, and soaring ambition. Was he, finally, more than merely a man who dishonored his office—was he a great man out of classical or Shakespearean tragedy, brought low by an excess of his own chief virtue, his stubborn belief in the rightness of his cause and of any means he used to promote it? Nixon appears to have thought so, and he had ample time to make the case.

For Nixon lived another 20 years after leaving office, writing many books about world affairs and about his eventful life. When he died, in 1994, four former presidents attending his funeral lauded his many achievements, including the famous "opening to China" in 1972. Hardly the cartoon villain of the liberals, he was also a more thoughtful man than the tapes usually reflect, as well as a self-conscious creator of his own legend who wrote with insight about the manufacture of images: "Legends are often an artful intertwining of fact and myth," he said, "designed to beguile, to impress, to inspire, or sometimes simply to attract attention." Nixon conceived of the presidency in terms of an institution characterized, in Jeffrey Kimball's words, by "an aura of meaning, mystery, drama, and mystical power." Leadership required, above all, strength of purpose and commitment; those who served the president, Nixon said, should share his "sense of history and of drama." Significantly, Nixon insisted that he and his entourage all had to be bold, to be "hardnosed," to "take risks." To temporize and compromise with opponents led to failure.

Clearly Nixon thought of himself as a great leader in the sense of doing resolute, uncompromising battle with his enemies. But he was apparently little troubled by ethical and moral qualms, and, successful as his *Realpolitik* approach had been in his early career—for example, with Alger Hiss—it ultimately led to disaster when he tried even more extreme means to discredit Ellsberg. In the end, he was not, in fact, a tragic figure. Truly tragic figures must have a moment of illumination, like the blinded Oedipus or the tortured Lear, when they can see how their own flaws of character led to their fate. Nixon, for all his intelligence, experience, and undoubted achievements, never acknowledged the irony or the poetic justice of having brought himself down by the same means he used to raise himself up.

10

Men Are Not the Enemy

*Betty Friedan, Phyllis Schlafly,
and the Equal Rights
Amendment*

Between 1972 and 1982 America's preeminent advocate of women's rights, Betty Friedan, warred with her most influential opponent, Phyllis Schlafly, over words. The conflict originated in a proposed amendment to the Constitution declaring that "equality of rights under the law shall not be denied or abridged by the United States or by any State on account of sex." Claiming that these seemingly innocent words literally threatened American civilization, Phyllis Schlafly ultimately prevailed.

During that ten-year span, Schlafly and Friedan repeatedly confronted one another in public debates. Her upswept hair immaculately coiffed, Schlafly always appeared cool, poised, and elegant even at her most combative. "The small number of women in Congress," she declared on a typical occasion, "proves only that most women do not want to do the things that must be done to win elections. . . . To most women, it isn't worth the price. They like to devote their energy to other things—like having

babies." Such remarks led Friedan to brand Schlafly "a traitor to
your sex." "I'd like to burn you at the stake," Friedan exploded at
one debate. Schlafly responded with a trademark comeback about
how Friedan's outburst revealed the true character of "the intem-
perate, agitating proponents" of the Equal Rights Amendment
(ERA). "Phyllis Schlafly is such a fake," Friedan once complained.
"Anyone who smiles that much has got to be a fraud. It's enough
to make you want to punch her in the mouth."

Friedan's temper, her gravel-voiced rapid-fire blasts of words,
her agitating hands and fly-away hair, all stamped her as the sort
of feminist that traditionalists loved to ridicule. Yet Friedan's outward manner also concealed a woman who had longed since adolescence for a successful marriage and family. "There I was,"
Friedan later wrote, "paired up with Phyllis Schlafly again and
again. It always just killed me that she would go on and on about
feminism and the ERA being against the family. . . . She was no
sweet little housewife rushing home to make dinner." Schlafly
polarized people, inspiring extreme reactions of admiration or
rage. So did Friedan. And in very different ways, the lives of both
Betty Friedan and Phyllis Schlafly embodied what women mean
today when they say they want to have it all.

✧   ✧   ✧

The story of the Equal Rights Amendment goes back to the
1920s, the decade during which Betty Friedan and Phyllis
Schlafly were born. By the beginning of that decade, 70 years of
effort had finally culminated in adoption of the Nineteenth
Amendment to the Constitution, granting women the vote in all
federal and state elections. Together with earlier suffrage measures
at the state level, this literally doubled the number of Americans
who were eligible to cast ballots. It was the greatest democratic
transformation in America of the twentieth century.

Then women's rights advocates had a falling out. Liberal
"social feminists" pushed for special protective legislation that
would distinctly benefit working women and children—by

exempting women from compulsory overtime or night work, for example, or limiting the amount of weight a woman must lift on the job, or banning child labor. Meanwhile, other women devoted themselves to securing total equality under the law. The new Woman's Party single-mindedly advocated the Equal Rights Amendment as a means of wiping out every trace of discrimination. ERA supporters tended to be well off, politically conservative, and sympathetic to business. Outraging social reformers, the Woman's Party fought protective laws as merely one more form of discrimination. There was a certain logic to this; notions about women as the weaker sex helped inspire protective legislation. At a time when few unions would accept women or bargain for them, though, a more important rationale was that only legislation could protect women from workplace exploitation. Professional women who demanded the ERA found themselves denounced for selfishly cutting poor working women adrift.

The Equal Rights Amendment was introduced in Congress in 1923. It read: "Men and women shall have equal rights throughout the United States and every place subject to its jurisdiction." Most women's groups opposed the ERA for fear of wiping out protective laws. One of the amendment's most prominent opponents was Eleanor Roosevelt. Like other strong believers in protective legislation, she regarded the ERA as essentially conservative.

Had women united behind the ERA, it might have seen adoption during the 1920s. Instead, for decades, the amendment languished in Congress. In 1940, the Republican Party finally endorsed it. Despite the continuing opposition of Eleanor Roosevelt, the Democrats followed suit in 1944. Between 1946 and 1953, the Senate voted in favor of various versions of the ERA on three separate occasions. The House consistently balked; while numerous employer groups endorsed the amendment, organized labor (including virtually all union women) and northern Democratic liberals successfully fought to defeat it.

For 40 years—roughly, from the time the women's suffrage amendment was adopted in 1920 until the early 1960s—the feminist movement in America sank from public view. While efforts to secure equality did persist, endorsement of the ERA in national Party platforms was one of the few visible reminders that the issue remained alive at all. Reflecting prevailing attitudes, most historians wrote their textbooks as if, with the Nineteenth Amendment, women had already achieved equality.

✦   ✦   ✦

Just five years after she was born Phyllis Stewart in 1924, the Depression began to shape Phyllis Schlafly's St. Louis suburban childhood in unexpected ways. Her father lost his engineering job with Westinghouse. In order to put food on the table, her mother, previously a homemaker, had to find work. Schlafly later recalled that as a teenager, "I felt a compulsion to get myself trained to support myself, which my mother had done." Schlafly admired her father, and her father despised FDR. While most Catholics, along with the country at large, went Democratic during the 1930s, the solidly Catholic Stewart family remained loyally Republican. Schlafly attended a strict Catholic girls' high school. She had plenty of friends and abundant good looks—blue eyes, golden hair, perfect posture, a flawless complexion. Classmates remembered her as extremely competitive and unusually self-confident. She graduated with the nuns' assurance that she could accomplish anything.

Schlafly then attended Washington University in St. Louis. To pay her way through and save money for graduate school, for 2 years she worked 48 hours a week at a night job at the St. Louis Ordnance Plant. This was no stint waiting tables in the company cafeteria. Blazing away with rifles and machine guns, on each eight-hour shift she test-fired up to five thousand .30- and -.50-caliber rounds. Weaponry would become a lifelong interest. She graduated from Washington University Phi Beta Kappa.

Schlafly proceeded to Radcliffe on a fellowship. In June, 1945, only 20 years old and having studied just 7 months, she completed a Master's degree in political science. "Political science," she wrote at the time, "really turned out to be my chosen field." One of her Radcliffe-Harvard professors called her "brilliant."

Like Phyllis Schlafly, Betty Friedan was a product of the American heartland. She was born Bettye Naomi Goldstein in 1921 in Peoria, Illinois. Friedan's father, a Russian immigrant, owned a successful jewelry store. Her mother, the daughter of Hungarian immigrants, had been a journalist when she married; but her husband put a stop to her career, insisting that she focus on their growing family. The parents fought continuously, and from an early age, Friedan displayed a volatile temper of her own. Her mother ridiculed Friedan's looks. Like Eleanor Roosevelt, Bettye Goldstein, a lumpish five-foot-two asthmatic, grew up feeling homely. As a teenager she dated misfits from the family's Reform temple. (Ultimately she became an agnostic. She also dropped the letter *e* from her first name.)

Friedan wrote for the Peoria High School newspaper, gave speeches, and read so voraciously that her family consulted a therapist to find out what was wrong with her. Declaring that "it doesn't look nice for a girl to be so bookish," her father slapped a quota on the number of books she could check out of the library. Unlike Schlafly's parents, Friedan's family enthusiastically backed the New Deal. What Friedan later called her personal "passion against injustice," though, apparently originated in her painful encounters with anti-Semitism, notably rejection for membership in a high school sorority on account of her religion. Spirited and rebellious, Friedan was determined not to relive her mother's life. "I want to fall in love and be loved and be needed by someone," she wrote. "I want to have children." But "I don't want to marry a man and keep house for him and be the mother of his children and nothing else." "I want success and fame."

In 1938 Friedan left Peoria for Smith College in Northampton, Massachusetts, the private women's school that her frustrated mother had wanted to attend. Like Schlafly, Friedan proved an exceptional student—"extremely intelligent," in the words of one of her professors. "For the first time," Friedan said afterward, "I wasn't a freak for having brains." Her confidence rose and her friendships multiplied.

Influenced by left-wing faculty mentors and by her study of Marx and Freud, Friedan became politically engaged and radicalized—a passionate supporter of the downtrodden, free speech, labor unions, and women's rights (including the unionization of Smith's maids). Like Herbert Hoover at Stanford, she butted heads with the student power structure. She relished the adversarial role. Writing nonstop for student publications, like FDR at Harvard she became the editor of the campus newspaper. A dedicated anti-fascist and not a pacifist, she nevertheless opposed U.S. intervention in World War II right up until Pearl Harbor. She graduated in 1942 with a degree in psychology and a Phi Beta Kappa key to match Phyllis Schlafly's. An abridgement of her senior honors thesis was published in a scholarly journal. A college administrator remarked that "Betty has the most outstanding record of any student ever matriculated at Smith."

Like Schlafly at Radcliffe, Friedan headed straight to graduate school, at Berkeley, to study psychology. Her political commitments traveled with her, and she made numerous radical acquaintances. "I was that girl with all A's," Friedan later remarked, "and I wanted boys worse than anything." David Bohm, a young doctoral candidate in physics, met the need. A student of J. Robert Oppenheimer, Bohm was working on the top-secret atomic bomb project. Bohm also belonged to the Communist Party. Government agents monitored him as a potential security risk.*

Deciding not to pursue a Ph.D., after a year at Berkeley Friedan turned down a graduate fellowship. In and out of psy-

---

*On Friedan's own possible bid to join the Communist Party, see Horowitz (in Bibliography), pp. 93–94.

chological therapy, for a time she considered training as a psychiatrist. Instead, from 1943 to 1952, she became a leftist labor journalist, first for Federated Press in New York and then for the Communist-led United Electrical, Radio and Machine Workers of America (UE). Immersed in labor-oriented feminism, she espoused the rights of minority women, supported government-sponsored day care for the children of working women, and backed universal health care. Along with Communist Party members, she lived in a world populated by socialists, pacifists, and civil rights supporters. Later on, she would drastically play down these onetime connections.

Meanwhile, Phyllis Schlafly was establishing herself in a far different world. In 1945 she went to work for the conservative think tank known today as the American Enterprise Institute. The following year, in St. Louis, she took part in a successful campaign to oust a New Deal Democrat from the House of Representatives.

✧   ✧   ✧

By 1945 the country was entering what has been called the neo-Victorian era. From the last half of the 1940s through the first half of the 1960s, Americans devoted a tremendous amount of idealism and energy to the nuclear family. The marriage rate shot up from its Depression-era low. Family size rebounded too. By the 1950s, when the "baby boom" peaked, the average married couple was having three or more children. At the very same time, though, millions of women were also entering the work force. Between 1940 and 1960, the proportion of women holding paying jobs rose from 25 percent to 35 percent. In 1940, 15 percent of wives worked outside the home; by 1960, nearly thirty-one percent did. When such women had young children, they often played down their earnings as "pin money," even when the family really needed a second income. This dismissal represented a hangover from the Victorian world, when respectable middle-class urban wives were not supposed to take paying jobs and any husband who could not support his family was regarded as a failure.

During the 1950s, other Victorian-era attitudes persisted. Banks routinely denied women loans under their own name. Women who became pregnant were commonly compelled to quit their jobs—without unemployment benefits. Sexist language was as common as cigarette smoking, along with sexist jokes featuring stewardesses, nurses, or women drivers. History and other scholarly disciplines came close to ignoring women altogether, merging their story invisibly into men's.

In October, 1949, at the relatively advanced age (for the time) of 24, Phyllis Stewart married Fred Schlafly, an intense, Harvard-educated lawyer 15 years her senior. "Fred rescued me from the life of a working girl," she remarked. Marriage "is the best deal for women the world has yet devised." Like Phyllis, Fred was politically conservative and a devout Catholic. In her battle against the ERA, she would count on him for constitutional arguments and legal support. Phyllis firmly believed that the traditional division of labor between married partners— male = career, female = children—anchored civilization. As she put it: "God intended the husband to be the head of the family." "Fred is the boss . . . and that's the way it is."

Over time the Schlaflys had six bright children. Phyllis taught all of them to read before they started school. "I think of my marriage and family as my No. 1 career," she said. Yet in 1952, with a year-and-a-half-old toddler scampering around the house, she ran for Congress. Referred to by the press as the "housewife," "the powder-puff candidate" or "the good-looking blond," she won the St. Louis-area Republican primary. It was a blue-collar district, though, and she lost the general election to a perennially popular incumbent Democrat.

By 1952 Betty Friedan had already been married for five years and had a second child on the way. Her husband, Carl, who had dropped out of Massachusetts State, was an advertising and public relations man. During the first half of the 1950s, the growing family lived in suburban Queens. Betty invested most of the income she earned as a journalist in child care. When she published a pamphlet titled *UE Fights for Women Workers* (1952), in which she advocated an end to job discrimination, she was writing from first-hand experience—while working at the Federated Press, a man with more seniority had bumped her out of her position. Then, the very year that *UE Fights for Women Workers* appeared, she was bumped out again—from UE—because she was pregnant.

Though the 1950s was the golden age of suburban living, Betty Friedan's experience failed to match her expectations. Between 1948 and 1956, she bore three children who, like Phyllis Schlafly's, would make any parent proud. (The Friedans' oldest child, Daniel, a mathematician, would go on to win a MacArthur "genius" award.) Betty redecorated a big house that the family bought along the Hudson River. She struggled with stunning effectiveness to enrich the local school curriculum. She volunteered for the PTA. But she was not a typical housewife. She hired household help, and while the "soccer moms" of the era were carpooling their children around, Friedan got hers to school by taxi. Meantime, Betty and Carl fought. Sometimes they fought physically. Having dreamed for years of a romantic marriage that would combine children with career, Friedan felt trapped.

During the late 1940s and early 1950s, the American left, including its feminist cohort, was hammered by the FBI, congressional investigations, purges of left-leaning federal employees, and Senator Joe McCarthy. In 1949 the House Committee on Un-American Activities summoned David Bohm, Friedan's Berkeley boyfriend, for a grilling by (among others) Congressman Richard Nixon. Bohm was innocent of espionage, but by the time his ordeal had ended, his academic career in the U.S. was in ruins, and he left the country permanently.

Alarmed by McCarthyism, vulnerable to getting tarred like Bohm, and disenchanted with labor unions, Betty Friedan underwent a transformation. She began to write for mainstream, middle-class, mass-circulation magazines directed at suburban readers. By 1956, she had become a successful freelance journalist. Finally dropping the name Goldstein under which she had written for labor publications, she took her husband's last name as her professional one. As Betty Friedan, she broadly critiqued the conformism of middle-class suburban existence. Her articles appeared in *Reader's Digest, Harper's Magazine, Cosmopolitan, Parents' Magazine,* and *Good Housekeeping.* The articles paid well, and though their marriage was unraveling, the Friedans thrived financially. Repeatedly, though, editors toned down Friedan's more controversial passages. Much of what she wanted to say never made it into print.

In 1957, she began work on a book that no one would tone down. It appeared six years later as *The Feminine Mystique.*

✧   ✧   ✧

With their fifteenth reunion coming up in 1957, Betty Friedan's Smith College classmates had completed a questionnaire about the nature of their lives. Ninety-seven percent had married, 89 percent were housewives, and the women were generally quite happy about their family lives. As a group, though, they wished one thing had gone differently: that they had done more with their education. Friedan scrutinized the questionnaires with a focus on this one qualification. She identified a set of beliefs and constraints that had led middle-class women to eschew careers in favor of fulfillment strictly as mothers and homemakers. She termed this set of beliefs "the feminine mystique." Women, she argued, suffered from "the problem that has no name"— isolation, boredom, lack of fulfillment, a sense of incompleteness. Unaware that others shared these feelings, women tended to turn the blame inward. Friedan's cast of villains for consigning women to the home included educators, psychologists, sociologists, and advertisers, all of whom undermined women's self-identity and ability to grow. Her solution was not to abandon marriage or motherhood but to combine them with meaningful paying jobs and careers that would provide higher satisfaction than redecorating the kitchen or waxing the floors. Friedan dismissed the suburban home as a "comfortable concentration camp." The women she admired were married, achieving, salary-earning professionals with children—the sort of woman Friedan herself had always aspired to be. In fact, *The Feminine Mystique* is heavily autobiographical; in it, "all the pieces of my own life came together for the first time." Friedan was 42 when the book appeared in 1963.

Though well researched, *The Feminine Mystique,* like many influential tracts for the times, did distort reality. Friedan's Smith classmates, for example, were happier than she portrayed them. The first draft of the book read a lot more optimistically, too, than did the final, published version. Women transcended the feminine mystique in the draft; in the book, the mystique submerged them. The book focused narrowly on problems of the white suburban college-educated middle class at the expense of the working-class and minority women whom Friedan had written about as a labor journalist. Portraying herself as a victim of the feminine mystique, Friedan utterly played down her past. (This was not widely understood until the publication of Daniel Horowitz's *Betty Friedan and the Making of "The Feminine Mystique"* in 1998.) Friedan intended *The Feminine Mystique* to shock but to reveal only so much about its author.

It did shock. The publisher, W.W. Norton, initially printed 3,000 copies; ultimately the book sold, and continues to sell, millions. Friedan found herself deluged with fan mail. Today historians view *The Feminine Mystique* as another *Uncle Tom's Cabin,* the launching point of the modern women's movement. Like Harriet Beecher Stowe, Betty Friedan did not actually create a social movement; rather, she galvanized it at a crucial time by providing it with a central text.

Nineteen sixty-three would have been an important year for American women even had *The Feminine Mystique* never seen print. Prior to her death in 1962, Eleanor Roosevelt had been appointed by John F. Kennedy to chair the Presidential Commission on the Status of Women. The commission looked into women's relationship to the family, the economy, and the law. Strongly committed to the principle of "equality of rights under the law," the commission nonetheless concluded that an equal rights *amendment* was unnecessary; the Constitution already provided sufficient potential protection for women. This by no means meant, though, that women had actually achieved equality—the commission pointed out that they had not. Receiving its troubling report in 1963, President Kennedy quickly responded. He issued an order requiring gender-blind hiring in the civil service and signed the Equal Pay Act, which outlawed the time-honored practice of paying women less than men for performing identical jobs. All this occurred just as Betty Friedan was becoming a household name.

Though *The Feminine Mystique* reshaped the attitude of millions of people and altered millions of lives, Carl Friedan was upset. To friends he had grumbled that instead of fixing dinner, when he returned home after work "that bitch" was working on her book. The Friedans' relationship headed further downhill after the book made her a celebrity and he became Mr. Betty Friedan. After 22 years of marriage, in 1969 they went through a brutal divorce. Carl then married a beautiful blonde whom he called "no intellectual, thank God." Carl's new wife, in fact, bore a certain resemblance to Phyllis Schlafly.

✦   ✦   ✦

In 1964, just a year behind Betty Friedan, Phyllis Schlafly brought out her own first book. A self-published paperback running just 121 pages and costing 75 cents, *A Choice Not an Echo* hardly looked like a volume that would help change the course of American politics. But, as a campaign tract for presidential candidate Barry Goldwater, it did.

By this time Schlafly had become a Republican activist of note—an Eisenhower delegate to the 1956 national convention, a Nixon alternate delegate in 1960, president of the Illinois Federation of Republican Women, prominent in the Daughters of the American Revolution, and a frequent public speaker. With children born in 1955, 1957, 1958, and 1961, she nursed babies continually at home or on the road. In 1963, the year Betty Friedan became famous, Phyllis Schlafly testified before the Senate Foreign Relations Committee against the Nuclear Testban Treaty. She once called the atomic bomb "a marvelous gift that was given to our country by a wise God."

By 1964, weary of the me-too Republicanism that so dismayed Herbert Hoover, Schlafly was calling for the GOP to turn to the right. Over the coming decades she would publish a lot of books, but none packed the wallop of *A Choice Not an Echo*. Like Betty Friedan, Schlafly intended her book to shock. Though only a fraction of it was devoted to the ultraconservative Goldwater, he represented the title's "choice" against party moderates' "echo" of the New Deal. Since 1936, Schlafly claimed, northeastern internationalist "kingmakers" had picked every Republican presidential candidate in order to promote an "America last, pro-Communist foreign policy." (It came as news to a lot of people that Dwight Eisenhower or Richard Nixon—whom she had previously supported—were playing into Soviet hands.) Schlafly dismissed foreign aid as "foreign giveaways," lashed out at the United Nations, and called for mainstream Republicans to reclaim their party from the northeastern elite. Though she made no effort to advertise her book, it sold 3 million copies through hand-to-hand distribution. Without *A Choice Not an Echo*, Goldwater probably would not have won the California primary that year nor the GOP nomination for president. The book's title became his campaign slogan.

Despite her new prominence, or perhaps because of it, Schlafly's own political career failed to advance. In 1967 she made an unsuccessful bid for the presidency of the National Federation of Republican Women. "Many men in the party frankly want to keep the women doing the menial work," she observed, "while the selection of candidates and the policy decisions are taken care of by the men in the smoke-filled rooms." "The more we let . . . [women's] voices be heard in politics, the better off we are. . . . Women should have a role beyond stuffing envelopes and stirring coffee." Women, Schlafly claimed, not the party's male establishment, should pick their own leadership. The outgoing Federation president—unmarried, childless, and epitomizing the party's contemporary blue-hair image—declared that Schlafly should tend to her family instead of aspiring to leadership. "The party needs the image of youth," Schlafly shot back. "It's high time the Federation had a president who is the mother of young children."

That year, to spread her views, Schlafly began publishing a monthly newsletter, *The Phyllis Schlafly Report.* In 1970 she mounted her second run at an Illinois congressional seat. Together with more traditional Republican fare about cutting taxes and slashing the federal bureaucracy, her campaign played up the new social issues—race riots, crime, and illegitimacy. Her Democratic opponent, a former Marine, denounced her as a brainy snob who ought to "stay home with her husband and six kids." Schlafly lost the election, 53 percent to 47 percent. Although she afterward remained active in the GOP, her defeats, together with Goldwater's in 1964, marginalized her in party affairs. Increasingly, Schlafly would operate as a free agent. "I've run for office," she enjoyed repeating, "and I wouldn't wish it on Betty Friedan." In 1975 Schlafly, who loves American eagles, incorporated a competitor to the National Federation of Republican Women, the Eagle Forum. That year, at age 51 and already overextended, she started law school. Meanwhile, she went on publishing books that denounced, among other things, agreements by Republican administrations to limit nuclear arms.

✧   ✧   ✧

As Phyllis Schlafly focused her attention on weaponry, in 1970, Congresswoman Martha Griffiths of Michigan managed to pry the Equal Rights Amendment out of the House Judiciary Committee, where it had remained bottled up for close to half a century. In the wake of blacks' successful struggle for civil rights, gaining immediate and full gender equality had become an urgent matter of principle. Thus the amendment, once widely seen as conservative, had also become, like civil rights, a liberal cause (despite lingering concerns for protective laws). In August, 1970, the ERA passed the House 350–15. No action occurred in the Senate. The House passed it again the following year by a similar margin. In March, 1972, the Senate finally concurred, 84–8. Given these margins, the ERA's final incorporation into the Constitution as the Twenty-seventh Amendment seemed not just assured but easy. Polls showed that the public overwhelmingly favored women's equality. President Nixon endorsed the ERA, as did the League of Women Voters, Common Cause, the YWCA, and the American Association of University Women.

But the Constitution was written in a way that makes amending it exceptionally difficult. After two-thirds of each house of Congress ratifies, three-quarters of the states—38— must join them. Most states also require two-thirds legislative majorities. In order to kill an amendment, just 13 states—they can be the smallest ones, containing a tiny fraction of the nation's population—need do nothing more than refuse to vote at all. If states vote no, so much the worse. Amending the Constitution requires an extraordinary degree of consensus on both the national and local levels.

Beginning early in the twentieth century, Congress began setting a seven-year deadline for ratification by the states. The deadline for the ERA was accordingly set at March 22, 1979. Under the 7-year rule, successful amendments, which reflected national and local consensus, had required an average of just 16 months to clear the ratification gauntlet. The Twenty-sixth Amendment (1971), allowing 18-year-olds to vote, took only 4 months.

As things turned out, though, the ERA was terribly timed. Initiated by *The Feminine Mystique,* the modern women's movement had taken shape during the civil rights, antipoverty, and antiwar protests of the 1960s and early 1970s. By 1972 this ferment was waning. During the rest of the decade, the country passed through an era of political hesitation. Unless enough states ratified immediately, the amendment would succumb to drift and reaction.

At first, as predicted, states fell over one another to ratify. Hawaii led the way. Neither liberals nor even conservatives considered the amendment especially radical. It had been around, after all, since 1923. The GOP had endorsed it for over thirty years. Even legendary right-wing Senator Strom Thurmond of South Carolina supported it. The only people in opposition seemed to be scattered, ineffectual fringe elements. The John Birch Society, for example, labeled the ERA—along with a lot of other ideas—a communist plot. Concerns arose here and there about how the ERA might subject women to the draft, or compel housewives to go to work, or legitimate homosexuality. Some opponents dismissed the ERA as unnecessary, claiming that the Fourteenth and Nineteenth Amendments already granted women equality. No matter: by the end of 1972, 22 states, liberal and conservative, had ratified.

Easily the most famous living American feminist and at the height of her influence, Betty Friedan backed the ERA with gusto. As Mary Frances Berry has put it, "*The Feminine Mystique* had set the stage for the ERA movement." In 1966 Friedan cofounded the National Organization for Women (NOW) and became its first president. Almost immediately, she pressed NOW to back the ERA. As for protective legislation, she later wrote, "I thought those laws were probably important and necessary laws in the era of Eleanor Roosevelt." By the 1960s, though, they "were standing in women's way and denying them equal opportunity. It stood to reason that if the so-called protective laws were needed for women, they should also be applied to men." NOW actually challenged them in court. The ERA, Friedan wrote, "would give us the basis for all kinds of creative interpretation of the law that now didn't exist on behalf of women." "There would be enormous implications if it got ratified and established a woman's right to equality under the law. A whole new territory would present itself—pensions, insurance, property laws—for which there were no legal precedents."

The ERA promised to became one of the high points of Betty Friedan's career. Instead it became the absolute culmination of Phyllis Schlafly's. After decades of political setbacks, she finally met her moment. Had Schlafly not sunk it, the ERA would almost certainly have completed its smooth voyage to ratification. Yet at first, Schlafly—focused as she was on the Cold War and nuclear weapons—responded more or less indifferently to the amendment. "I don't even know which side I'm on," she remarked as late as December, 1971. "I'm not interested in ERA. How about a debate on national defense?" "I figured ERA was something between innocuous and mildly helpful," she later recalled.

Schlafly's attitude quickly changed. She was a liberated woman who despised feminism because she was also a traditionalist. She had raised two girls and four boys to excel within the time-honored expectations of their different genders. "Women's liberation," she declared, "teaches women to put their own goals above every other and therefore is destructive of the family." She concluded that the ERA, among other things, would encourage divorce, abortion, and homosexuality. She also claimed that the amendment was predicated on a false assumption, calling "the claim that American women are downtrodden and unfairly treated . . . the fraud of the century."

By the time the ERA had finally begun to arouse Schlafly's attention, it had already sailed through the House of Representatives. Inevitably the Senate would pass it too. That meant the only way of sinking it would be to line up 13 states in opposition. And that, in turn, would require selling the state legislatures on Schlafly's own version of "what [the] ERA really meant." "I knew from the start," she later remarked, "that I had found enough seriously wrong with ERA to stop it, or at least stall it, for an awfully long time, if only I could get the message out." From the start, she portrayed herself as an underdog. She *was* an underdog.

By late 1972 Schlafly was supplanting the snipers who had fired haphazard shots at the ERA with an army of sharpshooters recruited from scratch. That October she founded STOP ERA, organizing it hierarchically and assuming full control over strategy. Like Napoleon, she was the unrivalled commander and single indispensable figure. Her three home phones rang off the hook. Reaching deep into the public relations armory, she mounted a frontal attack on TV, in debates, via direct mail, and through her vividly written *Phyllis Schlafly Report*. After 1975 the *Eagle Forum Newsletter* blasted away as well. "My writing is designed," she declared, "to make people act." Her troops idolized her. They picketed the pro-ERA Gerald Ford Republican White House; then they picketed the pro-ERA Jimmy Carter Democratic White House. They pounded the pavement and rang doorbells. Schlafly demonstrated a remarkable flair for theater. Delegations of housewives wearing frilly dresses would present state legislators with homebaked apple pies or loaves of homemade bread and jam—while threatening them with defeat at the polls if they voted for the ERA.

Schlafly claimed that in reality the ERA was the "Men's Liberation Amendment." It would, she insisted, deprive women of old entitlements, load them up with new responsibilities, obliterate protective legislation, and give women nothing worth having in return. The amendment would nullify laws requiring men to support their wives; no more alimony. Ripping away obligatory male support would particularly jeopardize middle-aged homemakers who had never planned to take paid employment and lacked the needed skills. These very women became the backbone of STOP ERA.

Schlafly seized on the opportunities presented by the ERA's opaque meanings and uncertain outcomes. While Friedan delighted in such unpredictability, Schlafly abhorred it. Under the ERA, she claimed, women's colleges would have to admit men or face charges of discrimination. Homosexuals would become legally eligible to marry. Gays could even adopt children. And women would wind up with a constitutional right to abortion. (In 1973 the Supreme Court declared in *Roe v. Wade* that they already had this right.)

Ironically, congressional proponents of the ERA had inadvertently prepared the way for Schlafly's onslaught by wording the amendment so as to mandate complete, literal gender equality without exception. They refused, for example, to exempt women from the draft and combat duty. This meant, Schlafly insisted, that women *would* be liable to the draft and combat duty. Agreeing with her, the House Judiciary Committee stated that "not only would women, including mothers, be subject to the draft, but the military would be compelled to place them in combat units alongside of men." Schlafly the moralist argued that forcing men and women into foxholes together might turn the foxholes into bedrooms. Schlafly the national defense zealot argued that because women were physically less powerful than men, the ERA would undermine the country's battle readiness. Betty Friedan, on the other hand, felt ambivalent about the draft: "While I was not for anybody being drafted, if there were again such a thing as a just and necessary war like World War II, then there would be no reason for women not to be drafted." The public remained suspicious; 80 percent told pollsters that they did not want the U.S. sending women into combat.

If the ERA's first section, giving women equality, troubled Schlafly as a traditionalist, the second, which conferred enforcement power on Congress "by appropriate legislation," shocked her as a conservative—even though similar language appears elsewhere in the Constitution. Schlafly's warnings echoed Herbert Hoover and anticipated Ronald Reagan. "If you like ERA," she declared, "you'd better like congressmen and Washington bureaucrats and federal judges relieving you of what little power you have left over your own life." True enough, final interpretation of the amendment would rest with federal judges—ultimately, with the Supreme Court. Friedan and other feminists could dismiss the myriad objections Schlafly raised as scare tactics or red herrings, but individuals in black robes, most of them men, would ultimately decide which were fantasies and which weren't. Schlafly also reminded state legislators that in voting for the ERA, they would vote to deprive themselves of some of the last powers the states had not yet ceded to Washington, namely, highly sensitive powers affecting the family—marriage, divorce, adoption, child custody. Why would they want to do that?

Schlafly branded feminists "a bunch of anti-family radicals and lesbians and elitists." In truth, wide, largely moderate elements of the middle class comprised the foundation of the feminist movement. But a limited, highly visible fringe element did furnish her with plenty of ammunition. "The family, as that term is presently understood," declared one prominent feminist leftist, "must go." "A woman without a man is like a fish without a bicycle," went a memorable slogan of the era. The smug contempt in which a minority of feminists held the conventional family, along with their desire for a radical change in gender roles, left moderate ERA supporters feeling uneasy. Despite some appearances to the contrary, during the 1970s, the public remained committed to traditional family patterns. To the broad mass of Americans, assuring formal equal opportunity for women was one thing; radically overhauling the nature of the family or the meaning of gender represented quite another. This ambivalence became a political gold mine for Phyllis Schlafly. By attacking the ERA as pro-divorce, pro-lesbianism, and pro-abortion, Schlafly painted feminism *as a whole* as a conspiracy against the family. The doubts she sowed nurtured a desire to stay with the known by deepening fear about the amendment's many unknowns. (Would the ERA really lead to unisex toilets? Who but the courts could say for sure?)

Before Schlafly had completely deployed her army of housewives in 1973, 30 states had already ratified the ERA. Schlafly's counterattack cut the amendment's momentum to a slog, taking ERA proponents by surprise. Until now, it had all been so easy. The proponents had not bothered to stockpile resources for an extended fight, and following Senate ratification they wasted more than a year getting organized for a state-by-state campaign. By the time they realized they were in trouble, Schlafly had already seized the high ground, with forces that remained far better coordinated. Over the next eight years, STOP ERA's campaign failed in only five states. Five others which had already ratified voted to rescind on grounds that they had acted hastily or in error. Congress, though, did not recognize the right of any state to rescind.

Illinois, Betty Friedan's birthplace and Phyllis Schlafly's home state, became the goriest battleground of all. Though it had been the first state to ratify the woman suffrage amendment half a century before, Illinois became the one northern industrial state to hold out against the ERA. Calculating that if they could win in Illinois, other states would topple, the ratification leaders designated Illinois their Gettysburg and, like Robert E. Lee, poured in troops. Jimmy Carter lobbied more heavily in Illinois than anywhere else. Friedan and Schlafly faced off in debates. Again and again the Illinois legislature turned down the ERA.

By the end of 1977, 35 states had ratified—3 short of the necessary total. With progress stalling, Congress voted to extend the ratification deadline to June 30, 1982. Ninety thousand people had gathered in a single Washington demonstration to support extension. Schlafly dismissed them as "a combination of federal employees and radicals and lesbians." Never before had a deadline been lengthened. With scholars debating whether extension was even constitutional, Schlafly denounced the rule change as "wrong, crooked, and unfair"—then went right on fighting. In August, 1980, the Illinois legislature rejected the ERA for the eighth time. United in their loathing of Schlafly, labeling her a "witch," ERA backers accused her of gross hypocrisy for failing to practice what she preached. "If I had a daughter," remarked one feminist leader, "I'd want her to be a housewife just like Phyllis Schlafly." ERA supporters accused Schlafly of fronting for a mammoth right-wing conspiracy. They tried without success to trace her funding to the John Birch Society and the Ku Klux Klan.

✧   ✧   ✧

For all their differences over the ERA, the battle made clear that in certain important respects, Betty Friedan and Phyllis Schlafly actually agreed with one another. In order to get women into the economic and social mainstream alongside men, Friedan believed, feminism must become a movement with genuine mass appeal. Radical, male-bashing feminism threatened this, and Friedan found herself in an ongoing struggle with the separatists. Almost echoing Schlafly, she preached against "man-hating sex/class warfare" and "a female chauvinism that makes a woman apologize for loving her husband and children." "Men are not the enemy," she insisted.

"I am nasty, I'm bitchy, I get mad," Friedan declared, "but by God I'm absorbed in what I'm doing." Always by nature an outsider, Friedan proved a divisive leader. She ran NOW in an abrupt, highhanded manner that was suitable to the political agitator she had always been but was inappropriate for leading a mass political movement. She considered sex a private issue, and so-called sexual politics (including "pushing lesbianism") a threat to the women's movement's public image. Calling lesbians a "lavender menace," Friedan built a fire wall between their issues and NOW's, inspiring many lesbians to quit the organization. Friedan's presidency of NOW ended in 1970. In order to promote the ERA, she would later try, with limited success, to mend fences with radicals and lesbians, but they continued to regard her as a mere "liberal" or even a reactionary. When the *Roe* decision came down in 1973, Friedan was serving as vice president of the National Association to Repeal Abortion Laws. By then, though she remained a feminist icon, her influence over the women's movement was dwindling.

In 1980 Friedan published a critique of the movement, *The Second Stage.* In a ringing endorsement of what are today called family values, she argued that modern feminism's first stage (the one to date) had been too divisive and simplistic. As a case in point, she emphasized "our own extreme of reaction against . . . [the] wife-mother role." Feminism's second stage must center on the family. Friedan called for an alliance between women and men against "feminist denial of the importance of family, of women's own needs to give and get love and nurture." Among other things, her book espoused parental leave, flexible work schedules, and day care. By this time, in response to Phyllis Schlafly's stinging rebukes linking them to feminist extremism, other ERA supporters had also begun to embrace family values.

Now Jimmy Carter, a man of limited political gifts, weighed in. After 1973, when all-volunteer armed forces had replaced the draft, the notion of drafting women was really a red herring *unless* conscription, or at least requiring registration for future conscription, came back. In his 1980 State of the Union Address, Carter asked Congress to restore draft registration for men—and to break all precedent by requiring women to register too. If Carter had been campaigning against the ERA instead of for it, he could hardly have done a more effective job of handing Schlafly a loaded gun. Seeing the president's proposal coming, she had already instituted a petition drive ingeniously titled "Dads Against Drafting Our Daughters." By the time Carter delivered his address, mail and phone calls had inundated congressional offices. Congress did vote to register men, but Carter's proposal for women was dead on arrival. Draft-age women who had previously been neutral on the ERA began attacking the amendment's backers for trying to qualify them for military service. "Women who hesitated to join us because they thought we were using scare tactics—like warning that Carter had it up his sleeve to draft women—are joining us now," Schlafly gloated. "The draft issue has lowered the average age of our movement by about 20 years."

Up to 1980, Phyllis Schlafly had assumed the role of an underdog taking on the political establishment and its favored constitutional amendment. To oppose the ERA was unfashionable. Portraying issues as black or white was unfashionable. Long, frilly dresses and homemade jam were unfashionable. So was calling homosexuals "perverts." Schlafly's solutions to problems were not fashionable either—the husbands of battered wives, she said, should be publicly flogged. Schlafly's constituency was not establishment; it consisted disproportionately of people who were less educated, older, religious, conservative-traditionalist, Republican, southern or midwestern, and rural. Many supporters were Christian fundamentalists, Orthodox Jews, conservative Catholics, or Mormons. But then, Schlafly had never belonged to the political establishment, or its Republican branch, herself. With her fervid anti-communism, her suspicion of internationalism, and her partiality to nuclear weapons and laissez-faire economics, she sounded too much like Hoover or Goldwater to fit the world of Nixon or Ford. In her own impeccably proper way, Phyllis Schlafly was a rebel.

When Ronald Reagan ran for president in 1980, though, a lot of Schlafly's unfashionable views, especially the black-and-white perspective on life and the nuclear-brandishing anti-communism, suddenly became very fashionable indeed. That year, in response to Schlafly's energetic lobbying and after four decades of support, the GOP suddenly declined to endorse the Equal Rights Amendment. The Democrats actually strengthened their endorsement. That November, for the first time in history, a "gender gap" split the electorate. Simply put, men liked Reagan significantly better than women did. He took 54 percent of male votes but just 48 percent of females. This gender gap has persisted between the two parties ever since.

Schlafly's Republican platform victory served as a portent. Not a single state had ratified the Equal Rights Amendment since 1977. Its backers prepared one last big push. A 1981 Gallup Poll indicated that nearly two-thirds of the American people supported the amendment and that despite Schlafly's relentless onslaught, support had actually been *rising*. Calling its quarter-million members to arms, NOW mounted a $15 million advertising campaign, together with a series of rallies headed by two presidential wives, Lady Bird Johnson and Betty Ford. Former campaign opponents Gerald Ford and Jimmy Carter made a joint plea for the amendment. All in vain: STOP ERA had stoked enough opposition and kept enough people neutral so that casting a vote for the amendment in some states had become too hazardous to a legislator's political career; it was simply safer to vote no than to face STOP ERA's wrath. In 1982, Florida, for which ERA supporters had held out hope, rejected the amendment. Although more than three-fifths of the people of Illinois favored the ERA, it fell just short of victory there as well—again.

Given the high threshold set by the Constitution's framers, all the apple pies and homebaked bread and threats had done their work. Had Schlafly not opposed it, the ERA would almost certainly have completed a smooth voyage to ratification. Instead, at last, it sank like a great torpedoed ship.*

✧   ✧   ✧

Following her victory over the ERA, Phyllis Schlafly turned the Eagle Forum toward fresh campaigns. She fought against freezing nuclear weapons, against pornography, against sex education to prevent teen pregnancy, and in favor of stripping all the alleged

---

*The following states declined to ratify: Alabama, Arizona, Arkansas, Florida, Georgia, Illinois, Louisiana, Mississippi, Missouri, Nevada, North Carolina, Oklahoma, South Carolina, Utah, and Virginia.

feminist bias out of school textbooks. She also criticized liberals for endorsing "the dogmatic teaching of evolution." Betty Friedan followed *The Second Stage* with *The Fountain of Age* (1993), exploring the later phases of life. During the 1990s, much as she had done half a century before, she called for a renewed democratic system that would "revitalize our vision of the common good, a humane vision that places the highest priority on people's lives and not on the stock market index and the corporate bottom line." In 2000 she published an autobiography, *Life So Far.* Meantime, Friedan's son and Schlafly's son pursued Ph.D.s in physics at Berkeley under the same professor. "Both of your mothers should sit next to each other the way you do," the professor teased them.

STOP ERA portended America's turn to the right over the past generation. Since the Reagan era, southern and western conservatives have increasingly supplanted northeastern moderates as the *new* Republican establishment. There is a remarkable overlap between Schlafly's supporters and the constituency of President George W. Bush. Family values, which both Schlafly and Friedan endorsed in different ways and seemed threatened during the 1970s, have become a national bipartisan concern, though the political parties differ on how to ensure them. Of both men and women, half say they support the traditional division of labor—wife = home, husband = breadwinner. To the modern mainstream, radical feminism seems as odd an historical artifact as hoop skirts or Prohibition. On all these counts, Phyllis Schlafly's view of the world has prevailed.

In other ways, though, so has Betty Friedan's. By the early twenty-first century, nearly fifty percent of the paid work force consisted of women, some of them in high positions (Supreme Court Justice, secretary of state, national security advisor, army general)—hard to imagine when *The Feminine Mystique* appeared. Friedan's consuming drive to combine marriage, family, and paid employment—to "have it all"—has become today's American reality. During the years while the ERA rose and fell, the percentage of children with mothers in the work force soared from 39 (1970) to 61 (1990). Eighty-five percent of women now expect to bear children during their careers. As many women as not want to work irrespective of whether they need the income. Having it all has led society in some of the experimental directions Phyllis Schlafly warned against. In 2003, for example, at the outset of the war in Iraq, two women volunteer soldiers with a noncombat unit were captured. A third—a Hopi Indian, the mother of two young children—was killed in action.

Though the ERA failed, legislation such as the 1963 Equal Pay Act, the 1964 Civil Rights Act, Title IX of the Education Amendments of 1972, and the 1993 Family and Medical Leave Act have passed. Ironically, gains made under such laws even while the ERA faced state ratification undermined the amendment's chances—why race for a train you've already caught?—and highlighted its unknowns. Court decisions throwing out certain protective laws (for example, limitation on work hours for women) had a similar effect. Yet today, old workplace conditions and glass ceilings persist that the ERA was intended to stop. Women still make less than men. Most women think a strong women's movement is needed. But only a minority regard themselves as "feminists," largely, no doubt, because the term itself became so tainted by the radical fringe of the movement and by counterassaults from right-wingers such as Rush Limbaugh against "femi-Nazis." If "feminist" in its broadest sense means an endorsement of equal opportunities for women and men, then the great majority of Americans are feminists today, just as they were during the ERA struggle.

This curious mixture of old attitudes and new realities suggests why, though the ERA failed, the debates and conflicts it aroused continue today. The amendment's supporters dream of reviving it. The ERA is regularly reintroduced into Congress and just as regularly bottled up, as it was for half a century before the 1970s.

11

Race Unfortunately Still Matters

Sandra Day O'Connor, Clarence Thomas, and Affirmative Action

When she opened the thin envelope from the University of Michigan campus at Ann Arbor, Jennifer Gratz was shocked. Her application for admission had been rejected. "I read probably the first three lines," she later recalled, "and started crying."

Gratz had submitted her application in the fall of 1994. Since her childhood in a Detroit suburb, she had always dreamed of going to Ann Arbor—the state university's flagship campus, generally referred to as "*the* University of Michigan" or simply "Michigan." She had achieved a 3.765 grade point average (GPA) in high school; had earned an ACT score in the eighty-third percentile; and had been a member of the National Honor Society, a volunteer math tutor, an athlete, a varsity cheerleader, vice president of the student council, and class historian. Michigan was the only campus to which she even applied.

Initially the university had relegated her to the wait list; then it rejected her. Jennifer Gratz, as it happened, was white.

Two years later Barbara Grutter, 43 and also white, applied to the University of Michigan Law School. A 1978 honors graduate of Michigan State University with a 3.8 GPA, Grutter had put herself through college working night jobs. She had spent the years since graduation as a health care consultant and business-woman, and was raising two children. She had scored a respectable 161 on the Law School Admission Test (LSAT). The law school turned her down.

Both Jennifer Gratz and Barbara Grutter sued the University of Michigan and its president, Lee Bollinger,* claiming that they had been discriminated against because the university had a double standard—one admissions policy for whites of both genders, another for African Americans, Latinos, and American Indians. These policies, the two women held, violated the Fourteenth Amendment to the Constitution, which guarantees all citizens "equal protection of the laws," as well as the Civil Rights Act of 1964. The university, Grutter claimed, "had no compelling interest to justify their use of race in the admissions process." "The University of Michigan is treating people differently based on skin color," Gratz told CNN, "and that's unconstitutional." Another unsuccessful white undergraduate applicant, Patrick Hamacher, joined Gratz in her lawsuit. All three litigants were represented in a class action by the Center for Individual Rights, a conservative, activist law firm.

By the time the *Gratz* and *Grutter* cases finally reached the United States Supreme Court, lower courts had rendered conflicting verdicts. When the Supreme Court handed down its own decision in June, 2003, it too was sharply divided. Jennifer Gratz won. Barbara Grutter lost. And the high court's sole African

---

*Gratz v. Bollinger, et al., 123 S. Ct. 2411, 156 L. Ed. 2d 257 (2003); *Grutter v. Bollinger, et al.*, 123 S. Ct. 2325, 156 L. Ed. 2d 304 (2003).

American, Justice Clarence Thomas, lashed out against a majority opinion written by one of the Court's two women justices, Sandra Day O'Connor. Thomas—who had personally benefited time and again from affirmative action—sided with Gratz and Grutter.

✧　　✧　　✧

Sandra Day O'Connor is the first woman ever to sit on the Supreme Court. When Ronald Reagan nominated her in 1981, both liberals and conservatives criticized the choice. Liberals wanted a woman on the Court, but not this woman, a conservative with scant credentials as a feminist. Conservatives lambasted her lack of experience in the federal judicial system; they also harbored doubts about her position on abortion. Eventually O'Connor would confirm her reputation for conservatism—but with an independent, pragmatic streak.

Born in 1930 to Harry and Ada Mae Day, O'Connor grew up on her family's 155,000-acre Lazy B Cattle Ranch, which straddled the border between southeastern Arizona and southwestern New Mexico. A grandfather had established the ranch during the 1880s—the Geronimo era. Parched and treeless, the land was broken up into mesas. Life revolved around a predictable rhythm of roundups and brandings. Sandra was seven before the ranch had running water or electricity, and eight before siblings began to come along. By that time, her parents had already sent her to live with her maternal grandparents in El Paso, where she attended an exclusive private girls' school. Her grandmother encouraged the tiny girl to learn to excel in a man's world. During the summers, Sandra would return to the ranch. At seven she could drive cattle; at eight she could fire a rifle. One of her pets was a bobcat.

Sandra Day went to Stanford, where she majored in economics—a "man's" subject (unlike, say, home economics). She took advantage of an option that allowed a student to pursue bachelor's and law degrees in a simultaneous six-year program. The law class had hardly any women, but some faculty thought even one woman was too many. O'Connor had to contend with this. She might be elfin, with a subdued voice, but in her own quiet way, she could also be staunch. And she was smart. In 1952 she graduated third in her law school class of 102.

Despite her stellar record, with one exception not a single law firm to which she applied in San Francisco or Los Angeles offered her a position. As she later wrote, "none had ever hired a woman before as a lawyer, and they were not prepared to do so" now. Her sole offer was a job as a legal secretary. Half a century ago, only husbands with their own firms or government agencies were receptive to hiring female lawyers. She ended up as a deputy county attorney.

When her husband, John Jay O'Connor III (a fellow Stanford Law alumnus whom she had married after graduation) was drafted into the army and sent to Germany, both newlyweds practiced law there, he in the Judge Advocate General's Corps, she as a civilian with the Quartermaster Corps. In 1957 the couple settled in Phoenix, where they began raising a family that would eventually include three boys. Since established law firms still didn't want her, she opened her own small firm after arriving in Phoenix, which let her combine a part-time practice with motherhood. Then, beginning in 1960, she devoted five years to full-time parenthood. Meanwhile she became a prominent volunteer for a variety of causes, among them the Republican Party; in 1964 she organized precincts for fellow Arizonan Barry Goldwater.

Her role in party politics brought rewards. When O'Connor did return to practicing law full time in 1965, it was through an appointment as an assistant state attorney general. Four years later, the Republican governor appointed her to fill a vacancy in the state senate. Running on the GOP ticket, she held the office through two elections, and in 1972 she became the first woman majority leader of a state senate in American history. Her voting record generally ranged between conservative and moderate; she was for the death penalty, for containing government spending, and against gun control. On the subject of discrimination against women, she took a modestly liberal direction. She battled to overhaul community property laws, leaned toward freedom of choice on abortion, and voted for the Equal Rights Amendment. Apparently her gender and independence isolated her to some degree in the senate; "I was never one of the boys," she has recalled.

In 1974 O'Connor won election as a trial judge on the Maricopa County Superior Court. Five years later, Arizona's Democratic governor nominated her to the state court of appeals—possibly to sideline her as a potential political rival. On the bench she was noted as exceedingly meticulous and businesslike. Her judicial philosophy was hard to define. She examined cases (most involving run-of-the-mill criminal or commercial issues) on their particular merits and wrote practical, well-crafted decisions.

By this time O'Connor had become a prominent Reagan Republican. To deflect women's anger over his opposition to the ERA, during the 1980 campaign Ronald Reagan promised to nominate a woman to the United States Supreme Court. When a slot opened in 1981, he named O'Connor, even though she lacked any judicial experience at the federal level. An unlikely choice had she not been female, now she was perfectly positioned. Swallowing doubts, reluctant to vote against a woman, the Senate confirmed her unanimously.

O'Connor had arrived on the Court by a circuitous route. She had experienced discrimination; she had taken time off to raise her children; she had volunteered; and her volunteer work, notably of the political kind, had kindled an illustrious career. Her appointment to the high court has been called an act of affirmative action, and so it was. Reagan naturally wanted a conservative, but he had specifically promised to appoint a woman regardless of whether she was the most qualified candidate. For the first time in 192 years, a woman had finally made it to the nation's highest bench. One change occurred right away. In formal terms of address, the word "Mr." was dropped from "Mr. Justice."

Formalities aside, what did it mean to have a woman on the Court? "More and more writers have suggested that women practice law differently than men," O'Connor observed in 1991, adding teasingly: "One author has even concluded that *my* opinions differ in a *peculiarly feminine* way from those of my colleagues." On the evidence, one could argue either way.

✧   ✧   ✧

Clarence Thomas grew up in vastly different circumstances from Sandra Day O'Connor's. The second of three children, he was born in June, 1948, in a tiny hamlet appropriately called Pin Point, Georgia. Pin Point was so destitute that it had no paved roads or even a sewage system. His father soon vanished, and Thomas's mother had to scramble for income as a maid, supplemented by local charities. In 1955 she sent her two boys to Savannah, nine miles from Pin Point, to live with their grandfather and step-grandmother. The boys' lives brightened. They were properly fed, for one thing; and their grandfather, Myers Anderson, decisively shaped them, teaching them the importance of discipline, hard work, self-help, and education. There was a big obstacle to getting an education, though—the Savannah Public Library did not so much as allow blacks to walk in the door. Clarence had to do his reading elsewhere.

Myers Anderson, a convert to Catholicism who brought the boys up in his adopted faith, wanted Clarence to enter the priesthood. Clarence's Catholic elementary school education was followed by two years at an all-black Catholic high school. He then gained admission to a white seminary just outside Savannah as one of a small cadre of African American students whom he later termed "integrators"—"the first and the only" blacks that an educational institution let in. Shutting him out of social events, the white seminarians taunted Thomas about his color, one even writing in his yearbook: "Keep on trying, Clarence. Some day you'll be as good as us [sic]." After high school, Thomas entered Missouri's Immaculate Conception Seminary for further priestly training but dropped out almost immediately after encountering even worse racism.

In 1968 Thomas entered Holy Cross College in Worcester, Massachusetts. Holy Cross, a Jesuit institution, had accepted him and five other African Americans under a program that provided special financial aid. These were "my radical days," Thomas later remarked. He devoured the novels of Richard Wright, the *Autobiography of Malcolm X*—and the writings of Booker T. Washington—each with a powerful emphasis on black self-reliance. He sported an Afro hairstyle and a goatee, wore army surplus fatigues or bib overalls and military boots, and helped found the Black Students' Union. But having a white roommate blurred his public identity as an African American activist. As Thomas later remarked, "I don't fit in with whites, and I don't fit in with blacks."

After graduating cum laude in 1971, Thomas married a student at a neighboring women's college with whom he had a son, Jamal. By the time the couple divorced in 1984, Thomas had long since abandoned Catholicism. Three years later, he remarried. Like his college roommate, his second wife was white.

Thomas's 3.7 grade point average at Holy Cross resembled Barbara Grutter's GPA later that decade at Michigan State—excellent, though not off the charts. Yale Law School had begun an affirmative action program in 1969, giving admissions preference to minorities by setting aside up to a tenth of its openings for them. In 1971 Yale admitted Thomas, 11 other African Americans, and one Latino under this quota system. (Harvard and the University of Pennsylvania also admitted him, presumably on a similar basis.) Absent affirmative action, one cannot say whether Thomas would have gotten into Yale; the question haunts him to this day. In Thomas's perception, the white law students regarded the African Americans' presence as a matter of social policy, not academics. He later insisted that whites had told him flat out that he was among them purely because of quotas. As Thomas has put it, "You had to prove yourself every day because the presumption was that you were dumb and didn't deserve to be there on merit." As a result, "every time you walked into a law class at Yale it was like having a monkey jump on your back from the Gothic arches. . . . The professors and the students resented your very presence." As one of Thomas's biographers, John Greenya, observes, "Above all, Yale reinforced Thomas's belief that affirmative action taints every black's achievement and robs him of respect."

Even before Yale, Thomas had begun moving politically to the right, and his bitterness over the "stigma" of affirmative action—this "monkey on my back"—pushed him hard in that direction. As an undergraduate, he had already become troubled about affirmative action programs that accepted unqualified applicants, setting them up to fail. The experience at Yale, where even liberals condescended to him, played a key role in transforming him into a conservative.

A widespread assumption in academe and the legal profession was that affirmative action law graduates would wind up in practices that emphasized civil rights or legal aid. Clarence Thomas took no such direction. At least in part because he would have to pay off student loans, he focused on potentially lucrative tax and business courses. A hard-working student though not a top one—unlike his Yale contemporary Bill Clinton, who excelled without bothering to go to class—Thomas got good grades. (Contrary to the Stanford practice, Yale did not rank its graduates.)

As had Sandra Day O'Connor, when he finished Yale Law, Thomas failed to land a position with a private firm. Rejection letters poured in. "Prospective employers dismissed our grades and diplomas," he later remarked of himself and other affirmative action students, "assuming we got both primarily because of preferential treatment." Again like O'Connor, Thomas eventually secured a government job—in 1974, John Danforth, the Republican attorney general of Missouri, hired Thomas as assistant attorney general. Consistent with his training, Thomas focused on tax, not civil rights, cases. When Danforth left for the United States Senate in 1977, Thomas went to work as a corporate lawyer for Monsanto, the chemical giant. Two years later he rejoined the man who had become his mentor, as Danforth's legislative aide. Thomas soon came to the notice of the Reagan administration. In 1981, the president appointed Thomas assistant secretary for civil rights in the Department of Education, and, shortly thereafter, head of the Equal Employment Opportunity Commission (EEOC), positions far removed from Thomas's training and practice.

In 1990 Reagan's successor, George H.W. Bush, named Thomas to the highly influential U.S. Court of Appeals in Washington, D.C. The following year, Thurgood Marshall—the first African American to serve on the United States Supreme Court and a legendary advocate of civil rights in the W.E.B. Du Bois tradition—retired. Under pressure to nominate another black, Bush now named Thomas, the ideological descendant of Booker T. Washington, to succeed Marshall. Conservatives saw Thomas as a key to controlling the federal judiciary; they desperately wanted him on the Court to vote against affirmative action and abortion. Civil rights leaders and feminists wanted to keep him off the Court for the same reasons, but they had scant expectation of success. The calculus was that the Senate would never accept a white as conservative as Thomas but would have to accept Thomas because he was black.

Ignoring the odds, Thomas's opponents, among them feminist organizations, the AFL-CIO, and the NAACP, took to the battlefield. They charged that he was an extreme conservative, out of step with the great majority of African Americans and unfit to follow Marshall; and they pointed out that Thomas, just 42, had served only a year on the federal bench, without any particular distinction. During the confirmation hearings, under fire from Senate Democrats, Thomas declined to respond to key questions about his legal views, including his attitude toward the Supreme Court's 1973 abortion ruling.

Then a surprise witness appeared. Anita Hill, an African American who had worked for Thomas at the EEOC a decade earlier and was now professor of law at the University of Oklahoma, accused him in graphic detail of sexually harassing her. The televised confirmation hearings suddenly riveted national attention. Thomas recoiled, denying some charges, dodging others, and denouncing the hearings as a "high-tech lynching." Ultimately the Senate voted to confirm him, 52–48. The episode gave American feminism, wounded by the ERA debacle, a significant boost.

Thomas arrived on the high bench both angry and self-pitying. "Being on the Supreme Court," he declared, "is not worth it, and there is no amount of money . . . that can restore my name." Perhaps because of all this, Thomas developed a peculiarly defensive judicial strategy, apparently to avoid criticism: during oral arguments before the Court, he would virtually never ask a question.

✧   ✧   ✧

It was no accident that by the 1970s, universities such as Yale had begun to recruit promising "nontraditional" students like Clarence Thomas. Universities had much to atone for. Historically, blacks south of the Mason-Dixon line had been barred from admission to public campuses that their own taxes helped to support. During the 1960s, one civil rights battle after another erupted over integrating such institutions as the University of Mississippi and the University of Alabama.

Nor did blacks alone suffer discrimination. Currents of anti-Semitism had historically run deep in the Ivy League. The "legacy" approach to admissions constituted a preference system for white applicants of northern European descent. Early in the twentieth century, mounting applications from Jews of Eastern European origin raised anxieties about weakening the ancient tradition of clubby domination by Protestant elites. "We must," Dean Frederick S. Jones of Yale declared in 1918, "put a ban on the Jews." Harvard rejected the strict numerical quota system proposed by its president; instead, admissions officers turned to more indirect and informal screening methods—examining an applicant's personal appearance, for example, or inquiring into an applicant's background. Most other elite eastern universities also enforced limits. Some schools asked direct questions about one's religion or national origin; some asked the maiden name of one's mother (to reveal whether a family surname had recently been Anglicized, say, from Abrahams to Allen). Columbia succeeded in dropping its undergraduate Jewish enrollment from about 25 percent (1917) to 15 percent (1920s). Harvard cut its proportion from 21 percent to 10 percent. The first "action" systems in American higher education, then, were not affirmative but negative, intended to keep people *out*.

By the 1960s the goal, in higher education and throughout the economy, involved getting people *in*. Like southern segregation, informal discriminatory practices in the north (such as shutting minorities out of jobs) came under presidential attack. Lyndon Johnson ordered "affirmative action" in federal contracting with the private sector "for the prompt achievement of full and equal employment opportunity" for African Americans, Hispanics, Native Americans, and "Orientals." While ethnic census data and "specific goals and timetables" were required, however, there were as yet no numerical quotas. Ironically, Johnson's successor, Richard Nixon—whose "southern strategy" catered politically to the prejudices and anxieties of southern whites—did launch an affirmative action program that mandated quotas (or "set-asides"). Though Congress never voted its approval, by the mid-1970s practically any institution that got funds from the federal government came under the umbrella of affirmative action—including private businesses, colleges, and universities. Yale's quota system was typical.

But by the late 1970s, affirmative action, always controversial, had come under increasing criticism. Implementing the policy in the booming, job-rich economy of the mid-1960s had been one thing; now the nation's flat economy made jobs tougher to get. White workers resented hiring quotas that favored minorities. Opponents of affirmative action sardonically branded the policy "reverse discrimination" or "affirmative discrimination."

In 1978 the Supreme Court handed down a landmark decision on affirmative action. Allan Bakke, a white applicant to the medical school of the University of California, Davis, had been rejected. Bakke sued, claiming that weaker candidates had gained admission under the university's quota system, which set aside seats specifically for minorities. A fractured high court voted 5–4 in Bakke's favor, ordering the medical school to admit him. Race, Justice Lewis F. Powell wrote, could be taken into consideration in university admissions, but specific quotas were unconstitutional. Thurgood Marshall, who as a lawyer a quarter-century before had successfully argued for school desegregation in *Brown v. Board of Education,* filed a bitter dissent. In the wake of slavery and segregation, he claimed, affirmative action was just and appropriate. Affirmative action and other social programs, in other words, were legitimate means of compensation for historic wrongs that had left a legacy of injustice down to the present. Though it has been so often repeated that many regard it as a truism, Marshall's argument remains highly controversial; nowhere in the Constitution or its amendments can a provision be found for the redress of slavery.

Following the inauguration of Ronald Reagan in 1981, the White House demonstrated markedly less enthusiasm for enforcing affirmative action. As head of the EEOC, in charge of all federal programs against workplace discrimination, Clarence Thomas epitomized the new approach. Outraging civil rights organizations, he drastically altered EEOC practices involving numbers: suddenly, numerical goals and timetables, along with class action lawsuits based on statistical evidence of discrimination, were out. Thomas urged Reagan to jettison all "preferential treatment under *any* guise, and no matter . . . whether it is called quotas or goals and timetables." This alienated Thomas even further from other African Americans and opened him to vociferous charges of hypocrisy. As his biographer Andrew Peyton Thomas puts it, Clarence Thomas "had benefited from racial preferences at every stage of his career. From his admission to Yale Law School . . . to Danforth's race-based recruitment drive to Monsanto's search for a black lawyer to his meteoric promotions in Washington: all were premised largely on race." Now, as John Greenya observes, Thomas "didn't just *oppose* such concepts as quotas and racial set-asides, and affirmative action in general, he made his name by opposing them."

During the 1990s, it looked as though affirmative action might well collapse. The Supreme Court was steadily undermining it. In 1989, for instance, the Court threw out a Nixon-era program that set aside jobs for minority construction workers. In *Adarand Constructors, Inc. v. Peña* (1995), a 5–4 majority ruled that in general, governmental bias either for or against any ethnic group violated the Equal Protection Clause of the Fourteenth Amendment, and that any proposed exception must withstand "strict scrutiny." Justice O'Connor wrote the majority opinion. Concurring, Justice Thomas declared "that racial paternalism . . . can be as poisonous and pernicious as any other form of discrimination."

In 1996, California voters approved Proposition 209, which barred the use of race or gender preferences by the state or its university systems, by 54 percent to 46 percent. Leading the 209 campaign was a University of California regent, Ward Connerly, an African American out of the Booker T. Washington tradition, who argued that to ensure fairness to all, the state should be officially colorblind. Like other affirmative action opponents, Connerly echoed 1960s civil rights rhetoric to make his case. Siding with Connerly (and disagreeing with the overwhelming majority of African American voters) were a number of black intellectuals who shared Clarence Thomas's anxieties about the way affirmative action created an impression of unearned rewards. By and large, the American public echoed the voters of California: they told pollsters that they wanted minority access but did not approve of federally mandated preferences. By the time the Supreme Court handed down its 2003 decisions in *Gratz* and *Grutter,* the Center for Individual Rights had sued successfully to undo affirmative action in both Texas and Washington State.

✧   ✧   ✧

The United States Supreme Court has passed through massive ideological shifts over the past century; changes in society and the economy, together with the succession of new appointments, have transformed constitutional interpretation. Following its battle with FDR in 1937, the Supreme Court took a liberal turn, most famously under Chief Justice Earl Warren (1953-1969). The decisions of the Warren Court generated an uproar from the right about "judicial activism," along with a strong demand to place more conservatives on the bench. All but two of the nine members of the high court of 2003, which heard the Gratz and Grutter cases, had been appointed by Republican presidents. The Court's ruling in the case of *Bush v. Gore* (December, 2000) had awarded the presidency of the United States to a new Republican president.

Internally, though, the Court was divided into a strongly conservative bloc, a liberal bloc, and a swing bloc with conservative instincts. Chief Justice William Rehnquist was as indelibly identified with the right as Earl Warren had been with the left. Rehnquist had particularly close ties with O'Connor. Not only did they both come from Arizona but they had been classmates at Stanford, where they edited the law review together. Rehnquist graduated at the top of the class. Highly intelligent, witty, and canny, Rehnquist was not a man plagued by self-doubt.

In Clarence Thomas, Rehnquist could safely count on as conservative an ally as they came. Thomas's vote virtually always tracked that of Antonin Scalia, a federal judge and former University of Chicago Law School professor. Brilliant and famously abrasive, Scalia tested his colleagues' tempers (and egos) in brutally written opinions that often ridiculed their own.

The Court's more or less liberal bloc consisted of four justices. John Paul Stevens, a Gerald Ford appointee, might more fairly be referred to as a moderate with a strong streak of independence and a superb prose style. Ruth Bader Ginsburg, the first woman hired with tenure to teach at Columbia Law School and a former federal judge, was a renowned legal advocate of women's rights. Stephen G. Breyer, like Ginsburg, had been appointed to the Court by Bill Clinton. A federal judge who had taught law at Harvard, Breyer frequently departed from the opinions of his fellow liberals. The truly enigmatic member of the liberal cadre was David Souter, whom George H.W. Bush nominated to the Court in 1990, a year ahead of Clarence Thomas. A practically anonymous New Hampshire judge, Souter aroused fear in liberal circles that he was a stealth right-winger. The last laugh went to the liberals when Souter turned out to be exactly as he had appeared during his confirmation hearings—reflective and independent.

Finally, the Court had two swing votes, justices famous for their ability to vote either way. One was Anthony M. Kennedy of Sacramento, a former lawyer, lobbyist, and federal judge. The other was Sandra Day O'Connor. Though she generally sided with her friend Justice Rehnquist and had originally been identified with the conservative bloc, after a few terms she charted a more moderate and independent course. "What distinguishes her approach to judging," writes John Yoo in describing the consensus among Court scholars, "is her reluctance to draw bright-line rules, her effort to decide each case on its unique facts and context, her affinity for balancing the costs and benefits of a policy and her desire to leave issues open to be decided another day. This has the effect of making O'Connor the most important vote on contentious issues that are never really decided but instead are destined to reappear before the court again and again."

One final person figured prominently in the affirmative action suits that Jennifer Gratz and Barbara Grutter had brought before the Court. He was Lee Bollinger—president of the University of Michigan and a passionate believer in affirmative action—who was the cases' most noteworthy defendant. A graduate of Columbia Law, the former dean of Michigan Law, and a renowned scholar of the First Amendment, as a young man Bollinger had clerked for Chief Justice Warren Burger. By the time he came to national attention in 1997 as a result of the lawsuits, Bollinger had become one of the most effective university presidents in the country. Regardless of one's position on affirmative action, there was no denying that in Bollinger it had an extraordinary advocate. California's public universities had repeatedly fumbled their attempt to defend affirmative action. Bollinger intended to mount the most formidable legal defense it had ever had. Behind this defense he would mobilize dozens of major corporations (such as Microsoft, General Motors, Coca-Cola, Johnson & Johnson, and 3M), an array of military officers, former President Gerald Ford, and other notables. Bollinger also intended to educate the public about what affirmative action meant to society. Doing a feature on the dispute at Michigan, CBS's *60 Minutes* turned up one affirmative action student who had earned a 3.9 undergraduate GPA and a Phi Beta Kappa key, offering Bollinger just the kind of publicity he wanted. As *Newsweek* put it, "Bollinger's outspoken advocacy of affirmative action has made him the role model for those who would like to see more college presidents speak out on social issues."

The University of Michigan really had two separate affirmative action systems, one for undergraduate admissions, the other for the law school. *Gratz* contested the first and *Grutter* the second, so that both would undergo the scrutiny of the Supreme Court. The undergraduate College of Literature, Science, and the Arts typically accepted about half of the 25,000 who applied; some five thousand would actually enroll. From year to year, between 11 percent and 17 percent of the student body came from the "underrepresented" groups covered by affirmative action. The college had a 150-point numerical system on which to rate applicants. Candidates who totaled 100 points were guaranteed admission. A perfect grade point average earned 80 points. African Americans, Hispanics, and American Indians automatically received a 20-point bonus—the equivalent of a full grade point. Besides ethnicity, other nonacademic factors entered in— Michigan residency (10 points), or being a legacy (4 points). A distinguished application essay could earn up to 3 points; outstanding leadership or volunteer work, up to 5 points; a perfect SAT score, a firm 12 points. Nothing, though, measured up to ethnicity, with one exception—athletics, which could also garner 20 points. The result of all this was that practically every qualified minority applicant got into Michigan while a great many qualified whites did not.

The other University of Michigan affirmative action policy concerned admission to the law school. One of the nation's most prestigious, it received over three thousand, five hundred applications each year for a tenth that number of seats. In common with all selective institutions, large numbers of qualified, potentially successful students had to be turned away regardless of circumstances. As dean, Bollinger had had a faculty committee draft a diversity policy for the law school in 1992. This policy tightly conformed to the 1978 *Bakke* decision and mimicked the Harvard admissions policy that Justice Powell had cited then as a proper model. (Harvard set no quotas but instead used race as a "plus" factor.) The declared intent of Michigan Law's policy was to "achieve that diversity which has the potential to enrich everyone's education and thus make a law school class stronger than the sum of its parts."

Though it did not define diversity "solely in terms of racial and ethnic status," the law school policy did focus on African Americans, Hispanics, and Native Americans as groups that had been "historically discriminated against" and that, without affirmative action, "might not be represented in our student body in meaningful numbers." For members of these groups, race or ethnicity was a "plus" factor; if they fell into the broad midrange of applicants, it might put them over the top. In court testimony, the law school insisted that it sought a "critical mass" of minority students—not some specific number or percentage but enough that students did not feel as though they were isolated or had been singled out (the way Clarence Thomas did at Yale). Why no mention of Jews or Asian Americans, who had also suffered discrimination? Because they already enjoyed sufficient admission rates. Admissions officers had to consider a whole range of variables in each applicant's file—undergraduate GPA, LSAT score, personal statement, essay, and letters of recommendation. The law school could show that it admitted white applicants with below-par grades or LSAT scores but with unusual profiles based, for example, on past hardships or particular abilities. The policy also stated that "no applicant should be admitted unless we expect that applicant to do well enough to graduate with no serious academic problems."

Had the law school's admissions policy been race-blind in 2000, members of the three protected minority groups would have been admitted at a rate of one in ten applicants, constituting a meager four percent of the entering class. Admitted at a rate of one in three applicants under affirmative action, though, these minorities made up 14.5 percent of the class.

When the Michigan cases came before the Court for oral arguments on April 1, 2003, both Barbara Grutter and Jennifer Gratz sat in the audience. The Bush administration weighed in against the university. In an unsteady presentation, its solicitor general, Theodore Olson, contended that the 20-point bonus amounted to "an admissions ticket," and that the law school program was nothing more than "a thinly disguised quota." Outside the Supreme Court building, thousands of demonstrators for and against affirmative action milled around. Everyone knew the stakes. A defeat for the university could dismantle affirmative action not just in higher education but to the degree it still survived in contracting and hiring as well.

✧   ✧   ✧

On June 23, 2003, the Supreme Court rendered its decisions. For the first time in a quarter-century, it squarely confronted the question of whether race could be considered in admitting students to public colleges and universities. Did such institutions in fact have a "compelling interest" in a diverse student body, as claimed, or did the Equal Protection Clause bar colleges from choosing along racial or ethnic lines?

On a 6–3 vote, the high court found in favor of Jennifer Gratz. The point system employed by Michigan's undergraduate college, wrote Chief Justice Rehnquist for the Court, failed the *Bakke* test because it lacked "individualized consideration." In concurring, Justice O'Connor described Michigan's undergraduate admissions process as "mechanized." The three dissenters were Justices Stevens, Ginsburg, and Souter.

The Court went differently in *Grutter.* It upheld Michigan Law's affirmative action program by 5–4—the same vote as in *Bakke,* but with the opposite result for the litigant. Sandra Day O'Connor wrote the majority opinion, joined by Justices Stevens, Ginsburg, Souter, and Breyer. On the other side of the decision were Justices Rehnquist, Scalia, and Kennedy, and Clarence Thomas, who filed an unusually bitter dissent.

Noting that the Supreme Court now had the responsibility of resolving disagreements among lower courts over the law school's affirmative action policy, Justice O'Connor committed the majority to deciding "a question of national importance: Whether diversity is a compelling interest that can justify the narrowly tailored use of race in selecting applicants for admission to public universities." O'Connor observed that Justice Powell—who had died in 1998 and whom she greatly admired—had voted against UC Davis in *Bakke,* but that Powell had also defended considerations of race in university admissions under certain circumstances. No other Justice had fully concurred with Powell at the time; four would have flatly upheld UC Davis, the other four would have upheld Allan Bakke. But among six separate opinions, not one of which could muster unequivocal majority support, Powell's opinion had represented a common denominator for the narrow five-vote majority because Powell had had it both ways, upholding *Bakke* but *also* upholding affirmative action. Therefore Powell's was the controlling opinion, the baseline standard of law. "Since this Court's splintered decision in *Bakke,*" O'Connor declared, for public and private universities alike, "Justice Powell's opinion announcing the judgment of the Court has served as the touchstone for constitutional analysis of race-conscious admissions policies."

What, in detail, had Powell said? That, where race was concerned, public universities could treat people differently only in ways that were "*precisely tailored* to serve a *compelling governmental interest*" [emphasis added]. Remedying social discrimination or training more minority M.D.s did not meet this test. Just one goal did: "The attainment of a diverse student body." The "'nation's future,'" Powell averred, "'depends upon leaders trained through wide exposure' to the ideas and mores of students as diverse as this Nation of many peoples." A university had a fundamental right to select "those students who will contribute the most to the 'robust exchange of ideas.'" For all its importance, though, race or ethnicity "is only one element in a range of factors a university properly may consider in attaining the goal of a heterogeneous student body."*

"Today," Justice O'Connor declared for the Court, "we endorse Justice Powell's view that student body diversity is a compelling state interest that can justify the use of race in university admissions." "Race unfortunately still matters" in America, and "when race-based action is necessary to further a compelling governmental interest, such action does not violate the constitutional guarantee of equal protection so long as the narrow-tailoring requirement is also satisfied." Michigan Law had met this test. The school had concluded that it had a "compelling interest in securing the educational benefits of a diverse student body." But it had not put minorities "on separate admissions tracks" or resorted to "outright racial balancing, which is patently unconstitutional." Instead, it had used race as a "plus" factor while evaluating each candidate "as an individual and not in a way that makes an applicant's race or ethnicity the defining feature of his or her application. The importance of this individualized consideration in the context of a race-conscious admissions program is paramount." In convincing the Court that its sole justification for affirmative action was educational, the school had also succeeded in making its case for accepting a "critical mass" of underrepresented minorities in terms of "the educational benefits that diversity is designed to produce." It had shown such benefits to be "substantial" in terms of enlivening classroom dialogue, breaking down stereotypes, and preparing new lawyers to practice in a heterogeneous society.

"These benefits," wrote O'Connor, "are not theoretical but real." As evidence, she cited the corporate and military briefs that Bollinger and his colleagues had provided and which had clearly

---

*Double quotation marks indicate where Powell was quoting earlier judicial opinions.

influenced her. These briefs emphasized such considerations as diversity in global markets or the need for a heterogeneous officer corps. Bollinger had intended to demonstrate an overriding consensus in favor of affirmative action, and, as the *New York Times* put it, he met the challenge "brilliantly."

O'Connor added another explanation for her opinion, which ventured a long way from classroom dynamics. Stressing the connection between education and personal success, she echoed Powell's emphasis on the role of universities—especially law schools—as (in her words) "the training ground for a large number of our Nation's leaders." So as "to cultivate a set of leaders with legitimacy in the eyes of the citizenry, it is necessary that the path to leadership be visibly open to talented and qualified individuals of every race and ethnicity. All members of our heterogeneous society must have confidence in the openness and integrity of the educational institutions that provide this training." Even more expansively, O'Connor declared: "Effective participation by members of all racial and ethnic groups in the civic life of our Nation is essential if the dream of one Nation, indivisible, is to be realized."

Toward the end of her opinion, though, O'Connor revealed lingering qualms that she shared with Justice Powell. Affirmative action, she cautioned, must proceed in a way that did "not unduly harm members of any racial group." What did "unduly" mean? Certainly Barbara Grutter thought she had been unduly harmed. While a majority of the Court disagreed with Grutter, "race-conscious admissions policies must be limited in time," O'Connor went on, because "racial classifications" of any sort were "potentially . . . dangerous." A *permanent* system of minority preferences *would* violate the Equal Protection Clause. "All governmental use of race must have a logical end point." Since *Bakke,* O'Connor contended, the qualifications of minority applicants had risen. "We expect that 25 years from now, the use of racial preferences will no longer be necessary to further the interest approved today." Constitutional interpretations have changed a good deal over time; but in this instance, rather than looking backward, Justice O'Connor actually looked forward to a rather indefinite day when what the high court had just found constitutional it would be obliged to declare unconstitutional.

✧　　　✧　　　✧

One would have difficulty imagining two opinions more different than Sandra Day O'Connor's for the Court in *Grutter,* and Clarence Thomas's dissent for himself and, partially concurring with him, Justice Scalia. While Rehnquist (writing another dissent that spoke for Thomas, Scalia, Kennedy, and himself) was somewhat oblique, Thomas and Scalia were entirely direct. Both would clearly have been delighted to throw out the *Bakke* precedent.

Thomas opened his dissent by quoting the great black leader Frederick Douglass, who a century and a half before had declared: "If the negro cannot stand on his own legs, let him fall. . . . All I ask is, give him a chance to stand on his own legs! Let him alone! . . . [Y]our interference is doing him positive injury." "Like Douglass," Thomas wrote, "I believe blacks can achieve in every avenue of American life without the meddling of university administrators." "Racial classifications," he insisted, "are *per se* harmful and . . . almost no amount of benefit in the eye of the beholder can justify such classifications."

Thomas lambasted the Court's majority for "responding to a faddish slogan of the cognoscenti." The affirmative action program at Michigan Law, he asserted, amounted to pure and simple "racial discrimination." It violated the Equal Protection Clause now, and would still be violating it 25 years from now. The majority opinion had no grounding whatsoever on "any principle." "The Constitution," Thomas argued, "abhors classifications based on race. . . . Every time the government places citizens on racial registers and makes race relevant to the provision of burdens or benefits, it demeans us all."

Thomas ventured into the disturbing history of university admissions practices: "Columbia, Harvard, and others infamously determined that they had 'too many' Jews, just as today the [Michigan] Law School argues it would have 'too many' whites if it could not discriminate in its admissions process." None of the evidence presented to the Court suggested "that the purported 'beneficiaries' of this racial discrimination prove themselves by performing at (or even near) the same level as those students who receive no preferences." "The Law School tantalizes unprepared students with the promise of a University of Michigan degree and all of the opportunities that it offers. These overmatched students take the bait, only to find that they cannot succeed in the cauldron of competition." Thomas seemed particularly upset that the law school admitted both minority students who would not have gotten in without affirmative action and the few who would have gotten in regardless. "Who can differentiate between those who belong and those who do not? The majority of blacks are admitted to the Law School because of discrimination, and because of this policy all are tarred as undeserving." "When blacks take positions in the highest places of government, industry, or academia, it is an open question today whether their skin color played a part in their advancement. The question itself is the stigma. . . . Asking the question itself unfairly marks those blacks who would succeed without discrimination." One would have a hard time imagining a clearer instance of a judge's autobiography surfacing in his opinion.

In dismissing affirmative action as an unconstitutional fad, Thomas repeatedly attacked its goal as a matter of "classroom aesthetics." He argued that along with other state universities, "Michigan has no compelling interest in having a law school at all, much less an *elite* one." "The Law School should be forced to choose between its classroom aesthetic and its exclusionary admissions system—it cannot have it both ways." If blacks did not do as well as whites on the LSAT, Michigan could knock down one racial barrier by discontinuing its use of the LSAT. Yet, basing its decision on "platitudes rather than principle," Thomas complained, "the Court will not even deign to make the Law School try other methods, . . . preferring instead to grant a 25-year license to violate the Constitution." No evidence existed that performance gaps between racial groups would close within 25 years, "nor is the Court's holding that racial discrimination will be unconstitutional in 25 years made contingent on the gap closing in that time."

✧   ✧   ✧

The majority opinion in the *Grutter* case put affirmative action in university admissions on a stronger footing than ever before. Around the country, civil rights advocates sighed in relief. The University of Michigan quickly went to work to bring its undergraduate admissions policy into compliance with the law. President Bush issued a face-saving statement approving campus diversity.

Following her day in court, Barbara Grutter returned to running her business. She dismisses critical mass as "the functional equivalent of a quota," and believes she overcame discrimination against her as a woman only to lose out to discrimination as a white. In 1999 Jennifer Gratz graduated from the University of Michigan's campus at Dearborn. Two years later, Patrick Hamacher graduated from Michigan State. Lee Bollinger is now the president of Columbia University. In the summer of 2005, Sandra Day O'Connor announced her retirement from the high court at age 75. In a moment of perhaps unguarded candor, she characterized her designated successor, John Roberts, as a "brilliant legal mind, a straight shooter, articulate. . . . He's good in every way, except he's not a woman." (Shortly afterward, when Rehnquist died, Roberts became Chief Justice.)

The Michigan affirmative action cases exemplify the sort of legal confrontation in which both sides seem to be right—not an uncommon situation faced by the high court. Affirmative action has given special opportunities to thousands of minority students, many of them (like the Phi Beta Kappa Michigan undergraduate) highly qualified. By acknowledging that in the interest of a greater benefit it sought only to avoid *undue* harm, though, the majority opinion in *Grutter* implicitly acknowledged that affirmative action does come with a price that someone (white, Asian American) must pay. Academic credentials—one's degree and where one takes it—are, unfortunately, today's American equivalent of royal pedigrees, and only so many seats exist at selective institutions. The *Grutter* decision may have resolved the issue of affirmative action for a generation, but Justice O'Connor's unease with her opinion was a reminder that both society and constitutional interpretations change over time. As they tried to come to terms with this, both O'Connor and Thomas attempted to project from the present 25 years into the future. They simply saw different futures.

12

Reporting for Duty!

John Kerry, George W. Bush, Iraq, and the War on Terror

Physical vigor and a love of the great outdoors having become virtual prerequisites for the modern presidency, the Grand Canyon was a brilliantly conceived place for John Kerry to lay out his objections to President George W. Bush's environmental policies. The timing was right, too—late July, 2004, just after the Democratic convention had anointed the junior senator from Massachusetts as the only man likely to defeat the president that November. Fresh from an invigorating hike, standing before a bank of reporters with the canyon at his back and condors soaring overhead, Kerry exuded confidence and optimism. Though often short-tempered with the press, he showed no annoyance as a reporter ignored the subject of the environment and asked him a question about foreign policy. Knowing what he knew now, the reporter asked, would Kerry still have voted back in November, 2002 to give Bush the go-ahead to wage war in Iraq? "Yes," Kerry replied, adding: "I believe it was the right authority for the president to have."

Some two thousand miles to the east, at President Bush's campaign headquarters in Arlington, Virginia, Kerry's interview in Arizona was taped and carefully filed. This was the situation room, the war room, where Bush's political guru Karl Rove reigned supreme as the GOP field marshal. A model of military precision, Rove's political apparatus had prided itself on identifying the weaknesses of the president's opponents during the Democratic primaries. Now Senator Kerry was their sole target. Every move he made, every word he uttered, was being scrutinized for stumbles and slips of the tongue that they could exploit. This slip, Rove's operatives suspected, might prove to be the equivalent of a headlong dive from the rim of the Grand Canyon: the press quickly depicted Kerry's statement as confirming that Bush had had no other choice but to go to war in Iraq. Kerry's current aggressively critical posture on Bush's Iraq policies could now be portrayed as indecisive and opportunistic—crippling charges in an election where the electorate was vividly portrayed in primary colors, as living in "red" or "blue" states, Republican or Democratic. At the Grand Canyon, Kerry blithely concluded his interview, with no effort to take back or to explain his remark, and apparently no clue that he had made a mistake. In more normal times it would not have mattered so much. But these were not normal times, nor was this a routine election. John Kerry had assumed the Herculean task of persuading the American people to vote out an incumbent president in wartime. This had never happened before, and Kerry too would fail. Why and how did he fail? Or, more positively, what did it mean that he came so close to succeeding?

✧   ✧   ✧

John Kerry and George W. Bush shared some rather surprising similarities in terms of their background and education. Both were privileged members of what passes in America for an aristocracy. Bush's father, George H.W. Bush, was the nation's forty-first president, his paternal grandfather was the powerful Connecticut Senator Prescott Bush, and the family had extensive holdings in oil and real estate. Kerry's family tree included such names as Winthrop and Forbes on his mother's side, while his wife, Teresa, was the widow of Pennsylvania Senator John Heinz and heiress to one of the greatest fortunes in America. Both men went to elite prep schools (Kerry to St. Paul's, Bush to Philips Andover). They even overlapped as college students at Yale, where each was tapped for membership in the secretive Skull and Bones society, perhaps the country's most exclusive fraternity.

But they never wailed the Whiffenpoof song together at the tables down at Morey's, pledging eternal brotherhood with locked arms and lifted kegs. "He was two years behind me at Yale," Kerry said tersely of Bush during the campaign, "and I knew him, and he's still the same guy." Bush, for his part, could not dredge up any memory of Kerry at all.

Their separate paths at Yale were generally seen as those of the gregarious fraternity boy/cheerleader/campus cut-up (Bush) and the sober-sided loner whose diversions ran to flying lessons, sailing, and skiing (Kerry). Thirty years later, Bush disarmingly joked in a Yale commencement speech that all the C students in the audience should take heart because one of their number had become president; Kerry, for his part, was said to be worried that voters would learn he spoke fluent French.

By that time, Bush had de-classed himself: the New England Brahmin had become a cowboy, complete with drawl, boots, swagger, and a 1500-acre ranch in central Texas. Even more important, the frat-party hellraiser, binge drinker, and occasional drunk driver had gone on the wagon and found God as a born-again Christian. In the mid-1980s he sold out his share of a failing oil business and became part-owner of a professional baseball team, the Texas Rangers, gratifying his love of the game and confirming his image as a regular guy. His late turn to electoral politics as the surprise winner of the Texas governor's office in 1994 was viewed by political sophisticates in Washington as a fluke, like an infield fly. However, Bush soon proved to have not just a gift for campaigning but, once in the governor's office, an unanticipated degree of competence.

Even so, Bush was a distinct underdog in the 2000 presidential race against President Bill Clinton's vice president Al Gore. He won, but was severely hobbled during the first nine months of his term by the conditions of his victory—Gore's nearly 544,000 popular vote margin had been negated by Florida's electoral votes being awarded to Bush in a hotly disputed Supreme Court decision. Derided as an accidental president elected by only 48 percent of the votes cast, Bush faltered often during the first nine months of his term.

His fortunes—and, many said, his character—changed abruptly with the worst disaster ever perpetrated by an enemy on American soil, surpassing even Pearl Harbor: the terrorist attacks of September 11, 2001. Bush's response to 9/11 was visceral, emotional, and effective (after some initial missteps). It inspired all but the few Americans who met at the extreme fringe—leftists who said the United States must have behaved very badly in the world community to have incurred such hatred, and religious right-wingers who said the country was being punished for its sins against God. The president's vigorous prosecution of the war on the home base in Afghanistan of the al Qaeda terrorists, who were responsible for 9/11, won overwhelming popular support—including that of John Kerry and the great majority of his fellow Democrats in Congress.

By the middle of 2003, when the 2004 presidential campaign was already under way, George W. Bush had attacked Iraq. Saddam Hussein had remained a festering sore for the United States since his 1991 defeat at the hands of the first President Bush's American-led coalition in the Gulf War, the consequence of Iraq's attempted annexation of Kuwait. George Bush justified this new war as a preventive attack against terrorism, which, he claimed, could be dangerously empowered by Saddam's programs to produce weapons of mass destruction (WMDs). The war was initially a striking success: Iraq was conquered and Saddam chased into hiding in a matter of weeks in February and March, 2003. But by mid-year it had become clear that the Administration had misjudged the ferocity of die-hard Saddam supporters and Islamic radicals, as well as the havoc they would wreak. While the United States remained free from further attacks, arguably due in part to Bush's homeland security legislation, terrorism increased around the world. Iraq became a honey-pot for terrorists from throughout the Middle East, and even from Europe. When John Kerry locked up the votes needed in March, 2004, to become the Democratic nominee for president, close to half of the electorate agreed that George Bush had bungled the war in Iraq. Kerry's presumed strategy was obvious: the election would be a referendum on whether the president should be given another four years to fix the mess in Iraq. It was up to Kerry to explain why and how he would do a better job of thwarting terrorism and dealing with Iraq than the incumbent.

Or so it seemed afterward. In fact, mainstream Democrats initially tried to finesse the war issue, for fear of appearing unpatriotic and because of deep divisions within the party on how to react to Saddam. They knew that their real strength lay with the issue of the economy. Democrats had presented themselves, since FDR won in 1932, as the party of bread-and-butter issues, concerned with such practical problems of everyday life as jobs, health care, and education. And, especially since the 1960s, with civil rights. Theirs was said to be the "mommy party," nurturing—and often nagging. Fractious and splintered into opposing interest groups, the numerically superior Democrats could turn suicidal during presidential elections—most notably in 1968 when their candidate, President Lyndon Johnson's vice president Hubert Humphrey, lost the left wing of the party by refusing to condemn outright Johnson's conduct of the war in Vietnam.

During the 2004 primaries, Kerry managed to fight off a similar challenge by Vermont's Governor Howard Dean by claiming virtual agreement with President Bush's Iraq policies, though questioning their original justification and current implementation. Kerry saw the difficulty of explaining his complicated position on the war—he could have voted to let the United Nations continue its dithering over sanctions for Iraq, but chose instead to vote to strengthen the president's hand, an entirely defensible move.

He failed at first to make that case for himself, apparently hoping that the baneful effects of the war on Bush's candidacy would be self-evident. Instead, Kerry's initial focus, once he became the Democratic nominee, was on the economy: Kerry noted repeatedly that Bush was the first president since Herbert Hoover to preside over an economic decline that included a net job loss and a stock market dive.

The charge was demonstrably true and the tactic seemed sound. Incumbent presidents who had been defeated in part for presiding over weak economies included Hoover in 1932, Gerald Ford in 1976, Jimmy Carter in 1980, and George H. W. Bush in 1992. But as the daily headlines from Iraq and the Middle East suggested, the overriding issue in 2004 was the war, not the economy. Campaign strategists on both sides knew that wars in the past had destroyed incumbent presidents: Woodrow Wilson never fully regained his credibility after breaking his promise to keep America out of the First World War. Harry Truman's chances for a second full term went glimmering as the Korean War dragged on and after his dismissal of Douglas MacArthur. So too did Lyndon Johnson's in 1968, when he saw that he would lose because of the Vietnam War and declined to stand for a second full term. Richard Nixon's Watergate disaster was joined at the hip with his Vietnam policy. And Jimmy Carter lost to Ronald Reagan in 1980 not only because of a weak economy but because he couldn't free the American embassy hostages in

Iran—an early battle in what George Bush now argued was a continuing war on terrorism coming out of the Middle East.

Bush was clearly vulnerable on both fronts, the war and the economy. At least half of the electorate thought the country was "headed in the wrong direction," according to several polls. The war, however, posed a problem for Kerry as an issue: since the mid-1970s, after Vietnam, the GOP had successfully portrayed Democrats as national security weaklings, cautious, indecisive, and unassertive. Kerry hoped to counter this image by presenting himself as tested in battle, and his party as no less fervently patriotic than the GOP.

✧   ✧   ✧

John Kerry offered George W. Bush a formidable challenge. Not least important, he *looked* presidential. Six feet four inches tall, lean, and tanned from sailing and skiing, Kerry towered over most of his colleagues, including Bush. His full head of carefully coiffed gray hair seemed to add an inch or two to his height, and his long, creased face suggested resolute determination. His admirers frequently called attention to Kerry's similarity in appearance—and, it was suggested, in character—to Abraham Lincoln, another gangling, craggy American who came on the scene when the nation most needed a savior.

Kerry's record of public service was far longer than Bush's. After losing an early bid for a U. S. congressional seat in 1972, he had earned a law degree at Boston College and an appointment as prosecutor for the district attorney's office in Middlesex County, which includes Boston and Cambridge, from 1976 to 1979. Following several years of private practice, he won his first election as lieutenant governor of Massachusetts, serving from 1983 to 1985, when he was elected to the U. S. Senate. There he had become a prominent figure, especially for his work on the Foreign Relations Committee. To be sure, Kerry's legislative accomplishments were few, and most Americans, if asked to name a senator from Massachusetts, would have reflexively said, "Ted Kennedy, of course."

But Kerry had shown initiative and political courage in taking on the problem of missing American soldiers—those who, it was said, were still being held in Vietnamese prison camps, or hundreds of others missing in action and presumed dead, whose remains the United States wanted found and returned home for proper burial. Kerry and Republican Senator John McCain pursued and eventually resolved most of the POW/MIA issues with the Vietnamese, which allowed President Clinton to normalize ties with the nation's former enemy more than two decades after the war there had ended.

Kerry also brought to his campaign an inspiring story of personal heroism, both physical and moral, in the eyes of his admirers. His achievement with McCain in cutting the Gordian knot of the unaccounted-for American soldiers in Vietnam derived in part from his and McCain's roles there as fighting men. Additionally, Kerry's credentials with the communist government of Vietnam were enhanced by his testimony before Congress in 1971 against further American participation in the war, which he had by then condemned as immoral.

Kerry's managers knew that being liked by communists was not the best job recommendation; they hoped to place greater stress on their man's courage in battle than on his later opposition to the war. They presented him as a patriot who had volunteered for dangerous duty in a war that most of his social peers had done their best to avoid, including many now in prominent Administration posts such as Vice President Dick Cheney, and even President Bush himself. Kerry had performed nobly under fire, winning a Bronze Star "for heroic achievement" and the even more meritorious Silver Star "for conspicuous gallantry and intrepidity in action." And he had received three Purple Hearts for wounds suffered in action. Only five presidents in the twentieth century had been under fire as warriors: William McKinley,

Theodore Roosevelt, Harry Truman, George H. W. Bush, and John Fitzgerald Kennedy, whose initials Kerry pointedly shared. By means of his service and his association with these brave predecessors, Kerry sought to enhance his appeal with an electorate that respects personal courage. When he accepted the Democratic convention's nomination as candidate for the presidency, he did so as a good soldier fulfilling his obligation: he saluted smartly and declared that he was "Reporting for duty!"

The candidate was said to be modestly reticent, in the best New England tradition, about bringing up his war record. Philip Gourevitch, writing for the June 7, 2004 issue of the resolutely anti-Bush *New Yorker,* explained that few voters knew that Kerry had won his first medal for saving a comrade's life at risk to his own—not until "that man, a lifelong Republican named Jim Rassman," turned the Iowa primary race around "by describing how Kerry, wounded and under fire, pulled him, hand over hand, from the water after he was blown off another American boat." Gourevitch also noted that Kerry "resists speaking publicly" about the occasion that led to his Silver Star; it was left to his crewmates to describe how their leader turned directly into a rocket attack from the riverbank, beached the boat, and chased down and killed the enemy soldier who was firing on them. Kerry's commanding officer joked as he recommended him for the Silver Star that sailors were not supposed to jump ship during combat, and, according to Gourevitch, "wasn't sure whether he shouldn't court-martial him instead."

In fact, Kerry had called attention to his wartime service from the beginning of his public career, and it was the heart of a book by historian Douglas Brinkley called *Tour of Duty: John Kerry and the Vietnam War,* published in January, 2004. One newspaper reviewer naively (or ingenuously) suggested that Brinkley's book "was never intended as a political biography," even as he noted that the final chapter described the launching of Kerry's campaign for the Democratic nomination in

September, 2003—using as a backdrop the USS *Yorktown* in Charleston, South Carolina, complete with a military band playing "Anchors Aweigh" and Kerry's old shipmates in attendance. But at least the message of the setting was clear to the reviewer: "While George W. Bush was serving in the Texas Air National Guard, the future Massachusetts senator was winning a Silver Star for combat heroism as a young Navy lieutenant in Vietnam, along with a Bronze Star and three Purple Hearts." Oddly, the reviewer failed, like many, to call attention to the obvious model for the Kerry book: Robert J. Donovan's 1961 best-seller about the heroic adventures of another young naval officer, *PT 109: John F. Kennedy in World War II.*

Brinkley's book was based on journals kept by Kerry while he was doing his four-month tour in Vietnam, on letters he sent to family members which they kept, and on interviews that Brinkley conducted with men who served with Kerry. It was mostly in the journals that Kerry revealed his misgivings about the war in Vietnam, and about past wars: "Here's a young man, in his 20s," Brinkley told an interviewer, "talking about [World War I poets] Wilfred Owen, Siegfried Sassoon, Rupert Brooke and Robert Graves, whom he particularly loved. He had read all of Hemingway and could quote from T.S. Eliot's 'The Wasteland.' He was very aware of the so-called Lost Generation literature of World War I, and was infatuated with the anti-war soldier poets."

Kerry comes across in Brinkley's book as a thoughtful young man with a sense of ironic displacement, a certain gift for descriptive narrative, and a capacity for compassion. In one journal entry he described seeing a man running from what appeared to be a deserted village. A group of Vietnamese then emerged from the village, old men, women, and children, all sick and hungry. Kerry ignored radio instructions to leave the villagers where they were and return to the combat mission, instead taking them to an American base to get treatment and food. Recollecting the incident to Brinkley, he said that "for an afternoon it felt good to really be helping the Vietnamese instead of destroying their villages."

Kerry's published journals echoed the reminiscences of Daniel Ellsberg, another young intellectual and adventurer who went to Vietnam and came back to argue that American involvement there was a disaster. Testifying before the Senate Foreign Relations Committee in 1971 as a leader of the Vietnam Veterans Against the War, Kerry said that "many very highly decorated veterans" admitted that "war crimes" had been committed in Vietnam: Southeast Asia." They had occurred not as rare exceptions to the norm but "on a day-to-day basis with the full awareness of officers at all levels of command." To hear these veterans' stories, he said, was to understand "the absolute horror of what this country, in a sense, made them do": "At times they had personally raped, cut off ears, cut off heads, taped wires from portable telephones to human genitals and turned up the power, cut off limbs, blown up bodies, randomly shot at civilians, razed villages in a fashion reminiscent of Genghis Khan, shot cattle and dogs for fun, poisoned food stocks, and generally ravaged the countryside of South Vietnam in addition to the normal ravage of war and the normal and very particular ravaging which is done by the applied bombing power of this country."

A few days after his Senate testimony, Kerry said on *Meet the Press* that he had "committed the same kind of atrocities as thousands of other soldiers have committed in that I took part in shootings in free fire zones. I conducted harassment and interdiction fire. I used .50-calibre machine guns, which we were granted and ordered to use, which were our only weapon against people. I took part in search and destroy missions, in the burning of villages. All of this is contrary to the laws of warfare, all of this is contrary to the Geneva Conventions and all of this is ordered as a matter of written established policy by the government of the United States from the top down. And I believe that the men who designed these, the men who designed the free fire zone, the men who ordered us, the men who signed off the air raid strike areas, I think these men, by the letter of the law . . . are war criminals."

Like Ellsberg, Kerry won the attention of President Nixon. In a taped conversation with H. R. Haldeman, his chief of staff, and Henry Kissinger, his national security adviser, Nixon fretted that Kerry was turning into a "real star." He wasn't one of those "bearded weirdos" protesting the war but "extremely effective." Nixon soon assigned an underling to find some "dirt" on Kerry in order to discredit him, plaintively suggesting, "He is sort of a phony, isn't he?"

✦   ✦   ✦

War metaphors as well as war stories dominated the 2004 campaign from beginning to end. As one journalist noted after the election, it was like fighting in the trenches of World War I: "muddy and gassy, with neither side able to secure much ground and keep it." But a medieval metaphor might be more to the point: Bush was defending his well-provisioned castle with experienced, devoted troops, most of whom had been with him since his days as governor of Texas. Kerry as a senator had had no need or occasion to assemble a force equivalent to Bush's; he was besieging this fortress with a hastily assembled army of true believers and mercenaries, many of them recruits from the staffs of his Democratic primary opponents or Bill Clinton's former operatives.

As his apparent capture of the war issue suggested, Kerry did have the aggressor's advantage of seizing the initiative. It's generally the Republicans who claim warfare and foreign policy as their areas of expertise, as seen in this book's chapter on Henry Cabot Lodge's dismantling of what he regarded as Woodrow Wilson's woolly-minded hopes for a League of Nations. Especially since Vietnam, the GOP has positioned itself as the "daddy party," complementing the nurturing "mommy party" of the Democrats;

its patriarchal premise is that respect and fear are more effective than diplomacy and cooperation in dealing with other nations. In the 2000 campaign, it is true, George W. Bush had been a Republican with zero experience in foreign policy. But there were no critical foreign policy issues that year, or none regarded as critical. He won, instead, as the candidate of "compassionate conservatism" and "moral values," buoyed by evangelical Christians and the lingering widespread disgust left by former President Clinton's Monica Lewinsky affair. By 2004, Bush had a four-year record in foreign policy. He was now a wartime president, and he intended to capitalize on his role as commander-in-chief.

The Bush camp's first task was to neutralize the war credentials of the president's opponent. Its most effective weapon was Kerry's testimony opposing the Vietnam War, which had infuriated as many as it had inspired at the time. There was ample precedent for successful GOP attacks on men, Republicans or Democrats, who were more famous for their wartime sacrifices than was John Kerry. Arizona Senator John McCain, the son of an admiral and a Navy fighter pilot, was held as a POW in Vietnam for five and a half years. Despite being tortured and starved, he turned down chances to be repatriated ahead of his comrades. When McCain ran against George W. Bush for the presidential nomination in 2000, he was smeared as mentally unstable—from his imprisonment, no less!—and rumored to be the father of an unacknowledged black baby. That same year the Democratic senator from Georgia, Max Cleland, a Silver Star winner and a triple amputee from a grenade in Vietnam, was chided by his Republican opponent for lack of patriotism. As for his wounds, it was his own clumsy fault that he had been blown up. Cleland lost his race for reelection.

On March 8, 2004—just a few days after Kerry's "Super Tuesday" sweep of the primaries in California, Connecticut, Georgia, Maryland, Massachusetts, New York, Ohio and Rhode Island, as well as the Minnesota caucuses—a group calling itself the Swift Boat Veterans for Truth emerged with startling charges against Senator Kerry. If taken at their word, these veterans had apparently managed to dig up the dirt that Nixon never found and to prove that Kerry indeed was a "phony." They claimed Kerry had lied about his record, that he had shot a wounded and defenseless enemy soldier in the back, that one of his Purple Hearts was for a self-inflicted wound. Kerry thought the motive behind the attacks was so transparent—one major source of funding for the group was a Republican businessman from Texas—that he refused to dignify them with denials.

But Kerry had failed to gauge the lingering resentment among many veterans, not limited to those who had been in Vietnam, for his 1971 protests against the war, particularly for his gesture of publicly throwing away some of the ribbons he had won. The charges continued to swirl for months, at first an annoying distraction from the real issues but finally perceived, correctly, as a dangerous assault on Kerry's character. He took until August to address the allegations, charging that Veterans for Truth was obviously a front group for President Bush: "Of course," he said, "the president keeps telling people he would never question my service to our country. Instead, he watches as a Republican-funded attack group does just that. Well, if he wants to have a debate about our service in Vietnam, here is my answer: Bring it on."

The charges against Kerry were eventually dismissed (though not by everyone) as unfounded. Despite Kerry's assertion that Bush's team was behind Veterans for Truth, no smoking gun emerged to support him. Kerry's own team was less clever. In a pathetically clumsy riposte, it encouraged the airing in early September of a television news special that seemed to confirm old charges concerning President Bush's Texas National Guard service. The issue turned around the question of how assiduous Bush had been in fulfilling his obligation to the Guard in the 1960s and 1970s, and whether he had won his assignment through political pull in order to avoid being sent to Vietnam. It never caught fire in 2000, in part because Bush's appeal consisted largely in his being an average guy who could be engagingly frank about himself—"I've got a name and a cute smile." It was also impolitic to attack the National Guard and, by extension, the various reserve units, as havens for shirkers in the past, particularly when so many of them were now serving in Iraq.

There was a brief flurry of alarm in the Bush camp when the long-time CBS anchorman Dan Rather reported finding new documents that confirmed the old charges of favoritism and malingering on the part of young George Bush—and then a great sigh of relief when it turned out the documents were forged. The special's producers were deservedly fired (Rather shortly afterward "retired") as attention turned away from Bush's record toward the liberal bias supposedly shown by CBS and the other mainstream media. Forgotten in the tumult was the far more damaging, and equally spurious, attack on John Kerry's war record. If chess is the board game for war, then Bush had rescued a pawn while Kerry had lost his queen. His single greatest advantage over President Bush had been neutralized.

✦   ✦   ✦

For all the millions spent by the Bush and Kerry camps, during what would turn out to be the most expensive campaign in history, most of their supporters had made up their minds long before the nominating conventions. As in many close elections, though, a significant fraction of the electorate remained truly undecided until late in the game. John Kerry still retained two advantages over George Bush that should have helped him win over most of this group. On the personal level, he was generally regarded as a more thoughtful and articulate man—in a word, smarter—and likely to outshine the president in their three scheduled debates. And insofar as the issues were concerned, President Bush was stuck with defending his conduct of an increasingly controversial war in Iraq. Yet Kerry failed to convince the electorate that he should replace the president in office.

What went wrong? For one thing, the product was over-marketed: the more exposure Kerry had, the less in evidence his superior qualities seemed to be. The Democrats tried to show not only that George Bush had made mistakes, but that he was mentally lazy and impervious to ideas and facts that didn't suit him. He was a limited though (to many) likeable man who happened to have a peculiar gift as a campaigner and the power of incumbency. Kerry was represented as a brighter, more imaginative alternative to the president, but the margin of difference turned out to be less than it appeared.

Part of the problem was that those who deal with words for a living, including journalists and commentators, often confuse fluency with intelligence and lack of fluency with stupidity. These observers assumed that most thinking voters would share their scorn for a man whose malapropisms without question made him an easy target:

"I'm looking forward to a good night's sleep on the soil of a friend." On visiting Denmark, Washington, D.C., June 29, 2005.

"I was going to say he's a piece of work, but that might not translate too well. Is that all right, if I call you a 'piece of work'?" To the prime minister of Luxembourg, Washington, D.C., June 20, 2005.

"And the second way to defeat the terrorists is to spread freedom. You see, the best way to defeat a society that is—doesn't have hope, a society where people become so angry they're willing to become suiciders, is to spread freedom, is to spread democracy." Washington, D.C., June 8, 2005.

"It seemed like to me they based some of their decisions on the word of—and the allegations—by people who were held in detention, people who hate America, people that had been trained in some instances to disassemble—that means not tell the truth." On an Amnesty International report on prisoner abuse at Guantanamo Bay, Washington, D.C., May 31, 2005.

"See, in my line of work you got to keep repeating things over and over and over again for the truth to sink in, to kind of catapult the propaganda." Greece, N.Y., May 24, 2005.

But many voters discounted Bush's fractured grammar and syntax, some even finding it endearing, another proof that he was one of them. They were not even upset with his response to a press conference question: what mistakes, the reporter asked, did Bush think he had made since 9/11? The president pondered for a long moment, then admitted that he couldn't think of any. When Bush's ratings increased instead of falling after that remark, Kerry shook his head in wonder and muttered to an aide, "I can't believe I'm losing to this idiot."

Kerry's remark showed how little he understood Bush's shrewdness. The reporter's question was a snare, as in "when did you stop beating your wife?" Only a fool would have responded seriously, though a subtler intelligence might have offered up a few trivial examples to prove his humility.

Kerry was undoubtedly the more articulate of the two candidates, but the intellectual superiority his supporters claimed was more assumed than demonstrated. After the election it was learned that Kerry's cumulative grade-point average at Yale was one point below Bush's 77—they were both "gentleman C" students. Kerry could talk at length about issues from health care to foreign policy, whereas Bush preferred to use punchy one-liners. But unlike Bush, Kerry often rambled at excruciating length in what his frustrated staff called "Senate-speak." He seemed not to know, or care, that his listeners' eyes often glazed over.

Moreover, Kerry failed to provide any clear sense of what path he thought the country should take under his leadership. This problem, to be sure, had bedeviled Democrats seeking the presidency since Lyndon Johnson, nearly all of whom had trouble projecting what their party stood for in the larger sense—even so gifted a politician as Bill Clinton had succeeded substantially by co-opting Republican programs for reforming welfare and passing international trade legislation. By the time Kerry did finally develop a unifying campaign theme, in September, it was simply that Bush lacked judgment. But he failed to develop that charge with a coherent critique of the area in which Bush was most vulnerable, the Iraq war. Even as scandals broke about the mistreatment of Iraqi prisoners by American soldiers, Kerry offered no dramatic policy alternative to Bush's. He merely asked the voters to trust that he would somehow win over allied support, even from the uncooperative French and Germans, that would allow the country to solve its foreign policy difficulties.

Kerry also suffered by comparison with Bush in terms of personal relations, both on the campaign trail and off. Bush liked campaigning, liked pressing the flesh, especially the friendly flesh of the carefully-screened audiences with which his handlers surrounded him. He did less well in formally structured situations like the televised debates with the senator; his grimaces and grins and head-shaking put many viewers off, while Kerry maintained a polite and dignified stance. Kerry also benefited from having to observe the time constraints for his answers. He seemed presidential, as some other Democratic candidates during the primaries—Howard Dean or Dennis Kucinich or Al Sharpton— might not have in the same setting.

But Kerry could be emotionally tone-deaf, even obtuse. He hurt himself badly with his response to a debate question concerning the candidates' attitudes on homosexuality: was it an inherited condition or a matter of choice? Bush simply said he didn't know, the position of most people. Kerry unctuously said we were "all God's children," adding that "if you were to talk to Dick Cheney's daughter, who is a lesbian, she would tell you that she's being who she was, she's being who she was born as."

Even the Mafia usually avoids hits on its targets' family members. Kerry came across as more calculating than humane, a wily competitor chalking up a debate point. Voters of both parties reacted with disgust. Not one of the many commentators who had mocked Bush for failing to recall a mistake seems to have paired these two instances and come up with the obvious conclusion: displaying a certain amount of practical intelligence,

Bush had responded to a potentially dangerous question with apparent honesty and common sense. Kerry's response, by contrast, seemed contrived* and was jarringly clumsy.

Kerry also stumbled during the campaign on more substantive issues of legislation and public policy. Bush had asked Congress in 2003 to authorize an additional $87 billion to pay for the war in Iraq, arguing that to vote against it was to deny American troops the support they needed. Among the bill's provisions was a $300 million request by the Pentagon to buy body armor for all troops in Iraq, as well as additional combat pay and health benefits for reservists called to active duty. The Bush administration also piggy-backed a tax-cut provision onto the bill, reasoning that most Democrats would swallow hard and vote for it anyway.

Kerry said he voted against the bill because of the tax cuts, not because he wanted to deny troops the protection they needed. The Administration could have submitted the bill, minus the tax cut provisions, that Democrats said they would support. When it declined to do so, Kerry and another Democratic senator cosponsored a substitute measure, which would have provided the requested money and temporarily reversed the tax cuts for those making more than $400,000 per year. It was defeated, along party lines, 57–42. When Bush's bill passed, Republicans had Kerry on record as voting against body armor for troops in danger.

Kerry's original vote and his reasoning were both defensible. But when asked at a small gathering in West Virginia why he wanted to deny money for the troops, he said, "I actually did vote for the $87 billion, before I voted against it." His futile efforts to explain the context of his decision tangled him in knots for the rest of the campaign. The message to the electorate

---

*After the election, one of the senator's senior campaign aides assured John Broesamle that Kerry's slip was an unrehearsed, spontaneous blunder.

seemed to confirm the GOP charges that Kerry didn't know his own mind on key issues, going all the way back to his 1991 vote against authorizing the first President Bush to force Saddam out of Kuwait in the first Gulf War. Kerry was tagged with being indecisive: he was a "flip-flopper," a "waffler." The Bush campaign quickly revised an existing ad to include Kerry's $87 billion statement, calling it "Troops-Fog." A Kerry spokesman denounced the ad as misleading and said what Kerry should have said when he was first questioned about the vote: "John Kerry opposed a red inked, blank check on Bush's failed Iraq policy." Too late: a Bush aide later called this the "iconic moment" of the campaign; "it framed the race the way we wanted it framed," and Kerry "did it for us."

✧　　✧　　✧

"Framing" was a concept that had been defined by a liberal academic from Berkeley, George Lakoff, not by George Bush's opportunistic advisers. It was part of Lakoff's larger argument in a book he called *Moral Politics,* based on the old father/mother characterizations of the two main parties. The conservatives, according to this formulation, present themselves within the structure—the frame—of discipline, hard work, and goal setting. They teach their children that the virtuous are rewarded, the lazy are punished. Right and wrong are difficult to achieve and to avoid, but they are clear and unambiguous. For liberals, the key concept is caring; if children are loved unconditionally, nurtured more than they are admonished, they become open and generous citizens who want to help others and improve their world.

Over the past twenty-five years, Lakoff said in an interview in October, 2004, the Republicans had become more effective than the Democrats in framing their arguments. "Tax relief," for example, began to be pitched by the White House early in Bush's first term. The press adopted the phrase uncritically, "as if it were a neutral term, which it is not. First, you have the frame for 'relief.'" Relief means there must be an affliction. Whoever administers relief is a hero, and whoever resists the hero's ministrations is a villain.

The proper liberal response, Lakoff says, is ignored by Democrats who too easily sign on to the idea of "relief." They should be responding that taxes are the dues we all pay to maintain a country with a vast infrastructure of highways, communications, power systems, public education, health, and basic research, an infrastructure that wealthy Americans use more than anyone else and that they should be willing to support accordingly.

The Iraq war was a far more contentious issue than taxes, one presumably less easy and more essential for either candidate to "frame." In Kerry's case, he stated his position clearly in a December, 2003 speech to the Council on Foreign Relations: "Simply put," he argued, "the Bush Administration has pursued the most arrogant, inept, reckless, and ideological foreign policy in modern history. In the wake of the September 11th terrorist attacks, the world rallied to the common cause of fighting terrorism. But President Bush has squandered that historic moment. . . . He rushed into battle—and he went almost alone. . . . I believed a year ago and I believe now that we had to hold Saddam Hussein accountable and that we needed to lead in that effort. But this Administration did it in the worst possible way: without the United Nations, without our allies, without a plan to win the peace. So we are left asking: How is it possible to liberate a country, depose a ruthless dictator who at least in the past had weapons of mass destruction, and convert a preordained success into a diplomatic fiasco? How is it possible to do what the Bush Administration has done in Iraq: win a great military victory yet make America weaker?"

Kerry's key charge, that Bush had shown bad judgment in his handling of the war, was one that appealed to approximately half of the electorate. Most Americans had accepted the administration's assurance that Saddam was hiding WMDs—weapons of mass destruction. Given Saddam's history, they agreed with Bush that such weapons in Saddam's hands did mean great and imminent danger for the region, and for the United States itself. But those weapons were never discovered—it remains unclear whether Saddam destroyed or hid them, or even whether they ever existed. The American-led invasion, the Democrats said, was thus based on a misconception, compounded by a mistake in judgment. Either that or on a deliberate effort by the Administration to justify an invasion that it had already determined to undertake.

Kerry undercut that argument by asserting in August, at the Grand Canyon photo op, that he would have supported Bush even knowing that no WMDs would be found, because the president needed the leverage such support would give him when dealing with allies abroad.

If Kerry's frame was fuzzy, Bush's was clear and simple—so easy to comprehend that a professional wrestler warming up the crowd at a rally in Florida a week before the election was able to sum it up with a pointed question: "If your babies were left all alone in the dead of night, who would you rather have setting there on the porch—John Kerry and his snowboard or George W. with his shotgun?" The four corners of Bush's frame were vividly illustrated by the banner over the platform where he spoke: "STRENGTH! LEADERSHIP! CHARACTER! INTEGRITY!"

Fear of the unknown and security with the known was the key to Bush's campaign. In one ad dangerous wolves skulked across the screen as a deep voice intoned, "In an increasingly dangerous world. . . . Even after the first terrorist attack on America . . . John Kerry and the liberals in Congress voted to slash America's intelligence operations. By six billion dollars. . . . Cuts so deep they would have weakened America's defenses. And weakness attracts those who are waiting to do America harm."

The Bush frame held together better than Kerry's, for reasons explained and anticipated in Stephen Wayne's 2001 study, *The*

Road to the White House 2000: The Politics of Presidential Elections. Although Wayne was writing about Al Gore, not Kerry, two of his observations are helpful in comparing Kerry and Bush. The first is that voters look for two sets of traits in their presidential candidates: "Traits such as inner strength, decisiveness, competence, and experience are considered essential for the office, and others such as empathy, sincerity, credibility, and integrity are viewed as necessary for the individual." The final vote suggests that Bush seemed to a majority of voters to personify more of these qualities, both executive and personal, than did Kerry.

Wayne also provides some insights into the 1948 campaign of Bush's embattled predecessor, Harry Truman, who was at risk of losing his bid for election. Although Democrats would challenge the association, Harry Truman, of all Bush's recent predecessors in office, is the one he most resembles as a self-described no-nonsense, plain-speaking man of the people. Truman, taking the initiative, "whistle-stopped the length and breadth of the United States," speaking from train cabooses in one eight-week period to some six million people. His opponent, like John Kerry a former prosecutor with a long record in public office, was the New York State Governor Thomas E. Dewey. A stiff and reserved man who regarded the president with disdain, Dewey was noted mostly for "sonorous speeches" that "contrasted sharply and unfavorably" with Truman's hard-hitting attacks. Also like Senator Kerry, Dewey "was promising new leadership but providing few particulars." Despite the predictions of most columnists and newspapers, Truman defeated Dewey.

Bush's victory over Kerry was clear but narrow. For all Kerry's difficulties, the Democrats had, after all, mounted a remarkable effort in 2004, mobilizing eight million more voters than they had four years earlier. Karl Rove, however, had mobilized eleven million more for the GOP. This constituted the margin of victory, 2.5 percent of the popular vote, 35 electoral votes. If 60,000 voters in Ohio had gone Democratic, their man would have won.

The Democrats compared earlier Republican victories to Bush's, unfavorably: Ronald Reagan in 1984 had an 18 percent popular vote margin and 512 electoral votes. Even Richard Nixon had won in 1972 with a popular vote margin of 23 percent and 503 electoral votes. Bush's victory was yet another infield fly, a lucky fluke. Disgusted Kerry partisans threw up their hands, saying the election had shown that "wrong and strong beats bright and right." More objectively, a Democratic polltaker said that Bush had "bet the farm on a particular theory of war," while "voters never could get a sense of what Kerry believed."

✧   ✧   ✧

John Kerry complained in an interview just before the election that the Republicans suffered from a "bankruptcy of ideas." "They don't have a real economic plan, except for the tax cut. They don't have a real health-care plan. They don't have a plan for education, except the broken promise of No Child Left Behind. So, therefore, what do they do? They attack, they attack, they attack, they attack."

Kerry would have been well advised to remember the old Greek proverb, brought back to life by the philosopher Isaiah Berlin: "the fox knows many things, but the hedgehog knows one big thing." Kerry was the fox, with innumerable proposals for change. Bush was the hedgehog, who knew one thing: the nation was in danger, and polls consistently showed that the public approved of the way he was conducting the war on terrorism. In a kind of rhetorical ju-jitsu, he intertwined his greatest liability, the Iraq war, with his greatest strength, the war on terrorism, so intricately that they could not be pried apart—and he could not be thrown. Terror was terror, war was war, and he was the commander in chief. If this linkage was in error, Kerry never managed to persuade enough voters how it was wrong and what he would do instead.

So it was not true that Bush lacked ideas. Where he might have been vulnerable, having charged Kerry so effectively with

332 ◆ Reporting for Duty!

flip-flopping, was in having completely reversed himself in terms of the idea concerning foreign policy he had voiced before 9/11. This position, against "nation-building," was enunciated in both philosophical and practical terms by earlier Republican stalwarts, including former Secretary of State Henry Kissinger and the first President Bush.

In the early 1990s, Kissinger had usefully defined what he called "two contradictory attitudes toward foreign policy" in American history: "The first is that America serves its values best by perfecting democracy at home, thereby acting as a beacon for the rest of mankind; the second, that America's values impose on it an obligation to crusade for them around the world." Those who see America as a beacon of light for the world are sympathetic to isolationism and discourage foreign involvement except when it is essential for self-protection. Those who advocate the notion of America as a crusader for democracy and human rights around the world feel obliged to commit the nation abroad when its help is needed to achieve these goals.

The opposition described by Kissinger is more fully explained in this book's chapter on the Republican Henry Cabot Lodge, the pragmatic realist, and the Democrat Woodrow Wilson, the idealist. The earlier President Bush and his son had been firm advocates of the first position after the Gulf War ended in 1991, when Saddam Hussein was left in power. With his national-security adviser, Brent Scowcroft, the senior Bush wrote in *A World Transformed* that removing Saddam would have incurred "incalculable human and political costs." "We would have been forced to occupy Baghdad and, in effect, rule Iraq. The coalition would instantly have collapsed, the Arabs deserting it in anger and other allies pulling out as well. . . . Furthermore, we had been self-consciously trying to set a pattern for handling aggression in the post-Cold War world. Going in and occupying Iraq, thus unilaterally exceeding the United Nations' mandate, would have destroyed the precedent of international response to aggression we hoped to establish. Had we gone the invasion route, the United States could conceivably still be an occupying power in a bitterly hostile land. It would have been a dramatically different—and perhaps barren—outcome."

John Kerry could have argued more effectively than he did that the senior Bush's prediction of what happened to his son's program in Iraq was eerily accurate. But even so, the younger Bush's program can be explained as yet one more version of the old domino theory used to describe the seemingly relentless march of international communism after World War II. The war against terrorism is based, the Bush camp argues, not on fear but on optimism and a nobly self-sacrificing idealism. As a key part of that war, if Iraq can be turned into something approaching a democracy, other nations in the Middle East will be forced to liberalize their regimes.

Seen from this perspective, Bush's foreign policy of promoting democracy around the world is Wilsonian. During the campaign President Bush spoke continually of democratic values that were universally applicable, capable of taking root even in the sands of the Middle East. Commentators complained that Bush lacked a vision for his foreign policy and derided his comments as trite, not comprehending the degree to which Wilson's ideas had become part of the American psyche. In echoing the ideas of his great Democratic predecessor in the White House, Bush was actually enunciating a larger vision than was Kerry. If he is right, the turmoil caused by terrorism will end at some point, just as, finally, the threat posed by international communism was ended by American patience, persistence, and force.

To the contrary, say Bush's opponents. Although Kerry himself resisted likening Iraq to the American involvement in Vietnam, the words "quagmire" and "swamp" began by the end of the campaign to surface frequently. Bush's resurrection of the domino theory as now working in our favor was not noted by Kerry, but it might have been—as yet another instance of vastly over-simplifying the course of history, this time due to wishful thinking rather than to fear.

✧   ✧   ✧

How finally are we to understand this latest and in some ways most important clash of will, philosophy, and temperament? By looking back, perhaps, at this book's initial chapter on George Crook, Nelson Miles, and Geronimo. Geronimo was seen in his time as a terrorist, given to ruthless depredations and the murder of innocent civilians. George Crook was the humanist who thought he could apply his interest in Indian culture and psychology to Geronimo, to reason with him. When Crook failed, it was the hard-driving, tough-talking Nelson Miles who solved the problem of Geronimo by applying direct force. Equivalencies carry us only so far, but it seems clear that Crook and Kerry personify the man of thought, while Miles and Bush personify the man of action. In dire times, Americans are intensely pragmatic: if the national goal is seen as just and force is required to accomplish that goal, most of them will say, then let force be used, and worry later about nuances of justification and application. The question continues to be, are the times now as dire as they appear? We must wait for the answer.

Conclusion

This book is about the importance of personality; about the contrast between what should be and what can be; and about the virtue of compromise. None of the contentious issues it treats has yet been "solved." Hetch Hetchy still stirs debate, as it did between Theodore Roosevelt and John Muir; American attitudes toward the United Nations today have their roots in the quarrel between Henry Cabot Lodge and Woodrow Wilson over the League of Nations; most women now in college have no trouble understanding the positions so clearly set forth by Betty Friedan and Phyllis Schlafly.

Some of the figures depicted here took great joy in battle. But because nearly every contest produced a winner, it also produced a loser—for example, Geronimo subdued, Pullman disgraced, Hoover embittered. All fought for a belief, which made defeat particularly difficult. Winning, surprisingly, was often less than entirely satisfactory for the victors, because the democratic tendency toward compromise meant they still had to settle for less than they wanted.

Like the issues that divided them, the combatants' reputations live on; they blossom and they wither, depending on who is watering them. Some have been vindicated: Crook's military tactics reappeared in the American conquest of Afghanistan in 2002; Muir's defeat continues to motivate environmentalists today. Others, such as Oppenheimer and Nixon, tarnished their legacies. The one constant in this regard seems to be that it pays to outlive your opponent, as did, by many years, Miles, Debs, Du Bois, Hoover, Teller, and Ellsberg.

Readers will also have noticed the significance of class in these discussions. Birthplace, family, education, religion, profession, income, and wealth—each contributes to a person's sense of identity. Each is vital to understanding the issues represented.

Two final points stand out. The first is that ideas matter: they moved these people to action, shaping their lives and ours. We need only to consider the similarities between, for example, Hoover and Schlafly, or between Oppenheimer and Ellsberg, to see how ideas and attitudes pass from generation to generation. More broadly, ideas embodied in the Constitution by the Framers have shaped over half of our confrontations—the two-thirds rule for adoption of treaties by the Senate, the three-quarters of the states provision for passing an amendment, the designated role of the president as commander in chief, the impeachment provision, the Supreme Court's right to nullify or uphold public policies.

The second key point is that the opposition between "realists" and "idealists" is positive, not negative. They are married to each other, for better or for worse. The results of their union, like children, usually turn out satisfactorily. As in any family, without some conflict, resistance, and opposition, there can be no progress.

An optimistic conclusion? Only to a point, for today two of the great traditions portrayed in these chapters are imperiled. One is political leadership. The Preface notes that many of the legendary figures whom this book describes, such as Woodrow Wilson and the Roosevelts, have no current counterpart of equivalent stature. The 2004 contest between George W. Bush and John Kerry underscored the diminished state of American political leadership. One wonders whether the country's history of finding outstanding leaders when it desperately needs them will survive. Regardless, the nation will be harder to lead because of the second peril—the brass knuckles brawl between red state and blue state political cultures. This move toward "smashmouth politics"—an ugly neologism that echoes George Orwell's *1984*— threatens the tradition of compromise which allows democracy to work in the first place.

Bibliography

The literature on all of these subjects is vast. Following are the works that were most useful in the preparation of these chapters, with particular emphasis on the more recent titles.

Chapter 1

Peter Aleshire. *The Fox and the Whirlwind: General George Crook and Geronimo; A Paired Biography* (2000). Takes liberties in interpreting Geronimo's thoughts; from a factual standpoint, must be read with considerable caution.

John G. Bourke. *On the Border with Crook* (1891). A crucial eyewitness account.

General George Crook: His Autobiography, ed. Martin F. Schmitt (1946). Crook's memoirs, though revealing, were incomplete at the time of his death.

Angie Debo. *Geronimo: The Man, His Time, His Place* (1976). The standard biography.

Peter R. DeMontravel. *A Hero to His Fighting Men: Nelson A. Miles, 1839–1925* (1998). Solidly accompanies Wooster's treatment, listed below.

Personal Recollections and Observations of General Nelson A. Miles (1897); *Serving the Republic: Memoirs of the Civil and Military Life of Nelson A. Miles, Lieutenant-General, United States Army* (1911). Best read in conjunction with the DeMontravel and Wooster biographies listed.

Charles M. Robinson, III. *General Crook and the Western Frontier* (2001). The best of the recent works on Crook.

Sherry Robinson. *Apache Voices: Their Stories of Survival as Told to Eve Ball* (2000). Conveys the Apaches' perspective on their history and culture.

Edward H. Spicer. *Cycles of Conquest: The Impact of Spain, Mexico, and the United States on the Indians of the Southwest,*

1533–1960 (1962). Provides a good overall view of long-term cultural clashes in the Southwest.

Richard White. *"It's Your Misfortune and None of My Own": A History of the American West* (1991). The standard broad treatment of its subject, often biting in its revisionism (as the ambiguous title implies).

Robert Wooster. *Nelson A. Miles and the Twilight of the Frontier Army* (1993). A well-researched, well-written biography that should be used in conjunction with DeMontravel's, above.

Chapter 2

William Adelman. *Touring Pullman* (1993). Photos and maps of the town as it looked in the nineteenth century and more recently.

Stanley Buder. *Pullman: An Experiment in Industrial Order and Community Planning 1880–1930* (1967). Excellent description of Pullman's town and the strike.

Philip S. Foner. *The Great Labor Uprising of 1877* (1977). First published in the centenary year of the strikes described in his book, Foner's account has since become a classic.

Ray Ginger. *The Bending Cross: A Biography of Eugene V. Debs* (1949). The first full account of Debs's life and career, reliable and very readable.

Liston E. Leyendecker. *Palace Car Prince* (1992). The only full treatment of Pullman's life.

Almont Lindsay. *The Pullman Strike: The Story of a Unique Experiment and of a Great Labor Upheaval* (1964). The most thorough account of the strike.

Nick Salvatore. *Eugene V. Debs: Citizen and Socialist* (1982). The standard biography, somewhat more critical of Debs than Ginger's treatment.

Richard Schneirov, Shelton Stromquist, and Nick Salvatore. *The Pullman Strike and the Crisis of the 1890s: Essays on Labor and Politics* (1999). Very fine chapters by different scholars on a variety of topics, including a thorough bibliographical essay.

Colston E. Warne. *The Pullman Boycott of 1894: The Problem of Federal Intervention* (1955). Still relevant, this excellent discussion is one of a series of short texts in the D. C. Heath Problems in American Civilization series.

Chapter 3

W.E.B. Du Bois. *The Souls of Black Folk,* in *Three Negro Classics,* ed. John Hope Franklin (1965 [1940]). The book for which Du Bois is best known today by the general public; Washington's *Up From Slavery* is also included in this volume.

————. *Dusk of Dawn: An Essay Toward an Autobiography of a Race Concept* (1940). A three-volume compilation of Du Bois's critical and personal reflections.

Steven Hahn. *A Nation Under Our Feet: Black Political Struggles in the Rural South from Slavery to the Great Migration* (c. 2003). A thorough treatment of African American politics in the rural South between the Civil War and the early twentieth century.

Lewis R. Harlan. *Booker T. Washington: The Making of a Black Leader, 1856–1901* (1972), and *Booker T. Washington: The Wizard of Tuskegee, 1901–1915* (1983). The authoritative standard biography of Washington.

Martin Kilson. *The Annals of the American Academy of Political and Social Science* (2000), pp. 298–313. Useful opposition of the two leaders' characteristics, hostile to Washington and sympathetic to Du Bois.

David Levering Lewis. *W.E.B. Du Bois: Biography of a Race 1868–1919* (1993), and *W.E.B. Du Bois: The Fight for Equality and the American Century, 1919–1963* (2000). The authoritative standard biography of Du Bois.

Ross Posnock. *Color and Culture: Black Writers and the Making of the Modern Intellectual* (1998). Du Bois is the key figure in this important study.

Arnold Rampersad. *The Art and Imagination of W.E.B. Du Bois* (1976). Useful for its close examination of Du Bois as a writer.

Joel Williamson. *The Crucible of Race: Black-White Relations in the American South since Emancipation* (1984). Essential for an understanding of the conditions that shaped Washington and Du Bois.

Chapter 4

Edward Abbey. *The Monkey Wrench Gang* (1975). A fanciful but influential portrayal of environmentalism run amok.

H. W. Brands. *T. R.: The Last Romantic* (1997); Kathleen Dalton. *Theodore Roosevelt: A Strenuous Life* (2002). Among the recent biographies, these fine, lengthy studies are the ones to read.

Stephen Fox. *John Muir and His Legacy: The American Conservation Movement* (1981). Indispensable for linking Muir to the environmental history that followed his time.

Samuel R. Hays. *Conservation and the Gospel of Efficiency: The Progressive Conservation Movement, 1890–1920* (1969). A classic work on conservation for use.

Holway R. Jones. *John Muir and the Sierra Club: The Battle for Yosemite* (1965). Contains a detailed account of the Hetch Hetchy struggle, with excellent photographs of the valley as it was.

The Wilderness World of John Muir, ed. Edwin Way Teale (1954). Among the many collections of Muir's writings, this remains the best in one volume.

Roderick Nash. *Wilderness and the American Mind* (1986). A superb study of changing American attitudes toward wilderness.

Robert W. Righter. *The Battle over Hetch Hetchy: America's Most Controversial Dam and the Birth of Modern Environmentalism* (2005). A crucial account of the fight over the reservoir, its legacy, and the restoration issue today.

Theodore Roosevelt: An Autobiography (1913). A classic, colorful American autobiography and the best by any president, in part because Roosevelt (not some ghostwriter) actually wrote it.

Alfred Runte. *Yosemite: The Embattled Wilderness* (1990). Unlike most of the nostalgic, antiquarian histories that are sold in national park bookshops, this one is worth reading. It may be the most powerful critique of the way Yosemite has been managed since Muir's.

John Warfield Simpson. *Dam! Water, Power, Politics, and Preservation in Hetch Hetchy and Yosemite National Park* (2005). Together with Righter, above, the place to begin a study of the issue.

Ted Steinberg. *Down to Earth: Nature's Role in American History* (2002). A fine history of the United States with the environment as its focus.

Thurman Wilkins. *John Muir: Apostle of Nature* (1995). The most useful Muir biography.

Chapter 5

Lloyd E. Ambrosius. *Woodrow Wilson and the American Diplomatic Tradition: The Treaty Fight in Perspective* (1987); *Wilsonianism: Woodrow Wilson and His Legacy in American Foreign Relations* (2002). Two of the best studies of Wilsonian foreign policy and its legacy.

Kendrick A. Clements. *Woodrow Wilson: World Statesman* (1987). A particularly good, relatively brief biography.

John Milton Cooper, Jr. *Breaking the Heart of the World: Woodrow Wilson and the Fight for the League of Nations* (2001). A fine study of Wilson and the events covered by this chapter.

Alan Dawley. *Changing the World: American Progressives in War and Revolution* (2003). Examines the quest by American progressives (notably Woodrow Wilson) for peace and social justice from an international perspective.

John A. Garraty. *Henry Cabot Lodge: A Biography* (1953). The standard biography.

August Heckscher. *Woodrow Wilson* (1991). Distinguished among the more recent biographies for its depth and detail.

Thomas J. Knock. *To End All Wars: Woodrow Wilson and the Quest for a New World Order* (1992). An extraordinarily insightful look at Wilson's foreign policy and its fate at home.

Henry Cabot Lodge. *The Senate and the League of Nations* (1925). Lodge's own summary of the League fight, with the predictable biases.

Margaret MacMillan. *Paris 1919: Six Months that Changed the World* (2002). The best study of the peacemaking process from an international perspective.

Michael Mandelbaum. *The Ideas that Conquered the World: Peace, Democracy, and Free Markets in the Twenty-first Century* (2002). Traces the way Wilson's ideas have evolved and flourished since his time.

John A. Thompson. *Woodrow Wilson* (2002). An unusually insightful brief biography.

William C. Widenor. *Henry Cabot Lodge and the Search for an American Foreign Policy* (1983). The best account of Lodge and the treaty fight.

The Papers of Woodrow Wilson, ed. Arthur S. Link (1966–94). One of the great American historical projects of its era, this multivolume work brings together the vital Wilson documents.

Chapter 6

David Burner. *Herbert Hoover: A Public Life* (1979). The best single-volume biography.

James MacGregor Burns and Susan Dunn. *The Three Roosevelts: Patrician Leaders Who Transformed America* (2001). A fine multiple biography of Theodore, Franklin, and Eleanor.

Blanche Wiesen Cook. *Eleanor Roosevelt* (1992–). Once completed, this multivolume study may stand as the definitive work.

Frank Freidel. *Franklin D. Roosevelt: A Rendezvous with Destiny* (1990). A distillation and completion of Freidel's distinguished multivolume biography.

Herbert Hoover. *The Challenge to Liberty* (1934). The clearest statement of Hoover's opposition to the New Deal.

Herbert Hoover and Franklin D. Roosevelt: A Documentary History, ed. Timothy Walch and Dwight M. Miller (1998). Includes the two men's correspondence and the observations of contemporaries.

David M. Kennedy. *Freedom from Fear: The American People in Depression and War, 1929–1945* (1999). An excellent, compendious recent study.

William E. Leuchtenburg. *Franklin D. Roosevelt and the New Deal: 1932–1940* (1963). A classic treatment of the New Deal, brilliantly supplemented by the author's *The FDR Years: On Roosevelt and His Legacy* (1995).

George H. Nash. *The Life of Herbert Hoover* (1983–). The most detailed biography, a multivolume project that awaits completion.

Studs Terkel. *Hard Times: An Oral History of the Great Depression* (1970). A classic of oral history that captures the human impact of the Depression through first-person accounts.

Geoffrey C. Ward. *A First-Class Temperament: The Emergence of Franklin Roosevelt* (1989). Excellent on Roosevelt's prepresidential career and polio.

Chapter 7

Jeremy Bernstein. *Oppenheimer: Portrait of an Enigma* (2004). Excellent short biography by a *New Yorker* writer.

Kai Bird and Martin J. Sherwin. *American Prometheus: The Triumph and Tragedy of J. Robert Oppenheimer* (2004). Important recent book, one of several published in 2004, widely praised as the fullest account so far.

Stanley Blumberg and Gwinn Owens. *Energy and Conflict: The Life and Times of Edward Teller* (1976). Excellent, thorough biography with much attention to Oppenheimer and Teller's relationship.

David C. Cassidy. *J. Robert Oppenheimer and the American Century* (2004). An overview of Oppenheimer's achievements, by the author of a life of Werner Heisenberg.

Haakon Chevalier. *Oppenheimer: The Story of a Friendship* (1965). Chevalier's story of betrayal by his friend, which lacks evidence of awareness on the author's part of his own complicity in treason.

Peter Goodchild. *J. Robert Oppenheimer, "Shatterer of Worlds"* (1980). Text accompanying the excellent BBC documentary of that year.

———. *Edward Teller: The Real Dr. Strangelove* (2004). Highly critical of Teller, as the title suggests.

Gregg Herken. *Brotherhood of the Bomb: The Tangled Lives and Loyalties of Robert Oppenheimer, Ernest Lawrence, and Edward Teller* (2002). Thorough and authoritative treatment of Oppenheimer and Teller's association; includes link to the author's website.

Priscilla J. McMillan. *The Ruin of J. Robert Oppenheimer and the Birth of the Modern Arms Race* (2004). The most detailed analysis of the role Teller played in Oppenheimer's downfall, and the most damaging.

Robert S. Norris. *Racing for the Bomb: General Leslie R. Groves, the Manhattan Project's Indispensable Man* (2002). Reviewed by the *Bulletin of the Atomic Scientists* as "the defining, if not definitive, narrative of this tale."

Richard Polenberg, ed. *In the Matter of J. Robert Oppenheimer: The Security Clearance Hearing* (2002). Transcripts and commentary on the 1954 proceedings.

Richard Rhodes. *The Making of the Atomic Bomb* (1986). The fullest account, awarded a Pulitzer Prize and a National Book Award.

Alex Ross. "Countdown," *The New Yorker* (Oct. 3, 2005). Lengthy article describing rehearsals for a new John Adams opera about Oppenheimer at Los Alamos, "Doctor Atomic."

Philip M. Stern. *The Oppenheimer Case: Security on Trial* (1969). Still a useful summary of the case, very sympathetic to Oppenheimer.

Edward Teller, with Judith L. Shoolery. *Memoirs: A Twentieth-Century Journey in Science and Politics* (2001). Conveys a vivid sense of the personalities and events that shaped Teller's life.

Herbert F. York. *The Advisors: Oppenheimer, Teller, and the Bomb* (1976). Solid account by a scientist who worked with both men and later directed the Livermore Lab.

Chapter 8

Clay Blair. *The Forgotten War: America in Korea 1950–1953* (1987). The fullest account of the military aspects of the war.

T.R. Fehrenbach. *This Kind of War* (1963). The classic narrative account by a former officer in Korea.

Alonzo Hamby. *Man of the People: A Life of Harry S. Truman* (1995). The definitive biography, more probing and critical than McCullough's, cited below.

D. Clayton James. *The Years of MacArthur* (3 volumes, 1970–1985). The authoritative biography, to which Manchester, cited below, acknowledges his indebtedness.

William Manchester. *American Caesar* (1972). Compelling popular biography of MacArthur.

David McCullough. *Truman* (1992). Best-selling popular biography.

John W. Spanier. *The Truman–MacArthur Controversy and the Korean War* (1959). Clear presentation of the central issue, still useful.

William Stueck. *Rethinking the Korean War: A New Diplomatic and Strategic History* (2002). Places the war in a global context, explaining links between Korea and Vietnam.

Stanley Weintraub. *MacArthur's War: Korea and the Undoing of an American Hero* (2000). Perspective of a literary scholar who served in Korea and has written widely about war in the twentieth century.

Chapter 9

Robert Blum. *Drawing the Line: The Origins of the American Containment Policy in East Asia* (1982). Explains the rationale behind American policies and actions with regard to Vietnam, Korea, Taiwan, Japan, and elsewhere.

Daniel Ellsberg. *Secrets: A Memoir of Vietnam and the Pentagon Papers* (2002). Self-serving and egotistical account by a principal in the Pentagon Papers episode but nonetheless essential.

David Halberstam. *The Best and the Brightest* (1969). Early bestseller by a reporter profiling the personalities of influential Americans as well as the issues concerning the Vietnam War.

Harry R. Haldeman. *The Haldeman Diaries: Inside the Nixon White House,* with editorial assistance from Stephen Ambrose (1994). Perspective on key events through the eyes of Nixon's chief of staff.

Stanley I. Kutler. *Abuse of Power: The New Nixon Tapes* (1997). Further evidence of the systematic abuses that led to Nixon's resignation.

Robert J. McMahon, ed. *Major Problems in the History of the Vietnam War,* second edition (1995). Valuable compilation of original documents covering all phases of the war, including perspectives of both North and South Vietnam, as well as interpretive essays; part of D. C. Heath's Major Problems in American History series.

George Moss. "Chronology of U.S. Involvement in Vietnam, 1942–1975," in *Vietnam: An American Ordeal* (1998), 454–469. A thorough and clarifying outline of a confusing, decades-long series of events.

Herbert Parmet. *Richard Nixon and His America* (1990). Sympathetic but unsparing depiction of Nixon, particularly useful for its account of his pursuit of Alger Hiss.

Neil Sheehan, et al. *The Pentagon Papers* (1971). Sheehan and others edited and wrote section introductions covering various aspects of the Vietnam War and the unauthorized release of the Pentagon documents by Ellsberg.

Sanford Ungar. *The Papers and The Papers: An Account of the Legal and Political Battle over the Pentagon Papers* (1972, 1989). The clearest explication of the degree to which the freedom of the press was challenged during the Pentagon Papers controversy.

Tom Wells. *Wild Man: The Life and Times of Daniel Ellsberg* (2001). Exhaustive and essential study of Ellsberg's character by a biographer/reporter who grew to dislike him intensely.

Chapter 10

Mary Frances Berry. *Why ERA Failed: Politics, Women's Rights, and the Amending Process of the Constitution* (1986). One wishes for more, but this remains the best account to date.

Donald T. Critchlow. *Phyllis Schlafly and Grassroots Conservatism: A Woman's Crusade* (2005). Depicts the role that Schlafly and her fight against the ERA played in the evolution of modern conservatism.

Sara M. Evans. *Born for Liberty: A History of Women in America* (1989). A solid introduction to the subject.

————. *Tidal Wave: How Women Changed America at Century's End* (2003). Examines, from a feminist perspective, how feminism has altered American culture and politics since World War II.

Carol Felsenthal. *The Sweetheart of the Silent Majority: The Biography of Phyllis Schlafly* (1981). Despite its title, an even-handed account of Schlafly's life and impact.

Betty Friedan. *The Feminine Mystique* (1963). The greatest modern statement of the case for feminism.

————. *The Second Stage* (1981). This powerful early-1980s critique of feminism is striking for its strong emphasis on the family.

Sylvia Ann Hewlett. *A Lesser Life: The Myth of Women's Liberation in America* (1986). One of the most effective critiques of feminism.

Daniel Horowitz. *Betty Friedan and the Making of "The Feminine Mystique": The American Left, the Cold War, and Modern Feminism* (1998). A revealing scholarly biography that persuasively revises Betty Friedan's own account of her life.

Ruth Rosen. *The World Split Open: How the Modern Women's Movement Changed America* (2000). Useful companion volume to Evans's *Tidal Wave*, above.

Phyllis Schlafly. *A Choice Not an Echo* (1964). The book that made its author a national political figure.

Chapter 11

Terry H. Anderson. *The Pursuit of Fairness: A History of Affirmative Action* (2004). Traces the American experience since the administration of Franklin D. Roosevelt, with a diligent attempt at evenhandedness.

William G. Bowen and Derek Bok. *The Shape of the River: Long-Term Consequences of Considering Race in College and University Admissions* (1998). Oddly titled, but the most complete account to date of affirmative action in higher education and its impact on minorities. Bowen is the former president of Princeton University, Bok of Harvard.

Steven M. Gillon. *"That's Not What We Meant to Do": Reform and Its Unintended Consequences in Twentieth-Century America* (2000). Shows in Chapter 3 how the original intentions of affirmative action's proponents yielded to something quite different.

Hugh Davis Graham. *Collision Course: The Strange Convergence of Affirmative Action and Immigration Policy in America* (2002). Examines how affirmative action and a generous immigration policy have led to conflict over education, jobs, and housing between American-born minorities and immigrants.

John Greenya. *Silent Justice: The Clarence Thomas Story* (2001). Most useful for its summaries and quotations of other sources on Justice Thomas.

Ira Katznelson. *When Affirmative Action Was White: An Untold History of Racial Inequality in Twentieth-Century America* (2005). In advocating affirmative action, explores the ways in which federal social programs of the 1930s and 1940s, including Social Security and the GI Bill of Rights, discriminated against blacks in favor of whites.

Nancy Maveety. *Justice Sandra Day O'Connor: Strategist on the Supreme Court* (1996). An analysis of Justice O'Connor's judicial thought and decisions, with some biographical material.

Sandra Day O'Connor and H. Alan Day. *Lazy B: Growing Up on a Cattle Ranch in the American Southwest* (2002). Interesting mainly for its portrayal of the setting of Justice O'Connor's childhood and upbringing; less revealing about the Justice herself.

Sandra Day O'Connor. *The Majesty of the Law: Reflections of a Supreme Court Justice* (2003). A wide-ranging discussion of life on the Court, notable jurists and cases, and women in the law.

Philip F. Rubio. *A History of Affirmative Action: 1619–2000* (2001). Examines the subject beginning with its origins in slavery and English common law.

Thomas Sowell. *Affirmative Action Around the World: An Empirical Study* (2004). A bleak account of the outcome of affirmative action programs in such countries as India and Malaysia as well as the United States.

Andrew Peyton Thomas. *Clarence Thomas: A Biography* (2001). A sympathetic (though not uncritical), lengthy biography with a conservative slant.

Chapter 12

Douglas Brinkley. *Tour of Duty: John Kerry and the Vietnam War* (2004). The candidate's wartime autobiography.

Mark Danner. "How Bush Won," *New York Review of Books,* Jan. 13, 2004. Lengthy analysis argues that fear was Bush's best weapon.

Philip Gourevitch. "Damage Control," *The New Yorker,* July 7, 2004. Thorough analysis of Kerry's problems by a supporter.

"How Bush Did It." *Newsweek* Election 2004 Special Issue, Nov. 15, 2004. Especially helpful for conveying color and personalities involved.

Hal Larson. "George and John," *California Journal,* October 1, 2004. Useful comparison of the candidates' personality traits.

Bonnie Azab Powell. UC Berkeley NewsCenter, "Framing the Issues," Oct. 27, 2004 [online]. Interview with George Lakoff on use of language in politics.

Stephen J. Wayne. *The Road to the White House 2000: The Politics of Presidential Elections* (2001). Emphasizes "nuts and bolts" of elections.

Index